The World's Greatest Books
Vol.- X
Lives And Letters

by

J. A. Hammerton

The World's Greatest Books
Vol.- X Lives And Letters
by J. A. Hammerton

Copyright © 2025

All Rights reserved.

ISBN: 978-93-59951-02-7

Published by

DOUBLE 9 BOOKS
2/13-B, Ansari Road
Daryaganj, New Delhi – 110002
info@double9books.com
www.double9books.com
Tel. 011-40042856

This book is under public domain

ABOUT THE AUTHOR

Dictionary of National Biography Calls Sir John Alexander Hammerton "the most successful creator of large-scale works of reference that Britain has known" (he was born on February 27, 1871, in Alexandria, Scotland and died on May 12, 1949, in London). Hammerton first job as a journalist was in Nottingham, where he met Arthur Mee, who would become his lifelong partner and friend. He joined Alfred Harmsworth's Amalgamated Press in 1905. The Harmsworth Self-Educator was made by him and Mee. Hammerton helped with the first version of Mee's Children's Encyclopaedia. It came out every two weeks from 1908 to 1910 and was later collected in eight big books. Hammerton contributed by putting together pieces about "Poetry" and "Famous Books." Harmsworth's Universal Encyclopaedia was Hammerton's most important work. It was first released every two weeks from 1920 to 1922. Twelve million books of the Encyclopedia were sold all over the English-speaking world. Other parts of the text were changed and published as articles in Hammerton's later six-volume self-help series called Practical Knowledge for All.

CONTENTS

VICTOR HUGO

Deeds and Words

"Deeds and Words" ("Actes et Paroles"), which is dated June, 1875, is the record of Victor Hugo's public life, speeches and letters, down to the year of his death, which occurred on May 32, 1885; but it is most important as a defence of his political career from 1848 onwards. It does not, however, tell us how changeable his opinions had actually been. His inconstant attachments are thus summed up by Dr. Brandes: "He warmly supports the candidacy of Louis Napoleon for the post of President of the Republic ... lends him his support when he occupies that post, and is even favourable to the idea of an empire, until the feeling that he is despised as a politician estranges him from the Prince-President, and resentment at the coup d'etat drives him into the camp of the extreme Republicans. His life may be said to mirror the political movements of France during the first half of the century." (See FICTION.)

I.--Right and Law

All human eloquence, among all peoples and in all times, may be summed up as the quarrel of Right against Law.

But this quarrel tends ever to decrease, and therein lies the whole of progress. On the day when it has disappeared, civilisation will have attained its highest point; that which ought to be will have become one with that which is; there will be an end of catastrophes, and even, so to speak, of events; and society will develop majestically according to nature. There will be no more disputes nor factions; no longer will laws be made, they will only be discovered. Education will have taken the place of war, and by means of universal suffrage there will be chosen a parliament of intellect.

In that serene and glorious age there will be no more warriors, but workers only; creators in the place of exterminators. The civilisation of action will have passed away, and that of thought will have succeeded. The masterpieces of art and of literature will be the great events.

Frontiers will disappear; and France, which is destined to die as the gods die, by transfiguration, will become Europe. For the Revolution of France will be known as the evolution of the peoples. France has laboured not for herself alone, but has aroused world-wide hopes, and is herself the representative of all human good-will.

Right and Law are the two great forces whose harmony gives birth to order, but their antagonism is the source of all catastrophe. Right is the divine truth, and Law is the earthly reality; liberty is Right and society is Law. Wherefore there are two tribunes, one of the men of ideas, the other of the men of facts; and between these two the consciences of most still vacillate. Not yet is there harmony between the immutable and the variable power; Right and Law are in ceaseless conflict.

To Right belong the inviolability of human life, liberty, peace; and nothing that is indissoluble, irrevocable, or irreparable. To Law belong the scaffold, sword, and sceptre; war itself; and every kind of yoke, from divorceless marriage in the family to the state of siege in the city. Right is to come and go, buy, sell, exchange; Law has its frontiers and its custom-houses. Right would have free and compulsory education, without encroaching on young consciences; that is to say, lay instruction; Law would have the teaching of ignorant friars. Right demands liberty of belief, but Law establishes the state religions. Universal suffrage and universal jury belong to Right, but restricted franchise and packed juries are creatures of the Law.

What a difference there is! And let it be understood that all social agitation arises from the persistence of Right against the obstinacy of Law. The keynote of the present writer's public life has been *"Pro jure contra legem"*--for the Right which makes men, against the Law which men have made. He believes that liberty is the highest expression of Right, and that the republican formula, "Liberty, Equality, and Fraternity," leaves nothing to be added or to be taken away. For Liberty is Right, Equality is Fact, and Fraternity is Duty. The whole of man is there. We are brothers in our life, equal in birth and death, free in soul.

II.--Days of Childhood

At the beginning of this nineteenth century there was a child who lived in a great house, surrounded by a large garden, in the most deserted part of Paris. He lived with his mother, two brothers, and a venerable and worthy priest, who was his only tutor, and taught him much Latin, a little Greek, and no history at all. Here, at the time of the First Empire, the three boys played and worked, watched the clouds and trees and listened to the birds, under the sweet influence of their mother's smile.

It was the child's misfortune, though no one's fault, that he was taught by a priest. What can be more terrible than a system of untruth, sincerely believed? For a priest teaches falsehoods, ignorant of the truth, and thinks he does well; everything he does for the child is done against the child, making crooked that which nature has made straight; his teaching poisons the young mind with aged prejudices, drawing evening twilight, like a curtain, over the dawn.

That ancient, solitary house and garden, formerly a convent and then the home of his childhood, is still in his old age a dear and religious memory, though its site is now profaned by a modern street He sees it in a romantic atmosphere, in which, amid sunbeams and roses, his spirit opened into flower. What a stillness was in its vast rooms and cloisters. Only at long intervals was the silence broken by the return of a plumed and sabred general, his father, from the wars. That child, already thoughtful, was myself.

One night--it was some great festival of the empire, and all Paris was illumined--my mother was walking in the garden with three of my father's comrades, and I was following them, when we saw a tall figure in the gloom of the trees. It was the proscribed Victor du Lahorie, my godfather. He was even then conspiring against Bonaparte in the cause of liberty, and was shortly after executed. I remember his saying, "If Rome had kept her kings, she had not been Rome," and then, looking on me, "Child, put liberty first of all!" That one word outweighed my whole education.

III.--Before the Exile

It was not until the writer saw, in 1848, the triumph of all the enemies of progress that he knew in the depths of his heart that he belonged, not to the conquerors, but to the vanquished. The Republic lay inanimate; but, gazing on her form, he saw that she was liberty, and not even the sure fore-knowledge of the ruin and exile that must follow could prevent his espousal with the dead. On June 15 he made his protest from the tribune, and from that day he fought relentless battle for liberty and the republic. And on December 2, 1851, he received what he had expected--twenty years of exile. That is the history of what has been called his apostasy.

Throughout that strange period before his exile, the frightful phantom of the past was all-powerful with men. Every kind of question was debated--national independence, individual liberty, liberty of conscience, of thought, of speech, and of the Press; questions of marriage, of education, of the right to work, of the right to one's fatherland as against exile, of the right to life as against penal law, of the separation of Church and state, of the federation of Europe, of frontiers to be wiped out, and of custom-houses to be done away--all these questions were proposed, debated, and sometimes settled.

In these debates the author of this memoir took his part and did his duty, and was repaid with insults. He remembers interjecting, when they were insisting on parental rights, that the children had rights, too. He astounded the assembly by asserting that it was possible to do away with misery. On July 17, 1851, he denounced the conspiracy of Louis Bonaparte, unveiling the project of the president to become emperor. On another day he pronounced from the tribune a phrase which had never yet been uttered--"The United States of Europe." Contempt and calumny were poured upon him, but what of that? They called George Washington a pickpocket.

These men of the old majority, who were doing all the evil that they could--did they mean to do evil? Not a bit of it. They deceived themselves, thinking that they had the truth, and they lied in the service of the truth. Their pity for society was pitiless for the people, whence arose so many laws, so many actions, that were blindly ferocious. They were rather a mob than a senate, and were led by the worst of their number. Let us be indulgent, and let night hide the men of night.

What do our labours and our troubles and our exiles matter if they have been for the general good; if the human race be indeed passing from December to its April; if the winter of tyrannies and of wars indeed be finished; if superstitions and prejudices no longer fall on our heads like snow; and if, after so many clouds of empire and of carnage have rolled away, we at last descry upon the horizon the rosy dawn of universal peace?

O my brothers, let us be reconciled! Let us set out on the immense highway of peace. Surely there has been enough of hatred. When will you understand that we are all together on the same ship, and that the immense menace of the sea is for all of us together? Our solidarity is terrible, but brotherhood is sweet.

IV.--Republican Principles

The sovereignty of the people, universal suffrage, and the liberty of the Press are all the same thing under three different names. The three together constitute the whole of our public right; the first is its principle, the second its manner, and the third its expression. The three principles are indissoluble from one another. The sovereignty of the people is the life-giving soul of the nation, universal suffrage its government, the Press its illumination; but they are all really one, and that unity is the republic. It is curious to notice how these principles appear again in the watchword of the republic; for the sovereignty of the people creates liberty, universal suffrage creates equality, and the Press, which enlightens the general mind, creates fraternity.

Wherever these three great principles exist in their powers and plenitude there is the republic, even though it be known as monarchy. Wherever, on the other hand, they are betrayed, hindered, or oppressed, the actual state is a monarchy or an oligarchy, even though it goes under the name of a republic. In the latter case we see the monstrous phenomenon of a government betrayed by its proper guardians, and it is this phenomenon that makes the stoutest hearts begin to be doubtful of revolutions. For revolutions are vast, ill-guided movements, which bring forth out of the darkness at one and the same time the greatest of ideas and the smallest of men; they are movements which we welcome as salutary when we look at their principles, but which we can only call catastrophes when he consider the character of their leaders.

Let us never forget that our three first principles live with a common life, and mutually defend one another. If the Liberty of the Press is in danger, the suffrages of the people arise and protect it; and, again, if the franchise is threatened, it is safeguarded by the freedom of the Press. Any attempt against either of them is a treachery to the sovereignty of the people.

The movement of this great nineteenth century is the movement not of one people only, but of all. France leads, and the nations follow. We are passing from the old world to the new, and our governors attempt in vain to arrest ideas by laws. There is in France and in Europe a party inspired by fear, which is not to be accounted the party of order; and its incessant question is: Who is to blame?

In the crisis through which we are passing, though it is a salutary crisis which will lead only to good, everyone exclaims at the dreadful moral disorder and the imminent social danger. Who, then, is guilty of these ravages? Whom shall we punish? Throughout Europe, the party of fear answers "France." Throughout France, it answers "Paris." In Paris, it blames the Press. But every thoughtful man must see that it is none of these, but is the human spirit.

It is the human spirit that has made the nations what they are. From the beginning, through infinite debate and contradiction, it has sought, unresting, to solve the problem eternally placed before the creature by his Creator. It is the human spirit which takes from age to age the form of the great revolts of history; it has been in turn, and sometimes altogether, error, illusion, heresy, schism, protest, and the truth. The human spirit is ever the great shepherd of the generations, proceeding always towards the just, the beautiful, and the true, enlightening the multitude, ennobling souls, directing the mind of man towards God.

Let the party of fear throughout Europe consider the magnitude of the task which they have undertaken. When they have destroyed the Press, they have yet to destroy Paris. When Paris is fallen, there remains France. Let France be annihilated, there still remains the human spirit--a thing intangible as the light, inaccessible as the sun.

V.--In Exile

Nothing is more terrible than exile. I do not say for him who suffers, but for the tyrant who inflicts it. A solitary figure paces a distant shore, or rises in the morning to his philosophic labours, or calls on God among the rocks and trees; his hairs become grey, and then white, in the slow passing of the years and in his longing for home; his lot is a sorrowful one; but his innocence is terrible to the crowned miscreant who sent him there. From 1852 to 1870 I was in exile.

How pleasant are those islands of the Channel, and how like France! Jersey, perhaps, more charming than Guernsey, prettier if less imposing; in Jersey the forest has become a garden; the island is like a bouquet of flowers, of the size of London, a smiling land, an idyll set in the midst of the sea.

The exile soon learns that, though the tyrant has placed him afar, he does not release his hold. Many and ingenious are the snares laid for the banished. A prince calls on you, but though he is of royal blood, he is also a detective of police. A grave professor stays at your house, and you surprise him searching your papers. Everything is permitted against you; you are outside the law, outside of common justice, outside of respect. They will say that they have your authority to publish your conversations, and will attribute to you words that you have never spoken and actions that you have never done. Never write to your friends--your letters are opened on the way. Beware of all who are kindly to you in exile; they are ruining you in Paris. You are isolated as a leper. A mysterious stranger whispers in your ear that he can procure the assassination of Bonaparte; it is Bonaparte offering to kill himself. Every day of your life is a new outrage. Only one thing is open to the exile; it is to turn his thought to other subjects.

He is at least beside the sea; let its infinity bring him wisdom. The eternal rioting of the surges against the rocks is as the agitation of impostures against the truth. It is a vain convulsion; the foam gains nothing by it, the granite loses nothing, and only sparkles the more bravely in the sun.

But exile has this great advantage--one is free to contemplate, to think, to suffer. To be alone, and yet to feel that one is with all humanity; to consolidate oneself as a citizen, and to purify oneself as a philosopher; to be poor, and begin again to work for one's living, to meditate on what is good and to contrive for what is better; to be angry in the public cause, but to crush all personal enmity; to breathe the vast, living winds of the solitudes; to compose a deeper indignation with a profounder peace--these are the opportunities of exile. I accustomed myself to say, "If, after a revolution, Bonaparte should knock at my door and ask shelter, let never a hair of his head be injured."

Yes, an exile becomes a well-wisher. He loves the roses, and the birds' nests, and the flitting hither and thither of the butterflies. He mingles with the sweet joys of the creatures, and learns a changeless faith in some secret and infinite goodness. The green glades are his chosen dwelling and his life is April; he reclines amazed at the mysteries of a tuft of grass; he studies the ant-hills of tiny republicans; he learns to know the birds by their songs; he watches the children playing barefoot in the edge of the sea.

Against this dangerous man governments are taking the most strenuous precautions. Victoria offers to hand over the exiles to Napoleon, and messages of compliment are passed from one throne to the other. But that gift did not take place. The English royalist Press applauded, but the people of London would have none of it. The great city muttered thunder. Majesty clothed in probity--that is the character of the English nation. That good and proud people showed their indignation, and Palmerston and Bonaparte had to be content with the expulsion of the exiles.

During the whole long night of my exile I never lost Paris from my view. When Europe and even France were in darkness, Paris was never hidden. That is because Paris is the frontier of the future, the visible frontier of the unknown. All of to-morrow that can be seen to-day is in Paris. The eyes that are searching for progress come to rest on Paris, for Paris is the city of light.

VI.--After the Exile

This triology, "Before, During, and After the Exile," is no work of mine, it is the doing of Napoleon III. He it is who has divided my life in this way, observing, as one might say, the rules of art. Returning to my country on September 5, 1870, I found the sky more gloomy and my duty more clamant than ever.

Though it is sad to leave the fatherland, to return to it is sometimes sadder still; and there is no Frenchman who would not have preferred a life-long banishment, to seeing France ground beneath the Prussian heel, and the loss of Metz and Strasburg. This was an invasion of barbarians; but there is another menace that is not less formidable. I mean the invasion of our land by darkness, an invasion of the nineteenth century by the middle ages. After the emperor, the pope; after Berlin, Rome; after the triumph of the sword, the triumph of night. For the light of civilisation may be extinguished in either of two ways, by a military or by a clerical invasion. The former threatens our mother, France; the latter our child, the future.

A double inviolability is the most precious possession of a civilised people--the inviolability of territory and the inviolability of conscience; and as the soldier violates the first, so does the priest violate the other. Yet the soldier does but obey his orders and the priest his dogmas, so that there are only two who are ultimately culpable--Caesar, who slays, and Peter, who lies. There is no religion which has not as its aim to seize forcibly the human soul, and it is to attempts of this kind that France is given up to-day.

One may say, indeed, that in our age there are two schools, and that these two schools sum up in themselves the two opposed currents which draw civilisation, the one towards the future and the other towards the past. One of these schools is called Paris and the other Rome. Each of them has its book; the one has the "Declaration of the Rights of Man," the other has the "Syllabus"; and the first of these books says "Yes" to progress, but the second of them says "No." Yet progress is the footstep of God.

Paris means Montaigne, Rabelais, Pascal, Corneille, Molière, Montesquieu, Diderot, Rousseau, Voltaire, Mirabeau, Danton. Rome, on the other hand, means Innocent III., Pius V., Alexander VI., Urban VIII., Arbuez, Cisneros, Lainez, Guillandus, Ignatius.

To educate is nothing less than to govern; and clerical education means a clerical government, with a despotism as its summit and ignorance as its foundation.

Rome already holds Belgium, and would now seize Paris. We are witnesses of a struggle to the death. Against us is all that manifold power which emerges from the past, the spirit of monarchy, of superstition, of the barrack and of the convent; we have against us temerity, effrontery, audacity, and fear. On our side there is nothing but the light. That is why the victory will be with us. For to enlighten is to deliver. Every increase in liberty involves increased responsibility. Nothing is graver than freedom; liberty has burdens of her own, and lays on the conscience all the chains which she unshackles from the limbs. We find rights transforming themselves into duties. Let us therefore take heed to what we are doing; we live in a difficult time and are answerable at once to the past and to the future. The time has come, in this year 1876, to replace commotions by concessions. That is how civilisation advances. For progress is nothing other than revolution effected amicably.

Therefore, legislators and citizens, let us redouble our good-will. Let all wounds be healed, all animosities extinguished; by overcoming hatred we shall overcome war; let no disturbance that may come be due to our fault. Our task of entering into the unknown is difficult enough without angers and bitterness. I am one of those who hope from that unknown future, but only on condition that we make use from the first of every means of pacification that is in our power. Let us act with the virile kindness of the strong.

Let us then calm the nations by peace, and the hearts of men by brotherhood, and let us never forget that we are ourselves responsible for this last half of the nineteenth century, and that we are placed between a great past, the Revolution of France, and a great future, the Revolution of Europe.

MARTIN HUME

The Courtships of Elizabeth

Major Martin Andrew Hume, born in London on December 8, 1847, and educated at Madrid, comes of an English family, the members of which have resided in Spain for a hundred years. He began life in the British Army, from which he retired with the rank of major. Major Hume was appointed editor of the Spanish state papers published by the Record Office; he is also lecturer in Spanish History and Literature at Cambridge, and examiner and lecturer in Spanish at the Birmingham University. He has written numerous works on the history of Spain; but perhaps he is best known for his historical studies of the Tudor period, of which may be mentioned "The Courtships of Queen Elizabeth," "The Love Affairs of Mary Queen of Scots," and "The Wives of Henry VIII." In the first-named work, published in 1896, Major Hume has presented an exceedingly interesting human document, and classified a tangled mass of material. The epitome here presented has been prepared for THE WORLD'S GREATEST BOOKS by the author himself.

I.--Foreign Philandering

The greatest diplomatic game ever played on the world's chessboard was that consummate succession of intrigues which, for nearly half a century, was carried on by Queen Elizabeth and her ministers with the object of playing off one great Continental power against another for the benefit of England and Protestantism, with which the interests of the queen were inextricably involved. Those in the midst of the strife worked mostly for immediate aims, and neither saw, nor cared, for the ultimate results; but we, looking back, see that out of that tangle of duplicity there emerged a new era of civilisation and a host of vigorous impulses which move us to this hour.

The victory of England in that struggle meant the dominance of modern ideas of liberty and of the imperial destiny of our race, and it seems as if the result could only have been attained in the peculiar combination of circumstances and persons then existing. Elizabeth triumphed as much by her weakness as by her strength. Honest Cecil kept his hand upon the helm so long because the only alternative to him was the greedy crew of councillors eager for foreign bribes. Without Leicester as a permanent matrimonial possibility, the queen could never have held the balance between her foreign suitors; and, but for the follies of Mary Stuart, the English Catholics would not have been subjected so easily, whilst the religious dissensions in France and the character of Philip II. aided Elizabeth's diplomacy. Elizabeth was more than once betrothed in her childhood to aid her father's policy, but when Henry died, in 1547, his younger daughter was unbetrothed.

During her residence with the Queen-Dowager, Catharine Parr, who soon married Thomas, Lord Seymour, the fourteen-year-old girl was exposed to peril from the designs of the ambitious Seymour. The indecorous romping, perhaps innocent at first, that took place between her and her married host provided grave scandal which touched even the honour of the girl, and her keen wits alone saved her on this occasion from disgrace. Her crafty reticence served her well, when the intrigues of Wyat, Courtenay, and the French party threatened Mary's throne; but when Mary was married, the Spanish party at once became interested in securing Elizabeth to their side by her marriage. Mary's jealousy, and Elizabeth's own determination not to be made a tool, frustrated Philip's attempt to marry the princess to his cousin, the Duke of Savoy; and when the Protestant Swedes clandestinely offered her the hand of Prince Eric, her discreet wariness again protected her from the dangerous proposal.

When Mary lay dying, Feria, the Spanish ambassador, hurried to Hatfield to salute the rising sun, and hinted even thus early that Elizabeth might marry her powerful Spanish brother-in-law. But she resented his patronage, and though she coquetted, as usual, with the proposal of marriage, she took care not to pledge herself or submit England to foreign dictation. To Spain it was vital that England should be at her bidding. If the queen could not marry Philip, surely she could only wed one of his Austrian cousins; or, if not, then England must be conquered by the sword. All that Elizabeth wanted was time, and tardy Philip played into her hands. One English noble after the other was taken up and dropped, in the intervals of foreign philandering. Lord Arundel, foolish, old, and vain, had high hopes; Sir William Pickering's chances looked bright, and France and Spain sought to patronise each English candidate in his turn, especially Lord Robert Dudley, the queen's friend from childhood, though he was already married to Amy Robsart.

At length, after many days of dallying, great Philip decided to sacrifice himself for Spain and marry his enigmatical sister-in-law. She must, of course, renounce Protestantism and all the laws that made her legally a queen; which was absurd, as Feria soon saw, and frankly told his master. So then Philip half-heartedly patronised the suit of his Austrian cousin, the Archduke Charles. If the latter would be an obedient Spanish instrument he could have Philip's support; but German Lutherans and English Protestants had also to be considered, and Elizabeth's court was divided into those who feared any consort not wholly Protestant and those who were eager for any marriage that shielded England from Spanish attack.

Elizabeth thought she could avoid the latter danger without marriage at all, so she dexterously played with all her suitors, English and foreign, while strengthening her position and gaining popularity. Sometimes she swore she would never marry, and the next day would grow sentimental over the archduke, or flirted with Dudley--keeping them all in suspense and afraid of offending her. The French, having no marriageable prince of their own, supported Dudley, or any other English candidate whom they could use against Spain; whilst Dudley himself pretended to favour the archduke, till matters looked serious, and then found means of frustrating him, often to Elizabeth's rage, for she wished to play her own deep game unhampered. She knew she could always choke off the Austrian when she wished by making fresh religious demands. The English nobles were furious at Dudley's selfish manoeuvres to keep the queen unwed till he was free, and they planned to marry the queen to Arran, the next heir of Scotland. This looked promising for months, but Dudley and his sister, Lady Sidney, checked the plan.

II.--The Nine Years' Comedy

In September, 1559, Dudley and his sister warmly took up the archduke's cause, and assured Quadra, the Spanish ambassador, that if the suitor would flatter the queen by coming to England on chance, she would marry him. But Elizabeth and Cecil, though they hinted much, would not clearly confirm Dudley's promise, and Philip and the emperor dared not expose the archduke to the risk of being repulsed. The English nobles, in good faith, urged the archduke's suit, and said that Dudley was plotting to kill his wife and marry the queen; but they and the Spanish ambassador were outwitted at every point by Elizabeth's diplomacy, and through 1559 and 1560 all the rivals were kept between hope and fear.

Then, in September 1560, the long-predicted murder of Amy Robsart set Dudley free, and made the nobles and Cecil more anxious than ever that the archduke should be bold, take the risk, and come to England. The queen, to weaken the new friendship between France and Spain, herself again pretended eagerness for the Austrian's coming; but the trick was stale now, and neither Philip nor the emperor believed her. To checkmate Dudley the Protestants were actively urging the suit of Eric of Sweden, when, in January 1561, the former made a bold bid for Spanish support. He was, he said, quite innocent of his wife's death, and he promised Quadra that if the King of Spain would urge his (Dudley's) suit upon the queen, England should send envoys to the Council of Trent, receive a papal legate, and become practically Catholic. He might promise, but such a thing was impossible, and Cecil, when he learnt of the intrigue, promptly embroiled matters and spoilt the plan.

Elizabeth, too, saw whither she was drifting, and by pretended levity turned it into a joke. At one time she invited the old Spanish bishop to marry her to Dudley, and next day said she would never marry at all. But she never ceased to flirt with Dudley, who, when his intrigue with Spain fell through, cynically appealed to the French Protestants for support. They were in no position to help him, and by January 1562, he was cringing to Spain, and pretending to be Catholic. But English Catholics hated him, and he was now no fit instrument for Philip.

In her own court it was firmly believed that Elizabeth was secretly married to Dudley--it was high time, said the gossips; but in truth the international importance of her marriage was now (1562-63) partially obscured by that of the widowed Mary Queen of Scots. Before the latter were dangled Eric of Sweden, the Archduke Charles, the Earl of Arran, and Darnley; but the match which Mary most wished for, and the most threatening to Elizabeth, was that with the vicious young lunatic, Don Carlos, the heir of Philip of Spain. The match with Darnley, too, as he was in the English succession, was distasteful to Elizabeth; but in order to divert the Spanish match--which, really, though she knew it not, was out of the question--she pretended to favour Darnley's suit at first.

In order still more to avert the Catholic alliance, Elizabeth sent active help to the French Huguenots, and drew closer to the Protestants of Germany and Holland, where distrust of their Spanish sovereign was already brewing. In these circumstances, Elizabeth for the first time could defy Spain, and Quadra, accused of conspiring against the queen, was expelled the country. When the Darnley match for Mary Stuart looked too serious, Elizabeth diverted it for a time by proposing that Dudley--now Earl of Leicester--should marry Mary. It was, of course, but a trick, through which the Scottish queen saw, with the object of preventing the Darnley marriage and discrediting Mary in the eyes of foreign princes; but it served its turn for a time.

In July 1564, when the league of France and Spain again menaced her, Elizabeth set her cap at the boy Don Carlos, and even swore to the Spanish ambassador that she was really a Catholic.

The further to alienate the Catholic powers from each other, she simultaneously approached the emperor to revive the proposal of marriage with the Archduke Charles, and to Catherine de Medici to drop a hint that she--Elizabeth--might marry the young King of France, Charles IX., a youth barely half her age--anything to prevent a combination against her and the marriage of Don Carlos with Mary Stuart. Catherine de Medici had her own reasons at the time for smiling upon Elizabeth's suggestion. She did not wish to be bound too tightly to Spain and the Catholics, for fear of the Huguenots; and in February 1565, she wrote to Elizabeth, saying that she would be the happiest of mothers if she could see her dearly beloved sister of England married to her son, Charles IX.

Elizabeth was full of maidenly hesitation. She was too old for him; perhaps he would not think her beautiful, and so on; but she took care to say that there was no one else she could marry, as she would not wed a subject. The Huguenots actively pushed the proposal, and Leicester pretended to favour it, though Cecil was against it on many grounds. But it was never seriously meant. It brought the Huguenots to Catherine's side on the eve of her voyage to renew the Catholic league with Philip, and it brought the Archduke Charles once more forward as a suitor for Elizabeth's hand. When it had thus served its purpose, the idea of the mature English queen marrying the boy Charles IX. was dropped.

The Austrian's new advances were looked upon somewhat askance by Spain, until his attitude towards religion was assured, and, to have a second string, the Spanish ambassador, Guzman, affected to favour Leicester's suit. Cecil and the conservative nobles were sincere now in their advocacy of the archduke, and between the two parties Elizabeth steered coquettishly and diplomatically, modestly urging the archduke's coming, and yet flirting desperately with Leicester. The breach between the English nobles was profound, as all but Leicester wished the question of the queen's marriage and succession to be settled; and Leicester's chances were stronger than ever when it became clear, late in 1565, that the archduke would not come to England without a firm pledge. The French played off Leicester, too, against the archduke; sometimes even again suggesting their own king when Leicester's star waxed pale.

Later, in 1566, the Lords and Commons urged the queen to marry, even Leicester joining in the remonstrance. But Elizabeth wished to play the game in her own way, and soundly scolded them. She did not mean to marry the archduke, or perhaps anyone, but whilst she kept him dangling, she knew she need not fear the Catholic combination. Soon all danger from that quarter disappeared for a time. Philip was in death struggle with his Protestant subjects in Holland; civil war was again raging in France, and Mary Stuart was a disgraced prisoner in the hands of her enemies. In the nine years that Elizabeth had carried on the marriage comedy she had kept the balance whilst England was growing stronger. Now, in 1568, she could afford to rest from her labours until danger from abroad again loomed.

III.--Catholics and Heretics

The peace of St. Germain in 1570 ended the long religious war in France, and the Guises and Catholics there, free from the strife, planned the rescue of the imprisoned Mary Stuart by force, and her marriage with the Duke of Anjou, the heir and brother of Charles IX. This was a danger both to Elizabeth and to the Huguenots, and was at once counteracted by their bringing forward the suggestion that the Queen of England might marry Anjou. He was, it is true, a fanatical Catholic, but the Huguenots thought that with England as a bait, and the powerful mind of Elizabeth to guide him, the youth might change his views. Leicester offered his help--for he knew the match was unlikely--and soon Catherine de Medici's agents were busy by Elizabeth's side. Elizabeth, as usual, was coy and maidenly. She was too old, she said, the thought of marriage was shocking to her; but, withal, the courtship went on actively. Anjou's charms and rumoured gallantries were the staple gossip at her court, and Elizabeth never tired of hearing praises of her young suitor.

But soon the Guises and the Catholic League took fright, and urged Anjou not to be drawn into a match with a heretic too old for him. Better, said they, win England by force and marry Mary. To England the marriage, or a similar one, seemed really necessary. The Catholics at home and abroad were busily plotting against Elizabeth. Philip and Alba were ready to connive at her murder; the Protestants in Holland and France were powerless, and this match with Anjou seemed the only way to meet the danger. Anjou, under Catholic influence, was scornful, whilst Catherine, anxious for the greatness of her favourite son, was in despair at his "assottedness."

Lord Buckhurst went, as ambassador to Paris, to forward the match in March 1571; but it soon became evident that Elizabeth could never concede the terms demanded by the French on religion. For many months the Huguenots, and Walsingham, as Elizabeth's ambassador, tried to reconcile the differences; and Catherine's agents in England laboured hard in the same cause. Elizabeth herself was ambiguous, though loving, and sometimes even Anjou was almost persuaded by his mother to accept the English crown matrimonial at the price demanded. For Elizabeth it was necessary to keep up the pretence at all costs, for the Spaniards were plotting her murder; and to split the Catholic party whilst secretly aiding the rebel Netherlanders seemed her only chance of safety. On one occasion, when Spain and France drew together, Elizabeth professed to be willing to marry Anjou on his own terms; but the prince grew ever more opposed to the match, and in January 1572, Catherine suddenly suggested that, as Anjou was so bigoted on religion, her youngest son, Alençon, might marry Elizabeth on any conditions she liked.

The lad was but seventeen--a swarthy, pock-marked youth--and Elizabeth was inclined at first to resent the way in which Anjou had flouted her. She was thirty-nine, and her vanity was wounded; but yet the friendship or neutrality of France was vital to her. "How tall is he?" she asked Cecil. "About as tall as I am," replied the elderly minister. "As tall as your grandson, you mean!" snapped the queen. But Walsingham, Smith, and the French envoys plied her busily with descriptions of Alençon's manly charms, and a treaty between France and England was settled by which the Huguenots for a time became paramount in France conjointly with the marriage of the Huguenot Henry of Navarre with Margaret, the king's sister. Feasts and cordiality were the rules on both sides of the Channel now, and the Huguenot leaders urged the Alençon match with Elizabeth with all their force. In reply to all these offers, Elizabeth replied that, though the discrepancy of age was a great drawback, yet the pock-marks on the suitor's face were a greater objection still; yet if he would let her see him, without a pledge, she might like him. She would never, she said, marry a man she had not seen.

But already Charles IX. and his mother were chafing under the Huguenot yoke and cooling towards England. They were determined not to be drawn by their new treaty with England into war with Spain; so, under the pretence of keeping up the negotiations for the Alençon match, they sent the youth La Mole to England in the autumn of 1572, really for the purpose of dissociating France from the Huguenot-English aid to the Protestant Netherlanders. La Mole was a gallant young lover, with whom Elizabeth was charmed, and when he played the vicarious wooer for Alençon, she could not make enough of him. But whilst he was philandering with her at Kenilworth, and she was losing patience at his political mission, there fell like a thunderbolt the awful news of the massacre of St. Bartholomew at Navarre's fatal wedding. At once the scene changed. La Mole and the French envoy hurried away amidst curses upon all false Frenchmen. Elizabeth, in a panic, smiled upon Spaniards again, and, for a time, the project of a French consort for her slept.

But not for long. Alençon had no part in the massacre, and was known to favour Huguenots. He wrote a fervent love-letter to Elizabeth, and proposed to escape to England; whilst his agent Maisonfleur joined with Mauvissière, the official French ambassador, in wooing Elizabeth anew for Alençon and for France. Gradually the parties drew together again, for Catherine was already alarmed at the effect of St. Bartholomew. All the Protestant world was arming, the English ports were full of privateers to attack Catholic shipping, and aid in plenty was being sent from England to the Huguenots of Rochelle and the rebel Dutchmen.

France could therefore not afford to quarrel with England, but Anjou and Charles IX. took care to hold Alençon tight, that he might not escape and strengthen the Protestant cause in union with Elizabeth, whilst they still kept up the appearance of marriage negotiations. Elizabeth was ever on the alert to serve her cause, and in March 1573, said she would go no further in the Alençon match unless the Protestants in Rochelle were allowed fair terms and the siege raised. Anjou, already tired of the war, consented, and soon afterwards Catherine asked whether Elizabeth would now proceed with the Alençon plan. The lad had grown much, she said, and his budding beard covered some of his facial imperfections. It was settled that the prince should make a flying visit to Dover, but soon Catherine began to make fresh conditions. It would be such a shame to them, she said, if her son went and returned unmarried.

IV.--The Lovelorn Alençon

In the meanwhile, Alençon's love-letters to his mature flame grew warmer; but much as Elizabeth liked such attentions, she dreaded to go too far. Charles IX. was sinking fast, and the next heir was Anjou. With Alençon for heir-presumptive of France, the position would be changed; and once more the queen began to get doubtful about those unfortunate pock-marks on her lover's face. Once Alençon planned with Henry of Navarre to escape from his mother's custody and make a dash for England on his own account, but Catherine held him firmly.

Both the Huguenots and the French king wished for the marriage, but each party frustrated the other because their objects were different. When the French ambassador, therefore, asked Elizabeth when Alençon might come to see her, she refused to name a time, because she knew secretly that a great Huguenot movement in France was pending, and she wished Alençon to be there as figurehead at the time--the very thing that the official French Government wished to avoid. The projected movement was betrayed and suppressed, and Alençon's life was for a time in danger; but when Henry III.

(Anjou) was seated on the throne, Alençon kept openly a rival court to that of his brother, and the Huguenots around the prince were at deadly feud with the minions of the king.

At last the crisis came. Alençon escaped from Paris in disguise, pursued by his mother, and, joining the Huguenots in arms, defied the king and the Guises. France was not big enough to hold both brothers in peace, and Catherine told Alençon that as Elizabeth seemed so ready to help him and his Huguenots, he ought to reopen the marriage negotiations. But Alençon was useless to England as a counterbalance to Spain unless France herself could be pledged as well, and Elizabeth considered it safest for the time, since that could not be done, to feign a new cordiality with Philip.

The Catholic party in France was again paramount, and by bribery and Catherine's diplomacy, Alençon and his friends were bought over. For the next three years the young prince held aloof from affairs, but in 1578 the hollow truce ended; he was suspected and placed under arrest, all his friends being cast into the Bastille. In February, 1578, Alençon broke his prison and fled, and all France was plunged into turmoil. Elizabeth was profoundly moved. The keynote of English policy was the exclusion of France from Flanders, and if Alençon was secretly supported in his action by his brother, then Elizabeth must oppose to the death any interference in Flanders.

And so began the long and clever juggle by which she used Alençon's ambition to wed her as a means to compass her ends without marrying him. Huguenots flocked to Alençon's standard, whilst he sent by every post love-lorn epistles to Elizabeth, praying her to aid him to free Flanders from the bloodthirsty Spaniards. On July 7, 1578, Alençon entered Flanders with his army, and Elizabeth, still full of distrust of Frenchmen, feigned to Spaniards her deep disapproval, whilst she took care that many English and Germans in her pay slipped into Flanders at the same time, to prevent any French national domination. Presently, persuaded that Alençon had no secret pact with his brother, Elizabeth took Alençon and the Flemish revolt into her own hands, and effusively welcomed Alençon's envoys who came to promote his love suit.

He chose for his emissary one Jehan Simier, an experienced gallant, who soon wooed Elizabeth to such good purpose that she fell violently in love with the messenger, as well as with his absent master. Protestant England took fright at the pending marriage of the queen with a papist of half her age. Simier, whom she called her "monkey," had bewitched her, said the courtiers, and remonstrances from all sides came to the queen.

V.--The Battle of Wits

Alençon's demands were high, but Elizabeth seems really for once to have lost her head, and but for the strong opposition of her Council, might have been drawn into the marriage. Simier, seeing the deadlock, decided to bring Alençon over at all risks. Leicester, deadly jealous, tried to assassinate Simier, who revenged himself by divulging to the queen Leicester's secret marriage. Elizabeth was beside herself with rage, and more in love than ever with Alençon and his envoy. At length, in August 1579, the young French prince, in disguise, suddenly appeared at Greenwich. The queen's vanity was flattered, and though the visit was supposed to be secret, she hardly left her young lover, whilst he, to judge by his letters, was as badly smitten as she. But though she promised him marriage, he had to return with little else, and as soon as he had gone she found many good reasons for delay and hesitation.

In October 1580, a new Catholic combination forced Elizabeth's hands, and she promised greater help to Alençon's project, whilst trying to draw France also into open war with Spain. The combat of wits was keen and cynical, each party trying to pledge the other and to keep free himself. A great French embassy came to England in April 1581, to negotiate an alliance and the queen's marriage with Alençon, who had now re-entered Flanders and was immersed in the struggle against the Spaniards. The discussions in England were becoming interminable, for the French ambassadors asked hard terms, when Alençon, in June 1581, losing patience, suddenly rushed over to England to plead his own cause independently of his brother's envoys, whom he distrusted with good reason. This suited Elizabeth, for it made Alençon more dependent upon her, and again she sent her lover back full of great promises to help him.

In August Alençon again entered Flanders, depending entirely upon Elizabeth for support, and thenceforward he looked alone to his marriage with her for his salvation. She was sparing, and the poor prince retired to France in September. In desperation he came to England again to press for money and marriage in November 1581; and for months the love-making was fast and furious. Frantic prayers, sighs, and tears on his part were answered by kisses and promises on hers, but she gave as little money as would serve to get rid of him. On February 1, 1582, Alençon sailed for Holland to Elizabeth's professed grief and real joy; and thenceforward the prince, first in Flanders as sovereign, and afterwards in France a fugitive, supplicated and threatened his betrothed for money, and ever more money. But Elizabeth had now taken the Netherlands revolt into her own hands, and thenceforward her French lover was useless to her there. So, though she still kept up the pretence of her willingness to marry him on impossible conditions, and drove the poor creature to love-lorn despair, Alençon had served his matrimonial purpose before he died, in 1584, and Elizabeth's courtships with a political object came to an end. She and England were strong enough now to face her possible foes without fear.

The Love Affairs of Mary Queen of Scots

Mary Queen of Scots was one of the most remarkable women who ever presided over the destinies of a nation. She was born at Linlithgow on December 8, 1542, a few days before the death of her father, James V., thus becoming a queen before she was a week old. Her complex personality and varied accomplishments have inspired many and various historians, but it has remained for Major Martin Hume to demonstrate the historical fatality of Mary's love affairs. In "The Love Affairs of Mary Queen of Scots," published in 1903, Major Hume gives a convincing and logical reason for Mary's political failure, inasmuch as it did not spring from her goodness or badness as a woman, but from a certain weakness of character. This epitome has been prepared by Major Hume himself.

I.--Betrothed in her Cradle

When in the great hall at Worms, on that ever-memorable April day in 1521, before the panic-stricken princes, Luther insolently flung at the emperor his defiance of the mediaeval church, the crash, though all unheard by the ears of men, shook to their base the crumbling foundations upon which, for hundreds of years, the institutions of Europe had rested. The sixteenth century thenceforward was a period of disintegration and reconstruction, in which fresh lines of cleavage between old political associates were opened, new affinities were formed, and the international balance re-adjusted.

In the long struggle of the house of Aragon, and its successor, Charles V., with France for the domination of Italy, the only effectual guarantee against England's actively aiding its traditional ally, the ruler of Spain and Flanders, against its traditional enemy, France, was for the latter country to keep a tight hold of its alliance with Scotland, by means of which English force might be diverted at any time. The existence of the Scottish "back door" to England, with the ever probable enemy behind it, had long been a check upon English power, and a humiliation to English kings in their efforts to hold the balance between the Continental rivals. But with the spread of Lutheranism in Germany and Henry VIII.'s defiance of the Papacy, the Catholic powers, drawn together in the face of common danger, found a fresh bond of union in their orthodoxy which partially superseded old rivalries.

In these circumstances the English policy, which had aimed at the control of Scottish foreign relations to the exclusion of French influence, became not only desirable as it always had been, but vitally necessary to preserve England's independence.

Henry VIII.'s policy towards Scotland had been that of *divide et impera*, and a series of royal minorities and the greed and poverty of the semi-independent Scottish nobles had aided him. The rout of the Scots at Solway Moss, and the pathetic passing of the gallant James V., leaving his new-born daughter, Mary, as queen (December 1542), seemed at length to place Scotland in England's power. The murder of Cardinal Beaton, the bribery of the Douglases, and the marriage of Lennox with Henry's sister were all subsequent moves in the same game. Mary was betrothed in her cradle to the heir of England, and France, whose sheet anchor for centuries had been the "auld alliance" with the Scots, appeared to be helpless against a coalition of England and the emperor.

Thenceforward, England's main object was to keep a tight grip upon Scotland by religion or otherwise, while at first France, and subsequently the Catholic league, strove ceaselessly, with the help of Mary Stuart, to free Scotland from English influence. The marriage juggle of Elizabeth was largely inspired by her Scottish aims, and if the fortuitous adjustment of her qualities kept England Protestant, and France wavering for all those critical years, if she secured the inactivity of Spain, the resistance of Protestant Holland, and the freedom of navigation by her skilful statecraft, her rival Mary Stuart was a hardly less powerful factor in the final triumph of England by reason of certain defects in her character, the consequences of which are dealt with in this book.

Mary possessed a finer and nobler nature than Elizabeth; she was a woman of higher courage and greater conviction, more generous, magnanimous, and confiding, and, apart from her incomparably greater beauty and fascination, she possessed mental endowments fully equal to those of the English queen. But, whilst caution and love of mastery in Elizabeth always saved her from her weakness at the critical moment, Mary Stuart possessed no such safeguards, and was periodically swept along helplessly by the irresistible rush of her amorous passion.

French intrigue and money, aided by the queen-regent of Scotland, Mary of Guise, succeeded, after Henry's death and Somerset's invasion of Scotland, in gaining firm hold upon Scotland, and Mary, as the betrothed wife of the dauphin Francis, was carried to France in 1548, at the age of six, to be reared by her cunning kinsmen of Lorraine, and made, as it was hoped, a future powerful instrument to aid Catholic French objects against

England, and the reformation in France and elsewhere. As she grew towards womanhood in the bravest and most amorous court in Europe, the queen-dauphiness became a paragon of beauty, charm, accomplishments, the theme of poets, the despair of lovers innumerable worshipping her from afar.

The boy Francis de Valois, to whom she was affianced, was a poor, bilious, degenerate weakling, stunted in figure, uncomely of face. He was shy and timid, shunning active exercises, and though at the time of his marriage (1558) he was too young to have been actively engaged in the vices of the outwardly devout court, he appears to have been fully alive to the desirability of his bride. Mary was precocious and ambitious; she was surrounded by profligates, male and female, and, though she can hardly have been in love with her young husband, she appears to have been fully reconciled to the union.

With unsurpassed magnificence the wedding of Mary and Francis took place in Paris, but it signified to the world much more than the wedding of a boy and girl. So far as men could see, it meant the triumph of the papal Guises in France, and a death-blow to Protestant hopes of ranging Scotland on the side of the reformation.

II.--Intrigue, Plot, and Intrigue

Francis died after sixteen months reign, and Mary Stuart and her Guisan uncles, hated jealously by the queen-mother, Catharine de Medici, and by the reforming Bourbons, fell, for a time, into the background. Mary can hardly have loved her puny boy husband, but she nursed him night and day in his long sickness and his death so affected her that "she would not receive any consolation, but, brooding over her disasters with constant tears and passionate, doleful lamentations, she universally inspired deep pity." She had, indeed, lost much besides her royal husband; and in a poem written by her afterwards, the waste of her youth in widowhood, the loss of her great position as Queen of France, and her powerlessness any longer to enforce her rule in Scotland by French power, are the main burden of her complaints against Providence, not pity for the husband she had lost.

The Guises were loath to surrender power without a struggle, and as soon as Francis died they sought to sell their niece in marriage again. Their first idea was for her to marry her child-brother-in-law, the new King Charles IX., but Catharine de Medici at once stopped that plan, though the boy himself was anxious for it and Mary was not averse. That failing, Cardinal Lorraine turned to the heir of Spain, Don Carlos, as a husband for her. This would have been a death-blow to Elizabeth, and Philip feigned to listen to it; but all the strength and cunning of Huguenots and Protestants, joined by those of Catharine and Elizabeth, were brought into play against this threatening move, and Mary went to Scotland with a sinking, sad, and angry heart in 1561, fearing her uncouth subjects, foreign to her now, vexed with the Protestant party for standing in the way of her ambitious marriage, and determined to oppose Elizabeth to the utmost in her designs against the independence of Scotland.

With these views, gay and winsome though she was, it was not long before Mary was at issue with her dour Protestant subjects and their spokesman, John Knox. It was hoped by her brother, James Stuart (Murray), and Secretary Lethington that a *modus vivendi* might be found by persuading Elizabeth to secure to Mary the English succession in case she herself died childless, on the undertaking of Mary that her marriage and policy should be dictated by England; but it was not Elizabeth's plan to pledge the future of England, and her nimble evasiveness drove the Scottish statesmen to despair.

Brawls and bitterness grew in Mary's court around the Catholicism of the queen, and English money and intrigue were freely lavished to set Scotland by the ears. Half the nobles were disaffected, and Murray and Lethington, having failed to secure Scottish interests by moderate counsels and the conciliation of Elizabeth, were forced to take a strong course. Of foreign suitors Mary had many, some promoted by the Protestants, some by the Pope and the Guises, while the Catholics of England were secretly intriguing to force Elizabeth's hand by arranging Mary's marriage with young Henry Stuart, Lord Darnley, eldest son of Margaret, Countess of Lennox, niece of Henry VIII., who lived at Elizabeth's court. Cecil's spies were everywhere, and the plot was soon known and stopped by Elizabeth, violently angry with her kinswoman for listening to such a scheme.

But Murray and Lethington, in desperation, were aiming at higher game even than this. They were Protestant, they had tried their best to win Elizabeth's recognition; but they were Scotsmen first, and if their country was to be independent it must have a great ally behind it. France was out of the question while the Guises were in the shade and Catharine was queen-mother. So the ministers of Mary turned their eyes to the Protestant heir of the Catholic king. Elizabeth soon heard of this, too, and suddenly pretended to be in favour of the Darnley match for Mary, while she developed the most cordial friendship for Mary herself; for the Guises had again become paramount in France, and Elizabeth could not afford to flout all the Catholic interests at once.

That danger soon passed, for the Huguenots flew to arms, and Guise was murdered, Mary losing thus her principal prop abroad. And Lethington now pushed vigorously what seemed to be Scotland's only chance of safety--the marriage of Mary with the semi-idiot heir of Spain.

The English Catholics were drawn into the plot. "Only let Mary marry the heir of Spain, and we will salute her as our leader," said they. But Elizabeth soon gained wind of it, as usual, and was ready with her antidote--a most extraordinary one--the proposal that Mary should wed her own lover, Lord Robert Dudley, with the assurance of the English succession after Elizabeth's death without issue. It was a mere feint, of course, but it divided Scotland, and unsettled Mary herself.

Meanwhile, Philip, with his leaden methods, was pondering and seeking fresh pledges and guarantees from the English Catholics. Before his temporising answer came Elizabeth had frightened Mary's advisers into doubt, while she was holding the English Catholics in check by dangling Darnley and Dudley before Mary's eyes, and swearing deadly vengeance if she married the Spaniard.

Elizabeth's first aim was to embroil Mary's prospects by discrediting her in the eyes of foreign powers. To this end was directed the offer alternately of Dudley and Darnley as a husband, and Elizabeth's pretence of shocked reprobation of Mary in connection with Chastelard's escapade. It must be confessed that Mary's imprudence aided Elizabeth's object, and the sour bigotry of Knox, which looked upon all gaiety as a sin, served the same purpose. All this drove the unhappy queen more and more into the arms of the Catholic party as her only means of defence.

III.--Prudence Overcome by Passion

The intrigue to wed Mary to the Spanish prince was met by Elizabeth cordially taking up Lady Lennox, and her son, Darnley, who by many was now regarded as the intended heir of England, and was held out to Mary as an ideal husband for her. So long as she had hopes of the Spanish prince she gave but evasive answers; but late in 1564 the cunning diplomacy of Catharine and the falseness of Cardinal Lorraine had diverted that danger; and Philip gave Mary to understand that the match with his son was impossible, Mary's great hope had been founded upon this marriage. Unless she could have a foreign Catholic husband strong enough to defy Elizabeth she knew that she must make terms with Elizabeth's enemies, the English Catholics, and thus bring pressure to bear upon her by internal dissensions.

It was a dangerous game to play, for it meant conspiracy; and so long as the Lennoxes and their effeminate, lanky son were basking in Elizabeth's favour, the English queen held her trump card. But Lady Lennox was intriguing and ambitious, the head of English Catholic disaffection, and could only be held to Elizabeth's side by delusive hopes of the English succession for her son. Lennox himself, with some misgiving, was allowed to go to Scotland to claim his forfeited estates, and there, to Elizabeth's anger, was received with marked respect, which made the English queen hold Darnley and his mother more firmly than ever, and again push forward Dudley as a suitor for Mary's hand. Anxious to get Darnley to Scotland, not necessarily to marry him, but as a useful instrument, Mary feigned willingness to accept Dudley; and, in face of this, Elizabeth was induced to allow young Darnley to go to Scotland for a short time, ostensibly on business of the family estates.

In February 1565, Darnley, aged nineteen, crossed the border, to the dismay of the English agents in Scotland. It was soon after Mary had received news that the Spanish match was at an end, and she was ready for a new plan to circumvent Elizabeth. Darnley as a husband would bring to her the support of English Catholics, and a new claim to the English crown. So when her eyes first lit upon the fair stripling at Wemyss Castle, she looked upon him with favour as "the properest tall man she ever saw." He was on his best behaviour, and danced delightfully with the queen. Up to this time Mary had played her game with self-command and policy, but now for the first time her heart ran away with her, and she took a false step.

To have married Darnley as part of a transaction with Elizabeth, and with the approval of her own Protestant subjects, would have been a master-stroke. But she fell in love with the "long lad," and could not wait for negotiation; so she at once sent off to pray King Philip to support her with money and men against England and the Protestants if she married Darnley and became the tool of Spain. Philip, nothing loth, consented, and welcomed the coming union as a Catholic alliance and a powerful weapon against Elizabeth. Mary thus made herself the head of a vast Catholic conspiracy looking to Spain for support, and Elizabeth was furious both with Mary and Darnley for having apparently beaten her at her own cunning game.

How Elizabeth sought a diversion, at first by new matrimonial schemes of her own, has been told elsewhere, but her more effectual weapon was to arouse the fears of Scottish Protestants, and breed dissension in Mary's realm. "The young fool," Darnley, insolent and proud of his new greatness, offended all the nobles, whilst Mary grew daily more infatuated with him. They were married in July 1565, and the great conspiracy against Elizabeth and Protestantism was complete. Already the Scottish Protestant lords were in a panic, and after an abortive rising, they fled before Mary's bold attack, taking refuge in England.

The queen herself led her forces, armed and mounted, with her stripling husband by her side; but she was followed close by the shaggy, stern, martial figure of James Hepburn, Earl of Bothwell, just returned from exile to serve her; and upon him she looked with kindling eyes as a stouter man than the fribble she had wed. Mary had now apparently triumphed by her Darnley marriage, but the avalanche was gathering to crush her. She looked mainly to Spain and the Pope for help, and had all Protestantism against her, led by Elizabeth, whose hate and fury knew no bounds. It was a duel now of life or death between two systems and two women, one with a heart and the other without; and, as usual, the heartless won.

English money and skill honeycombed Scottish loyalty. Darnley, vicious, vain, and passionate, was an easy prey to intrigue. The tools of England whispered in his ear that his wife was too intimate with the Italian secretary Rizzio, who had conducted the correspondence with the Catholic powers. Darnley, who had earned his wife's contempt already, was beside himself with jealousy, and himself led the Protestant conspirators and friends of England, who murdered Rizzio in the queen's presence at Holyrood (March 1566). From that hour Darnley's doom was sealed.

He had thought to be king indeed now, but Mary outwitted him; for she recalled her exiled lords, welcomed her brother Murray, and threw herself into the arms of Darnley's Protestant foes, the very men who had risen in arms against the marriage. As she fled by night with Darnley after Rizzio's murder, to betray him, she swore over Rizzio's new-made grave that a "fatter one" than he should lie there ere long. Whether she knew of the plot of his foes to murder her husband is not proved, but she almost certainly did so, and welcomed the deed when it was done. She made no pretence of love for him after Rizzio's death, and her husband repaid her coldness by sulky loutishness and bursts of drunken violence. Mary's conduct toward Bothwell, too, began to arouse scandal. By November 1566, matters had reached a crisis, and Mary, at Kelso, said that unless she was freed from Darnley she would put an end to herself. She spoke not to deaf ears. Morton, and the rest of Rizzio's slayers and bitter enemies, were pardoned, and the deadly bond was signed.

IV.--Dire Infatuation

On February 9, 1567, as the doomed consort lay sick and sorry outside Edinburgh at the lone house of Kirk o' Field, he was, done to death by Bothwell and the foes of the Lennoxes; and Mary Stuart's first true love affair was ended in tragedy. But already the second was in full blast. Bothwell had recently married; he was disliked by the Scottish nobles, and the queen's constant association with him had already brought discredit upon her. There had been a good political excuse for her union with Darnley, but Bothwell could bring no support to her cause; for his creed was doubtful, and he had no friends. Nothing, indeed, but the infatuation of an amorous woman for a brutally strong man could have so blinded her to her own great aims as to make her take Bothwell, the prime mover of Darnley's murder, for her husband.

As soon as the crime was known, all fingers were pointed to Bothwell and the queen as the murderers, and Protestants everywhere hastened to cast obloquy upon Mary for it. But for the nobles' jealousy of Bothwell, and the religious animus, probably Darnley's death would soon have been forgotten or condoned; but as it was, Scotland blazed out in denunciation of it, and though Bothwell was put upon a mock trial and acquitted, the hate against him grew, especially when he arranged to divorce his wife in April 1567, and, ostensibly by force, but clearly by Mary's connivance, abducted the queen and bore her off to his castle of Dunbar.

On her return to Edinburgh a few weeks later Mary publicly married Bothwell--she swore afterwards against her will, but, in any case, to the anger and disgust of her subjects. She found her new husband an arrogant tyrant rather than her slave, and he watched her closely. The dire infatuation of the lovelorn woman soon wore off, and again she sighed to be free; but it was too late, for the Catholic powers stood aloof from her now that she had married a divorced man, and all her nobles had abandoned her. So Mary clung to Bothwell still, for he was strong, and all Scotland cried shame upon her.

In June, Mary and her husband, fearing attack or treachery, fled from Edinburgh Castle, which at once opened its gates to Morton and the rebel lords. A parley was sent to Mary offering submission if she would leave Bothwell to his fate. She indignantly refused, for she feared the lords and hated Morton. Bothwell was strong, she thought, and he was the father of her unborn child; he might protect her. So by Bothwell's side she rode out at the head of the border clansmen, and met the rebel army at Carberry Hill, hard by Edinburgh.

It was agreed that the dispute should be decided by the single combat between Bothwell and Lindsay, but before the duel began Mary's bordermen became disordered, and then she knew that all was lost. Kirkaldy of Grange came from her opponents to parley with her and offer safety for her, but not for Bothwell. Whilst they were speaking, Bothwell attempted to murder Grange; and when Mary forbade such treachery, he lost his nerve and began to whimper. In a moment the scales fell from Mary's eyes. This man was but a lath painted like steel. His strength was but a lie, and he was unworthy of her. She turned from him in contempt, and surrendered to the lords; while Bothwell fled, and unhappy Mary saw him no more.

V.--Langside and After

Cursed by crowds, who reviled her as a murderess and adulteress, Mary was led, a captive, to her capital. By night, to save her from the fury of the mob, she was smuggled out of Edinburgh and lodged, a prisoner, in the island fortress of Lochleven. During her long incarceration there the story of her wrongs and sufferings stirred the Catholics at home and abroad in her favour, and her friends and foes were again sharply divided according to their religious creeds. The rulers of Scotland, too, headed by her brother Murray, were far from easy; for the Catholics were strong, and foreign crowned heads looked black at those who kept a sovereign in durance. So attempts were made to conciliate her by proposing marriage with some harmless Scottish noble, conjoined with her abdication. But her heart was high still, and she would bate no jot of her queenship; rather would she exercise her glamour upon her gaolers and escape to power and sovereignty again. Her fascination was irresistible, and Murray's half-brother, young George Douglas, a mere lad, fell a victim to her smiles. Once more Mary fell in love, and proposed to marry the youth who had endeavoured to aid her escape.

Murray was shocked, and had his brother expelled the castle; but in April 1568 the faithful George planned her evasion of the guard and joyfully welcomed her on the shore of the lake. To her standard flocked the Catholic lords, and, safe at Hamilton, Mary, again a queen, swore vengeance upon her foes. On her way with her army to Dumbarton she met Murray's force at Langside, near Glasgow. She had been strong at Carberry Hill with Bothwell at her side. Here she was weak, for no man of weight or character was with her, and as her men wavered she turned rein and fled.

For sixty miles on bad roads she struggled on, almost without sleep, and living on beggar's fare. With no adviser or woman near her, in her panic and despair she took the fatal resolve and crossed the Solway into Elizabeth's realm, trusting to the magnanimity of the woman whom she had tried to ruin and supplant. Again her heart had deceived her. Elizabeth had no pity for a vanquished foe, and for the rest of her miserable life, well nigh a score of years, Mary Stuart was a prisoner. But in all those years she never ceased to plot and plan for the overthrow of Elizabeth and her own elevation to the Catholic throne of all Britain.

Amidst her many weapons, that of marriage and her personal fascination were not forgotten. Twice, at least, she tried to make her love affairs serve her political ambition. Poor, feckless Norfolk was drawn by his vanity and ambition into her net. Love epistles, breathing eternal devotion, passed between them, but murder was behind it all--the murder of Elizabeth, and the subjection of England to Spain to work Mary's vengeance on her foes, and Norfolk lost his head deservedly.

Again she dreamed of marrying the Christian champion, Don Juan of Austria, and conquering and ruling over a Catholic England. But this plot, too, was discovered, and Don Juan, like all the rest of Mary's lovers, died miserably. Mary thenceforward was the centre of Spain's great conspiracy against England's queen, but she sought the end no more by love; for that had failed her every time she tried. She and her cause were beaten because her heart of fire was pitted against a heart of ice, and she lost all because she loved too much.

WASHINGTON IRVING

Life of Christopher Columbus

Washington Irving, American historian and essayist, was born on April 3, 1783, in New York, of a family which came originally from Scotland. He knew Europe well, and was equally at home in London, Paris, and Madrid; he held the offices, in 1829, of Secretary to the American Embassy in London, and, in 1842, of American Minister in Spain. He was deeply interested in Spanish history, and besides the "Life and Voyages of Christopher Columbus," he wrote "The Voyages of the Companions of Columbus," "The Conquest of Granada," "The Alhambra," and "Legends of the Conquest of Spain." He was an industrious man of letters, having an excellent style, wide knowledge, and pleasant humour. His chief work was the "Life of George Washington," of which we give an epitome elsewhere. Other writings include "A History of New York, by Diedrich Knickerbocker," the celebrated "Sketch Book," "Bracebridge Hall," "Tales of a Traveller," and a "Life of Goldsmith." Irving did not marry, and died on November 28, 1859, in his home at Sunnyside on the Hudson River, and is buried at Tarrytown. The "Life of Columbus" was published in 1828 and is now obtainable in a number of popular editions.

The Years of Waiting

Christopher Columbus was born in Genoa about 1435, of poor but reputable parents. He soon evinced a passion for geographical knowledge, and an irresistible inclination for the sea. We have but shadowy traces of his life till he took up his abode in Lisbon about 1470. His contemporaries describe him as tall and muscular; he was moderate and simple in diet and apparel, eloquent, engaging, and affable. At Lisbon he married a lady of rank, Doña Felipa. He supported his family by making maps and charts.

Portugal was prosecuting modern discovery with great enthusiasm, seeking a route to India by the coast of Africa; Columbus's genius conceived the bold idea of seeking India across the Atlantic. He set it down that the earth was a terraqueous globe, which might be travelled round. The circumference he divided into twenty-four hours. Of these he imagined that fifteen hours had been known to the ancients; the Portguese had advanced the western frontier one hour more by the discovery of the Azores and the Cape de Verde Islands; still, about eight hours remained to be explored. This space he imagined to be occupied in great measure by the eastern regions of Asia. A navigator, therefore, pursuing a direct course from east to west, must arrive at Asia or discover intervening land.

The work of Marco Polo is the key to many of the ideas of Columbus. The territories of the Great Khan were the object of his search in all his voyages. Much of the success of his enterprise rested on two happy errors; the imaginary extent of Asia to the east, and the supposed smallness of the earth. Without these errors he would hardly have ventured into the immeasurable waste of waters of the Atlantic.

A deep religious sentiment mingled with his thoughts; he looked upon himself as chosen from among men, and he read of his discovery as foretold in Holy Writ. Navigation was still too imperfect for such an undertaking; mariners rarely ventured far out of sight of land. But knowledge was advancing, and the astrolabe, which has been modified into the modern quadrant, was being applied to navigation. This was the one thing wanting to free the mariner from his long bondage to the land.

Columbus now laid his great project before the King of Portugal, but without success. Greatly disappointed, he sailed to Spain, hoping to receive the patronage of Ferdinand and Isabella. It was many months before he could even obtain a hearing; his means were exhausted, and he had to contend against ridicule and scorn, but the royal audience was at length obtained. Ferdinand assembled learned astronomers and cosmographers to hold a conference with Columbus. They assailed him with citations from the Bible. One objection advanced was, that should a ship ever succeed in reaching India, she could never come back, for the rotundity of the globe would present a mountain, up which it would be impossible to sail. Finally, after five years, the junta condemned the scheme as vain and impossible.

Columbus was on the point of leaving Spain, when the real grandeur of the subject broke at last on Isabella's mind, and she resolved to undertake the enterprise. Articles of agreement were drawn up and signed by Ferdinand and Isabella. Columbus and his heirs were to have the office of High Admiral in all the seas, lands, and continents he might discover, and he was to be viceroy over the said lands and continents. He was to have one-tenth of all profits, and contribute an eighth of the expense of expeditions. Columbus proposed that the profits from his discoveries should be consecrated to a crusade.

The First Voyage
(August, 1492--March, 1493)

Columbus set out joyfully for Palos, where the expedition was to be fitted out. He had spent eighteen years in hopeless solicitation, amidst poverty, neglect, and ridicule. When the nature of the expedition was heard, the boldest seamen shrank from such a chimerical cruise, but at last every difficulty was vanquished, and the vessels were ready for sea. Two of them were light, half-decked caravels; the Santa Maria, on which Columbus hoisted his flag, was completely decked. The whole number of persons was one hundred and twenty.

Columbus set sail on August 3, 1492, steering for the Canary Islands. From there they were wafted gently over a tranquil sea by the trade wind, and for many days did not change a sail. The poor mariners gradually became uneasy at the length of the voyage. The sight of small birds, too feeble to fly far, cheered their hearts for a time, but again their impatience rose to absolute mutiny. Then new hopes diverted them. There was an appearance of land, and the ships altered their course and stood all night to the south-west, but the morning light put an end to their hopes; the fancied land proved to be an evening cloud.

Again the seamen broke forth into loud clamours, and insisted on abandoning the voyage. Fortunately, the following day a branch with berries on it floated by; they picked up also a small board and a carved staff, and all murmuring was now at an end. Not an eye was closed that night. Columbus took his station on the top of the cabin. Suddenly, about ten o'clock, he beheld a light. At two in the morning the land was clearly seen, and they took in sail, waiting for the dawn. The great mystery of the ocean was revealed.

When the day dawned, Columbus landed, threw himself upon his knees, kissed the earth, and returned thanks to God. Rising, he drew his sword, displayed the royal standard, and took possession in the names of the Castillian sovereigns, naming the island San Salvador. It is one of the Bahama Islands, and still retains that name, though also called Cat Island.

The natives thought that the ships had descended from above on their ample wings, and that these marvellous beings were inhabitants of the skies. They appeared to be simple and artless people, and of gentle and friendly dispositions. As Columbus supposed that the island was at the extremity of India, he called them Indians. He understood them to say that a king of great wealth resided in the south. This, he concluded, could be no other than Cipango, or Japan. He now beheld a number of beautiful islands, green, level, and fertile; and supposed them to be the archipelago described by Marco Polo. He was enchanted by the lovely scenery, the singing of the birds, and the brilliantly colored fish, though disappointed in his hopes of finding gold or spice; but the natives continued to point to the south as the region of wealth, and spoke of an Island called Cuba.

He set sail in search of it, and was struck with its magnitude, the grandeur of its mountains, its fertile valleys, sweeping plains, stately forests, and noble rivers. He explored the coast to the east end of Cuba, supposing it the extreme point of Asia, and then descried the mountains of Hayti to the south-east. In coasting along this island, which he named Hispaniola, his ship was carried by a current on a sandbank and lost. The admiral and crew took refuge in one of the caravels. The natives, especially the cacique Guacanagari, offered him every assistance. The Spanish mariners regarded with a wistful eye the easy and idle existence of these Indians, who seemed to live in a golden world without toil, and they entreated permission to remain.

This suggested to Columbus the idea of forming the germ of a future colony. The cacique was overjoyed, and the natives helped to build a fort, thus assisting to place on their necks the yoke of slavery. The fortress and harbour were named La Navidad.

Columbus chose thirty-nine of those who volunteered to remain, charged them to be circumspect and friendly with the natives, and set sail for Spain. He encountered violent tempests, his small and crazy vessels were little fitted for the wild storms of the Atlantic; the oldest mariners had never known so tempestuous a winter, and their preservation seemed miraculous. They were forced to run into Tagus for shelter. The King of Portugal treated Columbus with the most honourable attentions. When the weather had moderated he put to sea again, and arrived safely at Palos on March 15, having taken not quite seven months and a half to accomplish this most momentous of all maritime enterprises.

Columbus landed and walked in procession to the church to return thanks to God. Bells were rung, the shops shut, and all business suspended. The sovereigns were dazzled by this easy acquisition of a new empire. They addressed Columbus as admiral and viceroy, and urged him to repair immediately to court to concert plans for a second expedition. His journey to Barcelona was like the progress of a sovereign, and his entrance into that city has been compared to a Roman triumph. On his approach the sovereigns rose and ordered him to seat himself in their presence. When Columbus had given an account of his voyage, the king and queen sank on their knees, and a *Te Deum* was chanted by the choir of the royal chapel. Such was the manner in which the brilliant court of Spain celebrated this sublime event.

The whole civilised world was filled with wonder and delight, but no one had an idea of the real importance of the discovery. The opinion of Columbus was universally adopted that Cuba was the end of Asia; the islands were named the West Indies, and the vast region was called the New World.

The Second Voyage
(September, 1493--June, 1496)

Extraordinary excitement prevailed about the second expedition, and many hidalgos of high rank pressed into it. They sailed from Cadiz in September 1493; all were full of animation, anticipating a triumphant return. When they reached La Navidad they found the fortress burnt. At length, from some natives they heard the story of the brawls of the colonists between themselves, and their surprise and destruction by unfriendly Indians. Columbus fixed upon a new site for his colony, which he named Isabella. Two small expeditions were sent inland to explore, and returned with enthusiastic accounts of the promise of the mountains, and Columbus sent to Spain a glowing report of the prospects of the colony.

Soon, however, maladies made their appearance, provisions began to fail, and murmuring prevailed among the colonists. In truth, the fate of many of the young cavaliers, who had come out deluded by romantic dreams, was lamentable in the extreme. Columbus arranged for the government of the island, and set sail to explore the southern coast of Cuba, supposing it to be the extreme end of Asia. He had to contend with almost incredible perils, and was obliged to return. Had he continued for two or three days longer he would have passed round the extremity of Cuba; his illusion would have been dispelled, and a different course given to his subsequent discoveries.

During his absence from Isabella the whole island had become a scene of violence and discord. Margarite, the general left in charge of the soldiers, and Friar Boyle, the apostolical vicar, formed a cabal of the discontented, took possession of certain ships, and set sail for Spain, to represent the disastrous state of the country, and to complain of the tyranny of Columbus. The soldiers indulged in all kinds of excesses, and the Indians were converted from gentle hosts into vindictive enemies.

Meanwhile, a commissioner was sent out to inquire into the distress of the colony and the conduct of Columbus. He collected all complaints, and returned to Spain, Columbus sailing at the same time. Never did a more miserable crew return from a land of promise.

The vessels anchored at Cadiz, and a feeble train of wretched men crawled forth, emaciated by diseases. Contrary to his anticipation, Columbus was received with distinguished favour. Thus encouraged, he proposed a further enterprise, and asked for eight ships, which were readily promised; but it was not until May 1498, that he again set sail.

The Third Voyage
(May, 1498--October, 1500)

From the Cape de Verde Islands, Columbus steered to the south-west, until he arrived at the fifth degree of north latitude. The air was like a furnace, the mariners lost all strength and spirit, and Columbus was induced to alter his course to the northwest. After sailing some distance they reached a genial region with a cooling breeze and serene and clear sky. They descried three mountains above the horizon; as they drew nearer, they proved to be united at the base, and Columbus, therefore, named this island La Trinidad. He coasted round Trinidad, and landed on the mainland, but mistook it for an island. He was astonished at the body of fresh water flowing into the Gulf of Paria, and came to the conclusion that it must be the outpouring of a great unknown continent stretching to the south, far beyond the equator. His supplies were now almost exhausted, and he determined to return to Hispaniola.

He found the island in a lamentable situation. A conspiracy had been formed against his viceroy, and the Indians, perceiving the dissensions among the Spaniards, threw off their allegiance. After long negotiations Columbus was forced to sign a humiliating capitulation with the rebels. Meanwhile, every vessel that returned from the New World came freighted with complaints against Columbus. The support of the colony was an incessant drain upon the mother country. Was this compatible, it was asked, with the pictures he had drawn of the wealth of the island?

Isabella herself at last began to entertain doubts about Columbus, and the sovereigns decided to send out Don Francisco del Bobadilla to investigate his conduct. This officer appears to have been needy, passionate, and ambitious. He acted as if he had been sent out to degrade the admiral, not to inquire into his conduct. He threw Columbus into irons, and seized his arms, gold, jewels, books, and most secret manuscripts. Columbus conducted himself with characteristic magnanimity, and bore all indignities in silence. Bobadilla collected testimony sufficient, as he thought, to ensure the condemnation of Columbus, and sent him a prisoner to Spain.

The arrival of Columbus at Cadiz, in chains, produced almost as great a sensation as his first triumphant return. A general burst of indignation arose. The sovereigns sent orders that he should be instantly set at liberty, and promised that Columbus should be reinstated in all his dignities. But Ferdinand repented having invested such great powers in any subject, and especially in a foreigner. Plausible reasons were given for delaying his reappointment, and meanwhile Don Nicholas de Ovando was sent out to supersede Bobadilla.

The Fourth Voyage
(May, 1502--November, 1504)

Columbus's thoughts were suddenly turned to a new enterprise. Vasco da Gama had recently reached India round the Cape of Good Hope, and immense wealth was poured by this route into Portugal. Columbus was persuaded that the currents of the Caribbean Sea must pass between Cuba and the land which he had discovered to the south, and that this route to India would be more easy and direct than that of Vasco da Gama. His plan was promptly adopted by the sovereigns, and he sailed in May 1502, on his last and most disastrous voyage. He steered to Hispaniola, but was not permitted to land, and then coasted along Honduras and down the Mosquito Coast to Costa Rica. Here he found gold among the natives, and heard rumours of Mexico. He continued beyond Cape Nombre de Dios in search for the imaginary strait, and then gave up all attempt to find it.

Possibly he knew that another voyager, coasting from the eastward, had reached this point. He turned westward to search for the gold-mines of Veragua, and attempted unsuccessfully to found a settlement there. As his vessels were no longer capable of standing the sea, he ran them aground on Jamaica, fastened them together, and put the wreck in a state of defence. He dispatched canoes to Hispaniola, asking Ovando to send a ship to relieve him, but many months of suffering and difficulty elapsed before it came.

Columbus returned to Spain in November 1504. Care and sorrow were destined to follow him; his finances were exhausted, and he was unable, from his infirmities, to go to court. The death of Isabella was a fatal blow to his fortunes. Many months were passed by him in painful and humiliating solicitation for the restitution of his high offices. At length he saw that further hope of redress from Ferdinand was vain. His illness increased, and he expired, with great resignation, on May 20, 1506.

Columbus was a man of great and inventive genius, and his ambition was noble and lofty. Instead of ravaging the newly-found countries, he sought to found regular and prosperous enterprises. He was naturally irritable and impetuous, but, though continually outraged in his dignity, and foiled in his plans by turbulent and worthless men, he restrained his valiant and indignant spirit, and brought himself to forbear and reason, and even to supplicate. His piety was genuine and fervent, and diffused a sober dignity over his whole deportment.

He died in ignorance of the real grandeur of his discovery. What visions of glory would have broken upon his mind could he have known that he had indeed discovered a new continent! And how would his spirit have been consoled, amidst the afflictions of age and the injustice of an ungrateful king, could he have anticipated the empires which would arise in the world he had discovered; and the nations, towns, and languages, which were to revere and bless his name to the latest posterity!

Life of George Washington

This great historical biography was Washington Irving's principal work. It was founded chiefly upon George Washington's correspondence, which is preserved in manuscript in the archives of the United States Government. Irving worked at it intermittently for many years; and it was published in successive sections during the last years of his life, 1855 to 1859, while he was living in retirement with his nieces at Sunnyside, on the Hudson River.

The De Wessyngton family, of the county of Durham, in feudal times, produced many men of mark in the field and in the cloister, and at a later period the Washingtons were intrepid supporters of the unfortunate House of Stuart. Compromised by this allegiance, two brothers, John and Andrew, uncles of Sir Henry Washington, the gallant defender of Worcester, emigrated to Virginia in 1657, and purchased lands in Westmoreland County, by the River Potomac. John, who became military leader of the Virginians against the Indians, was great-grandfather of the illustrious George Washington.

George, born February 22, 1732, in a homestead on Bridges Creek, was the eldest son of Mary Ball, second wife of Augustine Washington. Two half-brothers, Lawrence and Augustine, survived from the first marriage; and Mary had three other sons and two daughters. George received his first education in an "old field school-house," taught by the parish sexton; but the chief influences of his boyhood were the morality of his home and the military ardour of the colonists against the Spanish and the French. Lawrence, his eldest brother, had a captaincy in the colonial regiment which fought for England in the West Indies, in 1740, and the boy's whole mind was turned to war.

His father died when he was eleven years old, and George was sent to live with his married brother Augustine. Here he attended school, was eager in the acquirement of knowledge, and became expert in all athletic exercises. He very nearly entered on a naval career, but at his mother's earnest entreaty renounced the project, and returning to school, studied land-surveying.

Lawrence, his brother, having married into the Fairfax family, George came under the notice of Lord Fairfax, owner of immense tracts of country, who was so pleased with the lad's character and accomplishments that he entrusted him with the task of surveying his possessions. At the age of sixteen George Washington set out into the wilderness, and acquitted himself so well that he was appointed public surveyor. He thus gained an intimate knowledge, and of the ways of the Indians.

The English and French governments were at this time making conflicting claims to the Ohio valley, and their agents were treating with the various Indian tribes. At length the French prepared to enforce their claim by arms, and Washington received, in 1751, a commission as adjutant-general over a military district of Virginia. In October, 1753, he was sent by Governor Dinwiddie on a mission to the French commander, from which he returned in the following January; and his conduct on this occasion, when he had to traverse great distances of unknown forest at midwinter, and to cope with the craft of white men and savages alike, marked him out as a youth fitted for the most important civil and military trusts.

Conflicts with the French

Washington was for the first time under fire in April, 1754, when he had been sent, as second in command of the colonial forces, to take charge of a fort on the Ohio. He fell in with a French party of spies, whom his small force, with Indian assistance, put to flight. His fort, named Fort Necessity, was defended by three hundred men, but was attacked in July by a greatly superior force of French and Indians, and Washington had to capitulate, marching out with the honours of war.

When it was determined, the same autumn, by the Governor and the British Secretary of State, that the colonial troops should be reduced to independent companies, so that there should no longer be colonial officers above the rank of captain, Washington, in accordance with the dawning republicism of America, resigned his commission, and settling at Mount Vernon, prepared to devote himself to agriculture. But in 1755, General Braddock was sent out to undertake energetic operations against the French, and Washington accepted the General's offer of a position on his staff.

It was now that the eminent Benjamin Franklin did such great service to the British arms by organizing transport, and listened with astonishment to Braddock's anticipations of easy victory. The young aide-de-camp also warned the English soldier in vain. On July 9 Braddock's force was utterly routed by the French and Indians, and the general himself was slain. This reverse did away with all belief, throughout the colonies, in the power of British arms, and prepared the way for the independence that was to follow.

On August 14 George Washington was appointed to the supreme command of the Virginian forces, with his headquarters at Winchester, and was occupied in the defence of a wide frontier with an insufficient force, until the expedition against Fort Duquesne in 1758, when he planted the British flag on its smoking ruins, and put an end to the French domination of the Ohio.

His marriage to Mrs. Martha Custis, a young and wealthy widow, was celebrated on January 6, 1759; he took his seat in the House of Burgesses at Williamsburg, and established himself at Mount Vernon to develop his estates. A large Virginia estate, in those days, was a little empire.

The Dawn of Independence

The definitive treaty of peace between France and England was signed at Fontainebleau in 1763; but the tranquility of the colonies was again broken by an Indian insurrection, known as Pontiac's war. Washington had no part in its suppression, but he was soon to be called again to the defence of his country.

He was in his place in the House of Burgesses on May 29, 1765, when the claims of Britain to tax the colony were first repudiated, and it was declared that the General Assembly of Virginia had the exclusive right to tax the inhabitants, and that whoever maintained the contrary should be deemed an enemy to the colony. These resolutions were the signal for general applause throughout the continent.

The repeal, in 1766, of the objectionable Stamp Act only postponed the crisis, which became acute when the port of Boston was closed by Parliament, because of the resistance of that city to the importation of East Indian tea. A General Congress of deputies from the several colonies was convened for September 5, 1773, at Philadelphia, in which Washington took part, and a Federal Union of the colonies was then established. The English commander, General Gage, struck the first blow against popular liberties, in the engagement at Lexington, April 18, 1775, and on June 15 Washington was unanimously elected commander-in-chief of the American forces.

Two days later was fought, outside Boston, the heroic battle of Bunker's Hill, and on the 21st Washington set out from Philadelphia to the seat of war, where he laid a strict siege about Boston, with a view to forcing the British to come out. An English ship having bombarded the American port of Falmouth, an act was passed by the General Court of Massachusetts, encouraging the fitting out of armed vessels to defend the coast of America, and granting letters of marque and reprisal. In October a conference of delegates was held, under Washington's presidency, of which Benjamin Franklin was a member, with regard to a new organisation of the army; and a new force of twenty-two thousand was formed, every soldier being enlisted for one year only.

Montreal had been captured by an American expedition, and Washington was now looking forward to equal success in an expedition against Quebec. He was further encouraged by the capture, by one of his cruisers, of a brigantine laden with munitions of war, including a huge brass mortar. His wife joined the camp before Boston, and the eventful year was closed with festivities.

But the gallant attempt on Quebec, in which Montgomery fell, was frustrated, and the siege of Boston dragged on uneventfully, until the Americans, in March, seized Dorchester Heights, and made the town no longer tenable. On the 17th there were in Boston Harbor seventy-eight ships and transports casting loose for sea, and twelve thousand soldiers, sailors and refugees, hurrying to embark. The flag of thirteen stripes, the standard of the Union, floated above the Boston forts, after ten tedious months of siege.

The eminent services of Washington throughout this arduous period, his admirable management by which, in the course of a few months, an undisciplined band of husbandmen became soldiers, and were able to expel a brave army of veterans, commanded by the most experienced generals, won the enthusiastic applause of the nation. A unanimous vote of thanks was passed to him in Congress.

Declaration of Independence

Despatches from Canada continued to be disastrous, and the evacuation of that country was determined on in June, 1776. The great aim of the British was now to get possession of New York and the Hudson, and to make them the basis of military operations. While danger was gathering round New York, and its inhabitants were in mute suspense and fearful anticipations, the General Congress at Philadelphia was discussing with closed doors the greatest question ever debated in America. A resolution was passed unanimously, on July 2, "that these United Colonies are, of right ought to be, free and independent States."

The fourth of July is the day of national rejoicing, for on that day the "Declaration of Independence," that solemn and sublime document, was adopted. Tradition gives a dramatic effect to its announcement. It was known to be under discussion, but the closed doors of Congress excluded the populace. They awaited, in throngs, an appointed signal. In the steeple of the state-house was a bell, bearing the portentous text from Scripture, "Proclaim liberty throughout all the land, unto all the inhabitants thereof." A joyous peal from that bell gave notice that the bill had been passed. It was the knell of British domination.

Washington hailed the Declaration with joy. It was but a formal recognition of a state of things which had long existed, but it put an end to all those temporizing hopes of reconciliation which had clogged the military action of the country. On July 9, he caused it to be read at the head of each brigade of the army. "The general hopes," said he, "that this important event will serve as a fresh incentive to every officer and soldier, to act with fidelity and courage, as knowing that now the peace and safety of his country depend, under God, solely on the success of our arms; and that he is now in the service of a state possessed of sufficient power to reward his merit, and advance him to the highest honours of a free country." and again: "The general hopes and trusts that every officer and man will endeavour so to live and act as becomes a Christian soldier, defending the dearest rights and liberties of his country."

The Winning of Independence

But the exultation of the patriots of New York was soon overclouded. British warships, under Admiral Lord Howe, were in the harbour on July 12, and affairs now approached a crisis. Lord Howe came "as a mediator, not as a destroyer," and had prepared a declaration inviting communities as well as individuals to merit and receive pardon by a prompt return to their duty; it was a matter of sore regret to him that his call to loyalty had been forestalled by the Declaration of Independence.

The British force in the neighbourhood of New York, under General Howe, brother of the Admiral, was about thirty thousand men; the Americans were only about twenty thousand, for the most part raw and undisciplined, and the sectional jealousies prevalent among them were more and more a subject of uneasiness to Washington. On August 27 the American force was defeated with great loss in the battle of Long Island, and was withdrawn from the island by a masterly night retreat; this led to the loss of New York and the Hudson River to the British. Reverse followed reverse; Washington was driven by the British arms from one point after another; many of the chief American cities were taken; and on September 26, 1777, General Sir William Howe marched into Philadelphia and thus occupied the capital of the confederacy. But Washington still maintained his characteristic equanimity. "I hope," he said, "that a little time will put our affairs in a more flourishing condition."

This anticipation was soon to be fulfilled. General Burgoyne had been advancing from the north with a large force of British and Hessian troops, but was compelled by General Gates, with a superior American force, to capitulate on October 17,1777. By this capitulation the Americans gained a fine train of artillery, seven thousand stand of arms, and a great quantity of clothing, tents, and military stores of all kinds; and the surrender of Burgoyne struck dismay into the British army on the Hudson River.

But the struggle for independence was still to continue for four years of incessant military operations, and it was not until the surrender of Yorktown, on October 19, 1781, by Lord Cornwallis, that Britain gave up hope of reducing her rebel colonies. When the redoubts of Yorktown were taken, Washington exclaimed, "The work is done, and well done!"

A general treaty of peace was signed in Paris on January 20, 1783; and in March of that year Sir Guy Carleton informed Washington that he was ordered to proclaim a cessation of hostilities by sea and land. On April 19, the anniversary of the battle of Lexington, thus completing the eighth year of the war, Washington issued a general order to the army in these terms--"The generous task for which we first flew to arms being accomplished, the liberties of our country being fully acknowledged and firmly secured, and the characters of those who have persevered through every extremity of hardship, suffering, and danger, being immortalised by the illustrious appellation of 'the patriot army,' nothing now remains but for the actors of this mighty scene to preserve a perfect, unvarying consistency of character through the very last act, to close the drama with applause, and to retire from the military theatre with the same approbation of angels and men which has crowned all their former virtuous actions."

Writing, on June 8, to the Governors of the several States, he said-- "The great object for which I had the honour to hold an appointment in the service of my country being accomplished, I am now preparing to return to that domestic retirement which, it is well known, I left with the greatest reluctance; a retirement for which I have never ceased to sigh, through a long and painful absence, and in which, remote from the noise and trouble of the world, I meditate to pass the remainder of life in a state of undisturbed repose."

The Years of Peace

Washington returned to Mount Vernon on Christmas Eve, 1783, and busied himself with the care of his estates. He had never ceased to be the agriculturist; through all his campaigns he had kept himself informed of the course of rural affairs at Mount Vernon. By means of maps on which every field was laid down and numbered, he was enabled to give directions for their several cultivation, and to receive accounts of their several crops. No hurry of affairs prevented a correspondence with his agent, and he exacted weekly reports. He now read much on agriculture and gardening, and corresponded with the celebrated Arthur Young, from whom he obtained seeds of all kinds, improved ploughs, plans for laying out farmyards, and advice on various parts of rural economy.

His active day at Mount Vernon began some time before dawn. Much of his correspondence was despatched before breakfast, which took place at half-past seven. After breakfast he mounted his horse and rode off to various parts of his estate; dined at half-past two; if there was no company he would write until dark; and in the evening he read, or amused himself with a game of whist.

The adoption of the Federal Constitution opened another epoch in the life of Washington. Before the official forms of an election could be carried into operation, a unanimous sentiment throughout the Union pronounced him the nation's choice to fill the presidential chair. The election took place, and Washington was chosen President for a term of four years from March 4, 1788. An entry in his diary, on March 16, says--"I bade adieu to Mount Vernon, to private life, and to domestic felicity; and with a mind oppressed with more anxious and painful sensations than I have words to express, set out for New York with the best disposition to render service to my country in obedience to its call, but with less hope of answering its expectations."

The weight and influence of his name and character were deemed all essential to complete his work; to set the new government in motion, and conduct it through its first perils and trials. He undertook the task, firm in the resolve in all things to act as his conscience told him was "right as it respected his God, his country, and himself." For he knew no divided fidelity, no separate obligation; his most sacred duty to himself was his highest duty to his country and his God.

His death took place on December 14, 1799, at Mount Vernon.

The character of Washington may want some of the poetical elements which dazzle and delight the multitude, but it possessed fewer inequalities and a rarer union of virtues than perhaps ever fell to the lot of one man. Prudence, firmness, sagacity, moderation, an overruling judgement, an immovable justice, courage that never faltered, patience that never wearied, truth that disdained all artifice, magnanimity without alloy.

JOSEPHUS

Autobiography

Flavius Josephus was born in Jerusalem in 37 A.D. His father, Matthias, was a priest, and his mother belonged to the Asmonean princely family. So distinguished was he as a student that, at the age of twenty-six, he was chosen delegate to Nero. When the critical juncture arose for his nation, through the rebellion excited by the cruelties of Gessius Florus, the Roman procurator, Josephus was appointed governor of Galilee The insurrection proved fatal, for Vespasian by his invasion rendered resistance hopeless. Subsequently he lived in Rome, and the date of his death is unknown. The works of this writer are monumental. He wrote his vivid "Wars of the Jews" in both Hebrew and Greek. His "Antiquities of the Jews" traces the whole history of the race down to the outbreak of the great war. Scaliger, one of the acutest of mediaeval critics, declares that in his writings on the affairs of the Jews, and even on those of foreign nations, Josephus deserves more credit than all the Greek and Roman writers put together. His fidelity and veracity are as universally admitted as his direct and lucid style is generally admired. His account of his own life and career is a masterpiece in this category of literature, for it is written with blended modesty and naïveté. In many passages of this "Autobiography" he does not hesitate to assume great credit for his own courage, probity, and skill, but in each case the justification is manifest, for he constantly refers to the tortuous and treacherous machinations of his virulent enemies. The "Autobiography" is from beginning to end a thrilling and wonderful romance of real life, for the hairbreadth escapes of this extraordinary man are among the most singular recitals in the whole world of adventure. The whole story is unique, as was the noble individuality of the man himself.

I.--Priest of the Blood-Royal

The family from which I, Flavius Josephus, am derived is not an ignoble one, but hath descended all along from the priests. I am not only sprung from a sacerdotal family in general, but from the first of the twenty-four courses of the Jewish priests, and I am of the chief family of that course also. With us, to be of the sacerdotal dignity is an indication of the splendour of a family. But, further, by my mother I am of the royal blood; for the children of Asmonaeus, from whom that family was derived, had both the office of the high-priesthood and the dignity of a king for a long time together.

My father Matthias, to whom I was born in the first year of the reign of Gaius Caesar, was not only eminent in Jerusalem, our greatest city, on account of his nobility, but had a higher commendation on account of his righteousness. I was brought up with my brother Matthias. As a child I gained a great reputation through my love for learning, and, when I was about fourteen years of age, was frequently asked by the high-priests and chief men of the city my opinion about the accurate understanding of points of the law.

In my twenty-sixth year I took a voyage to Rome. My object was to plead before Caesar the cause of certain excellent priests whom Felix, then procurator of Judaea, had put in bonds on a trivial pretext. I was desirous to procure deliverance for them, not only because they were of my own friends, but because I heard that they sustained their piety towards God under their afflictions, and that they simply subsisted on figs and nuts.

Our voyage was an adventurous one, for the ship was wrecked in the Adriatic Sea, and we that were in it, being about six hundred in number, swam all night for our lives. I and about eighty others were saved by a ship of Cyrene. When I had thus escaped, and was come to Puteoli, I became acquainted with an actor named Alityrus, much beloved by Nero, but a Jew by birth. Through his interest I became known to Poppaea, Caesar's wife, and having, through her, procured the liberty of the priests, besides receiving from her many presents, I returned to Jerusalem.

Now I perceived that many innovations were begun, and that many were cherishing hopes of a revolt from the Romans.

II.--The Prelude to the Great Crisis

So I retired to the inner court of the Temple. Yet I went out of the Temple again, after Menahem and the chief members of the band of robbers were put to death, and abode among the high-priests and the chief of the Pharisees. But no small fear seized upon us when we saw the people in arms, while we were not able to restrain the seditious. We hoped that Gessius Floras would speedily arrive with great forces. But on his arrival he was defeated with great loss.

The disgrace that fell upon him became the calamity of our whole nation, for it elevated the hopes of conquering the Romans on the part of those who desired war. But another cause of the revolt arose in Syria from the cruel treatment of the Jews in many cities, where they showed not the least disposition towards rebellion. About 13,000 were treacherously slain in Scythopolis, and the Jews in Damascus underwent many miseries; but of these events accounts are given in the books of the Jewish War.

I was now sent, together with two other priests, Joazar and Judas, by the principal men of Jerusalem, to Galilee, to persuade the ill men there to lay down their arms, and to teach them that it were better for us all to wait to see what the Romans would do. I came into Galilee, and found the people of Sepphoris in no small agony about their country, by reason that the Galileans had resolved to plunder it, because of their friendship with the Romans, and because they had made a league with Cestius Gallus, the president of Syria. But I quieted their fears. Yet I found the people of Tiberias ready to take arms, for there were three factions in that city.

The first faction, with Julius Capellus for the head, was composed of men of worth and gravity, and advised the city to continue in allegiance to the Romans; the second faction, consisting of the most ignoble persons, was determined for war. But as for Justus, the head of the third faction, though he pretended to be doubtful about war, yet he was really desirous of innovation, as supposing that he should gain power by the change of affairs.

By his harangues Justus inflamed the minds of many of the people, persuading them to take arms, and then he went out and set fire to the villages that belonged to Gadara and Hippos, on the border of Tiberias, and of the region of Scythopolis.

Gamala persevered in its allegiance to the Romans, under the persuasion of Philip, the son of Jacimus, who was governor of the city under King Agrippa. He reminded the people of the benefits the king had bestowed on them, and pointed out how powerful the Romans were, and thus he restrained the zeal of the citizens.

Now, as soon as I was come into Galilee, and had ascertained the state of affairs, I wrote to the Sanhedrin at Jerusalem asking for their direction. They replied that I should remain there; and that, if my fellow-delegates were willing, I should join with them in the care of Galilee. But these my colleagues, having gotten great riches from those tithes which as priests were their dues, and were given to them, determined to return to their own country. Yet when I desired them to stay to settle public affairs, they complied, and we removed from Sepphoris to Bethmanus, a village four furlongs from Tiberias, whence I sent messengers to the senate of that city, asking that the principal men should come to me.

III.--Governor of Galilee

When the chief men of Tiberias were come, I told them I was sent as a legate from the people at Jerusalem, in order to persuade them to destroy that house which Herod the tetrarch had built in Tiberias, and which, contrary to our laws, contained the figures of living creatures. I desired that they would give us leave to do so; but for a good while they were unwilling, only being overcome by long persuasion. Then Jesus, son of Sapphias, one of the leaders of sedition, anticipated us and set the palace on fire, thinking that as some of the roofs were covered with gold, he should gain much money thereby. These incendiaries also plundered much furniture; then they slew all the Greeks who dwelt in Tiberias, and as many others as were their enemies.

When I understood this state of things, I was greatly provoked, and went down to Tiberias and took care of all the royal furniture that could be recovered from such as had plundered it. Next I committed it to ten of the chief senators. From thence I and my fellow-delegates went to Gischala to John, to learn his designs, and soon discovered that he was for innovations, for he wished me to give him authority to carry off the corn that belonged to Caesar, and to lay it in the villages of Upper Galilee. Though I refused, he corrupted my colleagues with money, and so I, being out-voted, held my tongue. By various other cunning contrivances which I could not prevent, John gained vast sums of money. But when I had dismissed my fellow-delegates I took care to have arms provided and the cities fortified. My first care was to keep Galilee in peace, so I made friends of seventy of the principal men, and took them on my journeys as companions, and set them to judge causes.

I was now about thirty years of age, in which time of life it is difficult to escape from the calumnies of the envious. Yet did I preserve every woman free from injury; I despised and refused presents; nor would I take the tithes due to me as a priest. When I twice took Sepphoris by force, and Tiberias four times, and Gadara once, and when I had subdued and captured John, who had laid treacherous snares for me, I did not punish with death either him or others. And on this account I suppose it was that God, Who is never unacquainted with those that do as they ought to do, delivered me still out of the hands of my enemies, and afterwards preserved me when I fell into many perils.

At this time, when my abode was at Cana, a village of Galilee, John came to Tiberias and stirred a revolt against me, so that my life was in danger. I escaped only by fleeing down the lake in a ship to Taricheae, whence I proceeded to Sepphoris. John returned to Gischala, where he continued to cultivate bitter hatred against me. Through the machinations of himself and Simon, a chief man in Gadara, all Galilee was filled with rumours that their country was about to be betrayed by me to the Romans.

Hereby I again incurred extreme peril, but I took a bold course. Dressed in a black garment, with my sword hung at my neck, I went to face, in the hippodrome, a multitude of the citizens of Taricheae, and addressed them in such terms that, though some wished to kill me, these were overcome by the rest.

Although the multitude returned to their homes, yet the robbers and other authors of the tumult, afraid lest I might punish them, took six hundred armed men and came to burn the house where I abode. Thinking it ignoble to run away, I resolved to expose myself to danger; so I shut myself up in an upper room, and asked that one of them should be sent up to me, by whom I would send out to them money from the spoils I had taken.

When they had sent in one of their boldest, I had him whipped severely, and commanded one of his hands to be cut off and hung about his neck. In this case he was put out, and those who had sent him, affrighted at the supposition that I had more armed men about me than they had, immediately fled.

I dealt in like manner with Clitus, a young man of Tiberias, who was the author of a fresh sedition in that city. Since I thought it not agreeable to piety to put one of my own people to death, I called to Clitus himself, and said to him, "Since thou deservest to lose both thy hands for thine ingratitude to me, be thou thine own executioner, lest by refusal to do so thou undergo a worse punishment."

When he earnestly begged me to spare one of his hands, it was with difficulty that I granted it. So, in order to prevent the loss of both his hands, he willingly took his sword and cut off his own left hand; and this put an end to the sedition.

IV.--The Failure of His Foes

The people of Gamala wrote to me, asking that I would send them an armed force, and also workmen to raise up the walls of their city, and I acceded to each of their requests. I also built walls about many villages and cities in Upper and Lower Galilee, besides laying up in them much corn. But the hatred of John of Gischala grew more violent by reason of my prosperity. He sent his brother Simon to Jerusalem with a hundred armed men to induce the Sanhedrin to deprive me of my commission; but this was not an easy thing to do, for Ananus, one of the chief priests, demonstrated that many of the people bore witness that I had acted like an excellent general.

Yet Ananus and some of his friends, corrupted by bribes, secretly agreed to expel me out of Galilee, without making the rest of the citizens acquainted with what they were doing. Accordingly they sent four men of distinction down to Galilee to seek to supersede me in ruling the province.

These were to ask the people of Galilee what was their reason of their love to me. If the people alleged that it was because I was born at Jerusalem, that I was versed in the law, and that I was a priest, then they were to reply that they also were natives of Jerusalem, that they understood the law, and that two of them were priests. To Jonathan and his companion were given 40,000 drachmae out of the public money, and a large band of men was equipped with arms and money to accompany them.

But wonderful was what I saw in a dream that very night. It seemed to me that a certain person stood by me, and said, "O Josephus, put away all fear, for what now afflicts thee will render thee most happy, and thou shalt overcome all difficulties! Be not cast down, but remember that thou art to fight the Romans."

When I had seen this vision I arose, intending to go down to the plain to meet a great multitude who, I knew, would be assembled, for my friends, on my refusal had dispatched messengers all around to inform the people of Galilee of my purpose to depart. And when the great assembly of men, with their wives and children, saw me, they fell on their faces weeping, and besought me not to leave them to be exposed to their enemies.

When I heard this, and saw what sorrow affected the people, I was moved with compassion, and promised that I would stay with them, thinking it became me to undergo manifold hazards for the sake of so great a multitude. So I ordered that five thousand of them should come to me armed, and that the rest should depart to their own homes.

It was not long before Vespasian landed at Tyre, and King Agrippa with him. How he then came into Galilee, and how he fought his first battle with me near Taricheae, and how, after the capture of Jotapata, I was taken alive and bound, and how I was afterward loosed, with all that was done by me in the Jewish war, and during the siege of Jerusalem, I have accurately related in the books concerning the "Wars of the Jews."

When the siege of Jotapata was over, and I was among the Romans, I was kept with much care, by means of the great respect that Vespasian showed me. After being freed from my bonds I went to Alexandria, where I married. From thence I was sent, together with Titus, to the siege of Jerusalem, and was frequently in danger of being put to death. For the Jews desired to get me into their power to have me punished, and the Romans, whenever they were beaten, thought it was through my treachery. But Titus Caesar was well acquainted with the uncertain fortune of war, and returned no answer to the soldiers' solicitation against me.

When Titus was going away to Rome he made choice of me to sail along with him, and paid me great respect And when we were come to Rome I had great care taken of me by Vespasian, for he gave me an apartment in his own house.

When Vespasian was dead, Titus kept up the same kindness which his father had shown me, and Domitian, who succeeded, still augmented his respects to me; nay, Domitia, the wife of Caesar, continued to show me many kindnesses.

JOHN GIBSON LOCKHART

Life of Sir Walter Scott

John Gibson Lockhart was born in Scotland in 1794. He received part of his education at Glasgow, part at Oxford, and in 1816 he became an advocate at the Scotch bar. As one of the chief supporters of Blackwood's Magazine, he began to exhibit that sharp, bitter wit which was his most salient characteristic. In 1820 he married the eldest daughter of Sir Walter Scott, and for this reason, perhaps no one has been better qualified to write the biography of the great novelist. Lockhart's "Life of Sir Walter Scott" is a biography in the best sense of the word--one which has been ranked even with Boswell's "Johnson." It reveals to the reader the inmost personality of the man himself, and no life from first to last could better afford such complete revelation. Moreover, the "Life" was a labour of love, Lockhart himself receiving not a fraction of its very considerable proceeds, but resigning them absolutely to Scott's creditors. Published in seven volumes in 1838, in every respect it is the greatest of all Lockhart's books. Lockhart died in 1854.

Early Years

Sir Walter Scott was distantly connected with ancient families both on his father's and his mother's side. His father, Walter Scott, a Writer to the Signet in Edinburgh, was a handsome, hospitable, shrewd and religious man, who married, in 1758, Anne, eldest daughter of Dr. John Rutherford, professor of medicine in Edinburgh University. The Scotts had twelve children, of whom only five survived early youth.

The subject of this biography was born on August 15, 1771, in a house at the head of the College Wynd. He was a healthy child, but when eighteen months old was affected with a fever which left a permanent lameness in the right leg. With a view to curing this weakness he was sent to live with his paternal grandfather, at the farm house of Sandy-Knowe near Dryburgh Abbey, in the extreme south of Berwickshire.

Here, in the country air, he became a sturdy boy, and his mind was stored with the old Broder tales and songs. In his fourth year he was taken to London by sea, and thence to Bath, where he remained about a year for the sake of the waters, became acquainted with the venerable John Home, author of "Douglas," and was introduced by his uncle, Capt. Robert Scott, to the delights of the theatre and "As You Like It."

From his eighth year Scott lived at his father's house in George Square, Edinburgh. His lameness and solitary habits had made him a good reader, and he used to read aloud to his mother, Pope's translation of Homer and Allan Ramsay's "Evergreen;" his mother had the happiest of tempers and a good love of poetry. In the same year he was sent to the High School, Edinburgh, under the celebrated Dr. Adam, who made him sensible of the beauties of the Latin poets.

After his school years, the lad, who had become delicate from rapid growth, spent half a year with an aunt, Miss Janet Scott, at Kelso. He had now awaked to the poetry of Shakespeare and of Spenser, and had acquired an ample and indiscriminate appetite for reading of all kinds. To this time at Kelso he also traced his earliest feeling for the beauties of natural objects. The love of Nature, especially when combined with ancient ruins, or remains of our forefathers' piety or splendour, became his insatiable passion.

He was then sent to classes in the Faculty of Arts in Edinburgh University; and in 1785 was articled to his father and entered upon the wilderness of law. Though he disliked the drudgery of the office, he loved his father and was ambitious, and the allowance which he received afforded the pleasures of the circulating library and the theatre. His reading had now extended to the great writers in French, Spanish and Italian literature. Distant excursions on foot or on horseback formed his favorite amusement, undertaken for the pleasure of seeing romantic scenery and places distinguished by historic events.

In 1790, Scott determined, in accordance with his father's wishes, to become an advocate, and assumed the gown on July 11, 1792. His personal appearance at this time was engaging. He had a fresh, brilliant complexion, his eyes were clear and radiant, and the noble expanse of his brow gave dignity to his whole aspect. His smile was always delightful, and there was a playful intermixture of tenderness and gravity well calculated to fix a lady's eye. His figure, except for the blemish in one limb, was eminently handsome, and much above the usual stature; and the whole outline was that of extraordinary vigour, without a touch of clumsiness.

The Poet's Education

I do not know when his first attachment began; its object was Margaret, daughter of Sir John and Lady Jane Stuart Belcher, of Invermay. But after Scott had for several years nourished the dream of union with this lady, his hopes terminated in her being married to the late Sir William Forbes, of Pitsligo, a gentleman of the highest character, who lived to act the part of a generous friend to his rival throughout the distresses of 1826 and 1827.

After being admitted an advocate, Scott undertook many excursions to various parts of Scotland, gaining that intimate knowledge of the country, and its people and traditions, which appears in his poems and novels. Thus, he visited Northumberland, and made a close inspection of the battle-field of Flodden, and on another journey studied the Saxon cathedral of Hexam. During seven successive years he made raids, as he called them, into the wild and inaccessible district of Liddesdale, picking up the ancient "riding ballads" preserved among the descendants of the moss-troopers. To these rambles he owed much of the materials of his "Minstrelsy of the Border," and here he came to know Willie Elliot, the original of Dandie Dinmont. Another expedition, into Galloway, carried him into the scenery of Guy Mannering. Stirlingshire, Perthshire and Forfarshire became familiar ground to him, and the scenery of Loch Katrine especially was associated with many a merry expedition. His first appearance as counsel in a criminal court was at the Jedburgh assizes, where he helped a veteran poacher and sheep-stealer to escape through the meshes of the law.

In June, 1795, Scott was appointed one of the curators of the Advocate's Library and became an adept in the deciphering of old manuscript. His highlands and border raids were constantly suggesting inquiries as to ancient local history and legend, which could nowhere else have been pursued with equal advantage.

In the same year, a rhymed translation of Burger's "Lenore," from his pen, was shown by him to Miss Cranstoun, afterwards Countess of Purgstall, who was delighted and astonished at it. "Upon my word," she wrote in a letter to a friend, "Walter Scott is going to turn out a poet--something of a cross I think between Burns and Gray." This lady had the ballad elegantly printed in April, 1796, and Scott thus made his first appearance as an author. In October, this translation, together with that of the "Wild Huntsman," also from Burger, was published anonymously in a thin quarto by Manners and Miller, of Edinburgh. The little volume found warm favour: its free, masculine and lively style revealing the hand of a poet.

Marriage

In July, 1797, Scott set out on a tour to the English lakes, accompanied by his brother John and Adam Fergusson, visiting Tweeddale, Carlisle, Penrith, Ullswater and Windermere, and at length fixing their headquarters at Gilsland, a peaceful and sequestered little watering place.

He was riding one day with Fergusson when they met, some miles away from home, a young lady on horseback, whose appearance instantly struck both of them so much, that they kept her in view until they had satisfied themselves that she was staying in Gilsland. The same evening there was a ball, at which Scott was introduced to Charlotte Margaret Carpenter.

Without the features of a regular beauty, she was rich in personal attractions; a fairy-like form; a clear olive complexion; large, deep eyes of Italian brown; a profusion of silken tresses, raven-black; her address mingling the reserve of a pretty young Englishwoman with a certain natural archness and gaiety that suited well her French accent. A lovelier vision, as all who remember her youth have assured me, could hardly be imagined, and from that hour the fate of the poet was fixed.

She was the daughter of Jean Charpentier, of Lyons, a devoted royalist, who died in the beginning of the Revolution; Madame Charpentier had died soon after bringing her children to London; and the Marquis of Downshire had become their guardian. Miss Charpentier was now making a summer excursion under the care of the lady who had superintended her education.

In an affectionate and dutiful letter Scott acquainted his mother with his purpose of marriage, and Miss Carpenter remained at Carlisle until her destiny was settled. The lady had a considerable private income, amounting to about £500 a year; the difficulties presented by the prudence and prejudices of family connections were soon overcome; and the marriage took place in St. Mary's, Carlisle, on December 24, 1797. Scott took his bride to a lodging in George Street, Edinburgh, the house which he had taken not being quite ready, and the first fortnight convinced her husband's family that she had the sterling qualities of a wife.

Their house in South Castle Street, soon after exchanged for one in North Castle Street, which he inhabited down to 1826, became the centre of a highly agreeable circle; the evenings passed in a round of innocent gaiety; and they and their friends were passionately fond of the theatre. Perhaps nowhere else could have been formed a society on so small a scale as that of Edinburgh at this time, including more of vigorous intellect, varied information, elegant tastes, and real virtue, affection and mutual confidence.

In the summer of 1798, Scott hired a cottage at Lasswade, on the Esk, about six miles from Edinburgh, having a garden with a most beautiful view. In this retreat they spent several happy summers, receiving the visits of their chosen friends from the neighbouring city, and wandering amidst some of the most romantic scenery of Scotland.

Early Poems

In February, 1799, a London Bookseller named Bell, brought out Scott's version of Goethe's tragedy, "Goetz von Berlichingen of the Iron Hand," having purchased the copyright for twenty-five guineas. This was the first publication that bore Scott's name. In March of that year he took his wife to London, and met with some literary and fashionable society; but his chief object was to examine the antiquities of the Tower and Westminster, and to make researches among the manuscripts of the British Museum. He found his "Goetz" favourably spoken of by the critics, but it had not attracted general attention.

About this time Scott wrote a play entitled "House of Aspen" which, having been read and commended by the celebrated actress, Mrs. Esten, was put in rehearsal by Kemble for the stage. But the notion was abandoned; and discovering the play thirty years after among his papers, Scott sent it to the "Keepsake" of 1829.

His return to Scotland was hastened by the news of his father's death, and his mother and sister spent the following summer and autumn in his cottage at Lasswade. This summer produced his first serious attempt in verse, "Glenfinlas," which was followed by the noble ballads, "Eve of St. John," "The Grey Brother" and "Fire-King"; and it was in the course of this autumn that he first visited Bothwell Castle, the seat of Archibald, Lord Douglas, whose wife, and her companion, Lady Louisa Stuart, were among his dearest friends through life.

During a visit to Kelso, before returning to Edinburgh for the winter, Scott renewed an acquaintance with a classfellow of his boyhood, Mr. James Ballantyne, who was now printer and editor of a weekly paper in his native town. Scott showed him some of his poems, expressed his wonder that his old friend did not try to get some bookseller's printing and suggested a collection of old Border ballads. Ballantyne printed for him a few specimens to show to the booksellers; and thus began an experiment which changed the fortunes of both Scott and Ballantyne.

Soon after the commencement of the Winter Session, the office of Sheriff-depute of Selkirkshire became vacant, and the Duke of Buccleuch used his influence with Mr. Henry Dundas, afterwards Viscount Melville, to procure it for Scott. The appointment to the Sheriff ship was made on December 16, 1799. It brought him an annual salary of £300; the duties of the office were far from heavy; the small pastoral territory was largely the property of the Duke of Buccleuch; and Scott turned with redoubled zeal to his project of editing the ballads, many of which belong to this district. In this design he found able assistants in Richard Heber and John Leyden. During the years 1800 and 1801, the "Minstrelsy" formed his chief occupation.

The duties of the Sheriffship took him frequently to Ettrick Forest, and on such occasions he took up his lodging at the little inn at Clovenford, a favourite fishing station on the road from Edinburgh to Selkirk. Here he was within a few miles of the values of Yarrow and Ettrick. On one of his excursions here, penetrating beyond St Mary's Lake, he found hospitality at the farmhouse of William Laidlaw, through whom he came to know James Hogg, a brother poet hardly conscious of his powers.

The first and second volumes of the "Minstrelsy" appeared in January, 1802, from the house of Cadell and Davies in the Strand, and formed Scott's first introduction as an original writer to the English public. Their reception greatly elated Ballantyne, the printer, who looked on his connection with them as the most fortunate event in his life. The great bookseller, Longman, repaired to Scotland soon after this, and purchased the copyright of the "Minstrelsy," including the third volume; and not long afterwards James Ballantyne set up as a printer in Edinburgh, assisted by a liberal loan from Scott.

Scott's Chief Poems

The "Edinburgh Review" was begun in 1802, and Scott soon became a contributor of critical articles for his friend Mr. Jeffrey, the elder. His chief work was now on "Sir Tristram," a romance ascribed to Thomas of Ercildoune; but "The Lay of the Last Minstrel" was making progress in 1803, when Scott made the acquaintance of Wordsworth and his sister, under circumstances described by Dorothy Wordsworth in her Journal. In the following May, he took a lease of the house of Ashestiel, with an adjoining farm, on the southern bank of the Tweed, a few miles from Selkirk; and in the same month "Sir Tristram" was published by Constable of Edinburgh. Captain Robert Scott, his uncle, died in June, leaving him the house of Rosebank near Kelso, which Scott sold for £5000.

"The Lay of the Last Minstrel" was published in the first week of 1805, and its success at once decided that literature should form the main business of Scott's life. Its design arose originally from the suggestion of the lovely Countess of Dalkeith, who had heard a wild, rude legend of Border *diablerie,* and sportively asked him to make it the subject of a ballad. He cast about for a new variety of diction and rhyme, and having happened to hear a recitation of Coleridge's unpublished "Christabel" determined to adopt a similar cadence. The division into cantos was suggested by one of his friends, after the example of Spenser's "Faery Queen." The creation of the framework, the conception of the ancient harper, came last of all. Thus did "The Lay of the Last Minstrel" grow out of the "Minstrelsy of the Scottish Border." The publishers were Longman of London, and Constable of Edinburgh, and the author's share of profits came to £769.

It was at this time that Scott took over a third share in Ballantyne's business, a commercial tie which bound him for twenty years. Its influence on his literary work and his fortunes was productive of much good and not a little evil. Meanwhile, he entered with the zest of an active partner into many publishing schemes, and exerted himself in the interests of many authors less fortunate than himself.

With the desire of placing his financial position on a more substantial basis, Scott had solicited the office of Clerk of Session; and after some difficulties, during which he visited London and was received by the Princess of Wales, he was installed in that position on March 8, 1806, and continued to discharge its duties with exemplary regularity for twenty-five years.

The progress of "Marmion" was further interrupted by Scott's appointment as secretary to a Commission for the improvement of Scottish Jurisprudence, but the poems appeared at last in February, 1808. It received only very qualified praise from Jeffrey, but I think it may be considered on the whole Scott's greatest poem, and its popularity was from the very first extraordinary.

In April of the same year William Miller of Albemarle Street published Scott's great edition of Dryden, with a biography, in eighteen volumes; and the editor's industry and critical judgement were the subject of a laudatory article by Hallam in the "Edinburgh Review."

Scott was now engaged in a vast multiplicity of business. He was preparing an edition of Swift for Constable, establishing his own partner as a publisher in Edinburgh under the title of "John Ballantyne and Co., Booksellers," and was projecting a new periodical of sound constitutional principles, to be known as the "Quarterly Review," published by Murray in London and by Ballantyne in Edinburgh. In connection with the latter enterprise Scott and Mrs. Scott went up to London for two months in the Spring of 1809, and enjoyed the society of Coleridge, Canning, Croker, and

Ellis. The first "Quarterly" appeared while he was in London, and contained three articles from his pen. At this time also he prevailed on Henry Siddons, the nephew of Kemble, to undertake the lease and management of the Edinburgh Theatre; and purchasing a share himself, became an acting trustee, and for many years took a lively concern in the Edinburgh company.

Early in May, 1810, "The Lady of the Lake" came out, like her two elder sisters, in all the majesty of quarto, at the price of two guineas, the author receiving two thousand guineas for the copyright. The whole country rang with the praises of the poet, and crowds set off to view the scenery of Loch Katrine. The critics were in full harmony with one another and with the popular voice.

The Waverley Novels

On returning, in 1810, from an excursion to the Islands of the western Scottish coast, where he had been collecting impressions for "The Lord of the Isles," Scott was searching one morning for fishing-flies in an old desk at Ashestiel, when he came across a forgotten manuscript, written and abandoned five years before. It contained the first two chapters of "Waverley." He submitted it to Ballantyne, whose opinion was on the whole against completion of the novel, and it was again laid aside.

Although his publishing venture had begun to wear a bad aspect, Scott was now in receipt of £1300 a year as Clerk of Session, and when the lease of Ashestiel ran out in May, 1811, he felt justified in purchasing, for £4000, a farm on the banks of the Tweed above Galafoot. This farm, then known as "Garty Holes," became "Abbotsford," so called because these lands had belonged of old to the great Abbey of Melrose; and in his own mind Scott became henceforth the "Laird of Abbotsford."

The last days at Ashestiel were marked by a friendly interchange of letters with Lord Byron, whose "Childe Harold" had just come out, and with correspondence with Johanna Baillie and with Crabbe. At Whitsuntide the family, which included two boys and two girls, moved to their new possession, and structural alterations on the farmhouse began.

The poem "Rokeby" appeared in January, 1813. A month or two later the crisis in the war affected credit aniversally, and many publishing firms, including that of the Ballantynes, were brought to extremity. The difficulty was relieved for a time by the sale of copyrights and much of the stock to Constable, on the understanding that the publishing concern should be wound up as soon as possible. But Scott was preparing fresh embarrassments for himself by the purchase of another parcel of land; a yet more acute crisis in the Ballantyne firm forced him to borrow from the Duke of Buccleuch; and when planning out his work for the purpose of retrieving his position he determined to complete the fragment of "Waverley."

The offer of the post of poet-laureate was made to Scott at this time, but holding already two lucrative offices in the gift of the Crown, he declined the honour and suggested that it should be given to Southey, which was accordingly done. The "Swift" in nineteen volumes, appeared in July, 1814, and had a moderate success.

"Waverley," of which Scott was to receive half the profits, was published by Constable in July, 1814, without the author's name, and its great success with the public was assured from the first. None of Scott's intimate friends ever had, or could have, the slightest doubt as to its parentage, and when Mr. Jeffrey reviewed the book, doing justice to its substantial merits, he was at no pains to conceal his conviction of the authorship. With the single exception of the "Quarterly," the critics hailed it as a work of original creative genius, one of the masterpieces of prose fiction.

From a voyage to the Hebrides with the Commissioners of the Northern Lighthouses, Scott returned in vigour to his desk at Abbotsford, where he worked at "The Lord of the Isles" and "Guy Mannering." The poem appeared in January and the novel in February, 1815. "The Lord of the Isles" never reached the same popularity as the earlier poems had enjoyed, but "Guy Mannering" was pronounced by acclamation to be fully worthy of the honours of "Waverley." In March, Scott went to London with his wife and daughter, met Byron almost daily in Murray's house, and was presented to the Prince Regent, who was enchanted with Scott, as Scott with him. A visit to Paris in July of the same year is commemorated in "Paul's Letters to His Kinsfolk." Scott's reputation had as yet made little way among the French, but the Duke of Wellington, then in Paris, treated him with kindness and confidence, and a few eminent Frenchmen vied with the enthusiastic Germans in their attentions to him.

"The Antiquary" came out early in 1816, and was its author's favourite among all his novels. The "Tales of my Landlord," published by Murray and Blackwood, appeared in December, and though anonymous was at once recognized as Scott's. The four volumes included the "Black Dwarf" and "Old Mortality." A month later followed a poem, "Harold the Dauntless." The title of "Rob Roy" was suggested by Constable; and the novel was published on the last day of 1817.

During this year the existing house of Abbotsford had been building, and Scott had added to his estate the lands of Toftfield, at a price of £10,000. He was then thought to be consolidating a large fortune, for the annual profits of his novels alone had, for several years, been not less than the cost of Toftfield.

Having been asked by the Ballantynes to contribute to the historical department of the "Annual Register," I often had occasion now to visit Scott in his house in Castle Street, where I usually found him working in his "den," a small room behind the dining parlour, in company with his dog, Maida. Besides his own huge elbow-chair, there were but two others in the room, and one of these was reserved for his amanuensis, a portrait of Claverhouse, over the chimneypiece, with a Highland target on either side and broadswords and dirks disposed star-fashion round them. A venerable cat, fat and sleek, watched the proceedings of his toaster **and** Maids with dignified equanimity.

Abbotsford

The house of Abbotsford was not completed, and finally rid of carpenters and upholsterers, until Christmas, 1824; but the first time I saw it was in 1818, and from that time onwards Scott's hospitality was extended freely not only to the proprietors and tenants of the surrounding district, but to a never-ending succession of visitors who came to Abbotsford as pilgrims. In the seven or eight brilliant seasons when his prosperity was at its height, he entertained under his roof as many persons of distinction in rank, in politics, in art, in literature, and in science, as the most princely nobleman of his age ever did in the like space of time. It is not beyond the mark to add that of the eminent foreigners who visited our Island within this period, a moiety crossed the Channel mainly in consequence of the interest in which his writings had invested Scotland, and that the hope of beholding the man under his own roof was the crowning motive with half that moiety. His rural neighbours were assembled principally at two annual festivals of sport; one was a solemn bout of salmon fishing for the neighbouring gentry, presided over by the Sheriff; and the other was the "Abbotsford Hunt," a coursing field on a large scale, including, with many of the young gentry, all Scott's personal favourites among the yeomen and farmers of the surrounding country.

Notwithstanding all his prodigious hospitality, his double official duties as Sheriff and Clerk of Session, the labours and anxieties in which the ill-directed and tottering firm of Ballantyne involved him, the keen interest which he took in every detail of the adornment of the house and estate of Abbotsford, and finally, notwithstanding obstinate and agonizing attacks of internal cramp which were undermining his constitution, Scott continued to produce rapidly the wonderful series of the Waverley Novels. "The Bride of Lammermoor," "Legend of Montrose" and "Ivanhoe" appeared in 1819, "The Monastery," "The Abbot" and "Kenilworth" in 1820, "The Pirate" in 1821, "The Fortunes of Nigel" in 1822, "Peveril of the Peak," "Quentin

Durward" and "St. Ronan's Well" in 1823, and "Redgauntlet" in 1824. His great literary reputation was acknowledged by a baronetcy conferred in 1820, and by the most flattering condescensions on the part of King George IV on his visit to Edinburgh in 1822.

The End of All

Scott's Diary from November, 1825, shows dear forebodings of the collapse of the houses of Constable and Ballantyne. In a time of universal confidence and prosperity, the banks had supported them to an extent quite unwarranted by their assets or their trade, and as soon as the banks began to doubt and to enquire, their fall was a foregone conclusion. In December, Scott borrowed £10,000 on the lands of Abbotsford, and advanced that sum to the struggling houses; on January 16, 1826, their ruin, and Scott's with them, were complete. Scott immediately placed his whole affairs in the hands of three trustees, and by the 26th all his creditors had agreed to a private trust to which he mortgaged all his future literary labours.

On March 15, he left for the last time his house in Castle Street; on April 3; "Woodstock" was sold for the creditors' behoof, realising £8228; on May 15, Lady Scott died, after a short illness, at Abbotsford. "I think," writes Scott in his Diary, "my heart will break. Lonely, aged, deprived of all my family--all but poor Anne; an impoverished, embarrassed man, deprived of the sharer of my thoughts and counsels, who could always talk down my sense of the calamitous apprehensions which break the heart that must bear them alone. Even her foibles were of service to me, by giving me things to think of beyond my weary self-reflections."

An expedition to Paris, in October, to gather materials for his "Life of Napoleon." was a seasonable relief. On his return through London, the King undertook that his son, Charles Scott, then at Oxford, should be launched in the diplomatic service. The elder son, heir to the baronetcy, was now with his regiment in Ireland.

The "Life of Buonaparte" was published in June, 1827, and secured high praise from many, among whom was Goethe. It realised £18,000 for the creditors, and had health been spared him, Scott must soon have freed himself from all encumbrances. Before the close of 1829 he had published also the "Chronicles of the Canongate," "Tales of a Grandfather," "The Fair Maid of Perth" and "Anne of Geirstein," but he had been visited also by several threatenings of apoplexy, and on February 15, 1830, was prostrated by a serious attack. Recovering from this illness, Scott resigned his office as Clerk of Session, and during the rest of the year produced a great quantity of manuscript, including the "Letters on Demonology and Witchcraft," and the series of "Tales of a Grandfather" dealing with French history. April, 1831, brought with it a distinct stroke of paralysis, yet both "Castle Dangerous" and "Count Robert of Paris" were finished in the course of the year.

Sailing in October, in the "Barham," Sir Walter Scott visited Malta and Naples, and came to Rome in April, 1832. In May he set out for home by Venice, Munich and the Rhine, but his companions could hardly prevail on him to look at the interesting objects by the way, and another serious attack fell upon him at Nimeguen. He reached London on June 13, and on July 7 was carried on board the steamer for Leith, and was at Abbotsford by the 11th. Here the remains of his strength gradually declined, and his mind was hopelessly obscured.

As I was dressing on the morning of September 17, a servant came to tell me that his master had awoke in a state of composure and consciousness, and wished to see me immediately. I found him entirely himself, though in the last extreme of feebleness. "Lockhart," he said "I may have no more than a minute to speak to you. My dear, be a good man--be virtuous--be religious--be a good man. Nothing else will give you any comfort when you come to lie here." He scarcely afterwards gave any sign of consciousness, and breathed his last on September 21, in the presence of all his children.

His funeral was unostentatious but the attendance was very great. He was laid in the Abbey of Dryburgh, by the side of his wife, in the sepulchre of his ancestors.

The Life of Robert Burns

John Gibson Lockhart was born, a son of the manse, at Cambusnethan, Lanarkshire, on July 14, 1794. Receiving his early education in Glasgow, he went, at sixteen, with a scholarship to Balliol College, Oxford. In 1816 he was called to the Scottish Bar; but literature occupied him more than law, and as early as 1819 he wrote the once popular "Peter's Letters to his Kinsfolk." Next year he married Scott's eldest daughter, Sophia. Lockhart was a leading contributor to the early "Blackwood," where his fine translations of Spanish ballads first appeared, and he edited the "Quarterly Review" from 1825 to 1853. He died at Abbotsford on November 25, 1854, and was buried at Scott's feet in Dryburgh Abbey. Lockhart's forte was biography, and his "Life of Scott" ranks beside Boswell's "Johnson." The "Life of Burns" was published first in Constable's "Miscellany" in 1828, when the whole impression was exhausted in six weeks. It passed through five editions before the author's death. Though many lives of Burns have appeared since, with details unknown to Lockhart, his biography is in many respects the best we possess, and is never likely to be superseded. Even Mr. Henley is "glad to agree with Lockhart." It is this book that is the subject of Carlyle's famous essay on Burns.

I.--The Poet in the Making

Robert Burns was born on January 25, 1759, in a clay cottage at Alloway, two miles south of Ayr, and near the "auld brig o' Doon." His father, William Burnes, or Burness--for so he spelt his name--was from Kincardineshire. When Robert was born he had the lease of a seven-acre croft, and had intended to establish himself as a nurseryman. He was a man of notable character and individuality, immortalised by his son as "the saint, the father, and the husband" of "The Cottar's Saturday Night." "I have met with few," said Burns, "who understood men, their manners, and their ways, equal to my father." Agnes Brown, the poet's mother, is described as a very sagacious woman, with an inexhaustible store of ballads and traditionary tales, upon which she nourished Robert's infant imagination, while her husband attended to "the weightier matters of the law."

When Burns was between six and seven, his father removed to the farm of Mount Oliphant, two miles from the Brig o' Doon. But the soil was poor, and the factor--afterwards pictured in "The Twa Dogs"--so harsh and unreasonable, that the tenant was glad to quit. In 1777 he removed about ten miles to the larger and better farm of Lochlea, in the parish of Tarbolton. Here, after a short interval of prosperity, some trouble arose about the conditions of the lease. The dispute involved William Burnes in ruin, and he died broken-hearted in February, 1784.

Meanwhile, at the age of six, Robert, with his brother Gilbert, was learning to read, write, and sum under the direction of John Murdoch, an itinerant teacher, who has left an interesting description of his pupil.

"Gilbert always appeared to me to possess a more lively imagination," says Murdoch, "and to be more of the wit, than Robert. I attempted to teach them a little church-music. Here they were left far behind by all the rest of the school. Robert's ear, in particular, was remarkably dull, and his voice untunable. It was long before I could get them to distinguish one tune from another. Robert's countenance was generally grave and expressive of a serious, contemplative, and thoughtful mind. Gilbert's face said, 'Mirth, with thee I mean to live;' and, certainly, if any person who knew the two boys had been asked which of them was the more likely to court the muses, he would never have guessed that Robert had a propensity of that kind."

When Murdoch left the district, the father himself continued to instruct the boys; but when Robert was about thirteen he and Gilbert were sent, "week about, during a summer quarter," to the parish school of Dalrymple. The good man could not pay two fees, or his two boys could not be spared at the same time from the farm!

"We lived very poorly," says the poet. "I was a dexterous ploughman for my age; and the next eldest to me was a brother [Gilbert], who could drive the plough very well, and help me to thrash the corn. A novel-writer might perhaps have viewed these scenes with some satisfaction, but so did not I." Burns's person, inured to daily toil, and continually exposed to every variety of weather, presented, before the usual time, every characteristic of robust and vigorous manhood. He says himself that he never feared a competitor in any species of rural exertion; and Gilbert, a man of uncommon bodily strength, adds that neither he, nor any labourer he ever saw at work, was equal to him, either in the cornfield or on the thrashing-floor.

Before his sixteenth year Burns had read a large amount of literature. But a collection of songs, he says significantly, "was my *vade mecum*. I pored over them, driving my cart, or walking to labour, song by song, verse by verse; carefully noticing the true, tender, or sublime from affectation or fustian." It was about this date that he "first committed the sin of rhyme." The subject was a "bewitching creature," a partner in the harvest field, and the song was that beginning "Once I loved a bonnie lass."

After this, though much occupied with labour and love, he found leisure occasionally to clothe the various moods of his mind in verse. It was as early as seventeen that he wrote the stanzas which open beautifully, "I dream'd I lay where flowers were springing," and also the ballad, "My father was a farmer upon the Carrick border," which, years afterwards, he used to con over with delight, because of the faithfulness with which it recalled to him the circumstances and feelings of his opening manhood. These are the only two of his very early productions in which there is nothing expressly about love. The rest were composed to celebrate the charms of those rustic beauties who followed each other in the domain of his fancy, or shared the capacious throne between them. The excursions of the rural lover form the theme of almost all the songs which Burns is known to have produced about this period; and such of these juvenile performances as have been preserved are beautiful. They show how powerfully his boyish fancy had been affected by the old rural minstrelsy of his own country, and how easily his native taste caught the secret of its charm.

In 1781, despairing of farming, he went to Irvine to learn flax-dressing with a relative. He was diligent at first, but misfortune soon overtook him. The shop where he was engaged caught fire, and he "was left, like a true poet, not worth a sixpence." Gilbert Burns dates a serious change in his character and conduct from this six months' residence in the seaport town. "He contracted," he says, "some acquaintance of a freer manner of thinking than he had been accustomed to, whose society prepared him for overleaping the bounds of rigid virtue which had hitherto restrained him."

He had certainly not come unscathed out of the society of those persons of "liberal opinions" with whom he consorted in Irvine; and he expressly attributes to their lessons the scrape into which he fell soon after "he put his hand to plough again." He was compelled, according to the then all but universal custom of rural parishes in Scotland, to do penance in church, before the congregation, in consequence of the birth of an illegitimate child. But not the amours, or the tavern, or drudging manual labour could keep him long from his true calling. "Rhyme," he says, "I had given up [on going to Irvine], but meeting with Fergusson's 'Scottish Poems,' I strung anew my wildly sounding lyre with emulating vigour." It was probably this accidental meeting with Fergusson that in a great measure finally determined the Scottish character of his poetry.

II.--The Loves of a Peasant Poet

Just before their father's death, Robert and Gilbert took the cold and ungrateful farm of Mossgiel, in the parish of Mauchline, to which the family now removed. The four years of Burns's connection with this place were the most important of his life. It was then that his genius developed its highest energies; on the works produced in these years his fame was first established, and must ever continue mainly to rest; it was then also that his personal character came out in all its brightest lights, and in all but its darkest shadows; and indeed from the commencement of this period the history of the man may be traced, step by step, in his own immortal writings.

Burns now began to know that Nature had meant him for a poet; and diligently, though as yet in secret, he laboured in what he felt to be his destined vocation. He was never more productive than at this time, when he wrote such skits on the kirk and its associates as "The Twa Herds" (pastors), "Holy Willie's Prayer," "The Holy Fair," and "The Ordination." "Hallowe'en," a descriptive poem, perhaps even more exquisitely wrought than "The Holy Fair," also belongs to the Mossgiel period, as does an even more notable effort.

Burns had often remarked to his brother that there was something peculiarly venerable in the phrase, "Let us worship God," used by a decent, sober head of a family introducing family worship. To this sentiment we are indebted for "The Cottar's Saturday Night," the hint of the plan and title of which were taken from Fergusson's "Farmer's Ingle." It is, perhaps, of all Burns's pieces, the one whose exclusion from the collection, were such a thing possible nowadays, would be the most injurious, if not to the genius, at least to the character of the man. In spite of many feeble lines and some heavy stanzas, it appears to me that even his genius would suffer more in estimation by being contemplated in the absence of this poem than of any other single performance he has left us. Loftier flights he certainly has made, but in these he remained but a short while on the wing, and effort is too often perceptible; here the motion is easy, gentle, placidly undulating.

Burns's art had now reached its climax; but it is time to revert more particularly to his personal history. In this his loves very nearly occupy the chief place. That they were many, his songs prove; for in those days he wrote no love-songs on imaginary heroines. "Mary Morison," "Behind yon hills where Lugar flows," and "On Cessnock banks there lives a lass," belong to this date; and there are three or four inspired by Mary Campbell--"Highland Mary"--the object of by far the deepest passion Burns ever knew, a passion which he has immortalised in the noblest of his elegiacs, "To Mary in Heaven."

Farming had, of course, to engage his attention as well as love-making, but he was less successful in the one than in the other. The first year of Mossgiel, from buying bad seed, the second from a late harvest, he lost half his crops. In these circumstances, he thought of proceeding to the West Indies. Presently he had further cause for contemplating an escape from his native land. Among his "flames" was one Jean Armour, the daughter of a mason in Mauchline, where she was the reigning toast. Jean found herself "as ladies wish to be that love their lords." Burns's worldly circumstances were in a most miserable state when he was informed of her condition, and he was staggered. He saw nothing for it but to fly the country at once.

Meanwhile, meeting Jean, he yielded to her tears, and gave her a written acknowledgment of marriage, valid according to Scottish law. Her father's wrath was not appeased thereby. Burns, confessing himself unequal to the support of a family, proposed to go immediately to Jamaica in search of better fortunes. He offered, if this were rejected, to abandon his farm, already a hopeless concern, and earn at least bread for his wife and children as a day labourer at home. But nothing would satisfy Armour, who, in his indignation, made his daughter destroy the written evidence of her "marriage."

III.--Burns at His Zenith

Such was his poverty that he could not satisfy the parish officers; and the only alternative that presented itself to him was America or a gaol. A situation was obtained for him in Jamaica, but he had no money to pay his passage. It occurred to him that the money might be raised by publishing his poems; and a first edition, printed at Kilmarnock in 1786, brought him nearly £20, out of which he paid for a steerage passage from the Clyde. "My chest was on the road to Greenock," he tells; "I had composed the last song I should ever measure in Caledonia, 'The gloomy night is gathering fast,' when a letter from Dr. Blacklock to a friend of mine overthrew all my schemes, by opening new prospects to my poetic ambition."

Blacklock, the blind divine upon whom Johnson "looked with reverence," had read the newly published poems, and it was his praise of them that directly prevented Burns from expatriating himself. "His opinion that I would meet with encouragement in Edinburgh fired me so much that away I posted for that city, without a single acquaintance, or a single letter of introduction. The baneful star that had so long shed its blasting influence in my zenith for once made a revolution to the nadir." In Edinburgh, which Burns reached in November, 1786, he was introduced by Blacklock to all the *literati*, and within a fortnight he was writing to a friend: "I am in a fair way of becoming as eminent as Thomas à Kempis or John Bunyan; and you may expect to see my birthday inscribed among the wonderful events in the Poor Robin and Aberdeen Almanacks, along with the Black Monday and the Battle of Bothwell Bridge."

But he bore his honours in a manner worthy of himself. "The attentions he received," says Dugald Stewart, "from all ranks and descriptions of persons were such as would have turned any head but his own. I cannot say that I could perceive any unfavourable effect which they left on his mind." Scott, then a lad of fifteen, met him, and wrote a vivid description of his appearance:

"His person was strong and robust; his manners rustic, not clownish; a sort of dignified plainness and simplicity, which received part of its effect, perhaps, from one's knowledge of his extraordinary talents. His features are represented in Mr. Nasmyth's picture, but to me it conveys the idea that they are diminished as if seen in perspective. I think his countenance was more massive than it looks in any of the portraits. I would have taken the poet, had I not known what he was, for a very sagacious country farmer of the old Scotch school--*i.e.*, none of your modern agriculturists, who keep labourers for their drudgery, but the *douce gudeman* who held his own plough. There was a strong expression of sense and shrewdness in all his lineaments; the eye alone, I think, indicated the poetical character and temperament. It was large, and of a dark cast, which glowed (I say literally *glowed*) when he spoke with feeling or interest. I never saw such another eye in a human head, though I have seen the most distinguished men of my time. His conversation expressed perfect self-confidence, without the slightest presumption. He was like a farmer dressed in his best to dine with the laird. I do not speak in *malam partem* when I say I never saw a man in company with his superiors in station and information more perfectly free from either the reality or the affectation of embarrassment. I was told that his address to females was extremely deferential, and always with a turn either to the pathetic or humorous, which engaged their attention particularly. I have heard the late Duchess of Gordon remark this."

It needs no effort of imagination to conceive what the sensations of an isolated set of scholars, almost all either clergymen or professors, must have been in the presence of this big-boned, brawny stranger, with his great flashing eyes, who had forced his way among them from the plough-tail at a single stride; and it will always be a reflection in their honour that they suffered no pedantic prejudices to interfere with their reception of the poet.

Shortly after his arrival he arranged with Creech, the chief bookseller in Edinburgh, to undertake a second edition of his poems. This was published in March, 1787, the subscribers numbering over 1,500. Out of money thus derived, he provided a tombstone for the neglected grave of Robert Fergusson, his "elder brother in the muses," in the Canongate churchyard. Then he decided to visit some of the classic scenes of Scottish history and romance. He had as yet seen but a small part of his own country, and this by no means among the most interesting, until, indeed, his own poetry made it equal, on that score, to any other. Various tours were, in fact, undertaken, the chief being, however, in the Border district and in the Highlands. Usually he returned to Edinburgh, partly to be near his jovial intimates, and partly because, after the excitement attending his first appearance in the capital, he found himself incapable of settling down contentedly in the humble circle at Mossgiel.

IV.--The Clarinda Romance

During the winter of 1787--1788, he had a little romance with Mrs. McLehose, the beautiful widow to whom he addressed the song, "Clarinda, mistress of my soul," and a series of letters which present more instances of bad taste, bombastic language, and fulsome sentiment than could be produced from all his writings besides. It was the same lady who inspired the lines which furnished Byron with a motto, and Scott declared to be "worth a thousand romances ":

Had we never loved so kindly
Had we never loved sae blindly,
Never met--or never parted,
We had ne'er been broken-hearted.

At this time the publication of Johnson's "Scots Musical Museum" was going on in Edinburgh; and Burns, being enlisted as a contributor, furnished many of his best songs to that work. From his youth upwards he had been an enthusiastic lover of the old minstrelsy and music of his country; but he now studied both subjects with better opportunities and appliances than he could have commanded previously; and it is from this time that we must date his ambition to transmit his own poetry to posterity, in eternal association with those exquisite airs which had hitherto, in far too many instances, been married to verses that did not deserve to be immortal. Later, beginning in 1792, he wrote about sixty songs for George Thomson's collection, many of which, like "Auld Lang Syne" and "Scots Wha Hae," are in the front rank of popularity. The letters he addressed to Thomson are full of interesting detail of various kinds. In one he writes:

"Until I am complete master of a tune in my own singing, such as it is, I can never compose for it. My way is this. I consider the poetic sentiment correspondent to my idea of the musical expression--then choose my theme--compose one stanza. When that is composed, which is generally the most difficult part of the business, I walk out, sit down now and then, look out for objects in Nature round me that are in unison or harmony with the cogitations of my fancy and workings of my bosom, humming every now and then the air, with the verses I have framed. When I feel my muse beginning to jade, I retire to the solitary fireside of my study, and there commit my effusions to paper; swinging at intervals on the hind legs of my elbow-chair, by way of calling forth my own critical strictures, as my pen goes. Seriously this, at home, is almost invariably my way."

But to return. During his second winter in Edinburgh, Burns met with a hackney coach accident which kept him to the house for six weeks. While in this state he learned from Mauchline that his intimacy with Jean Armour had again exposed her to the reproaches of her family. The father sternly turned her out of doors, and Burns had to arrange about a shelter for her and his children in a friend's house. In the meantime, through the influence of some sympathisers, he had been appointed an officer of excise. "I have chosen this," he wrote, "after mature deliberation. It is immediate bread, and, though poor in comparison of the last eighteen months of my existence, 'tis luxury in comparison of all my preceding life." However, when he settled finally with Creech about his poems, he found himself with between £500 and £600; and he retained his excise commission as a *dernier ressort*, to be used only if a reverse of fortune rendered it necessary.

He decided now to exchange Mossgiel for Ellisland farm, about six miles from Dumfries. As soon as he was able to leave Edinburgh, he had hurried to Mossgiel and gone through a justice-of-peace marriage with Jean Armour. Burns, with all his faults, was an honest and a high-spirited man, and he loved the mother of his children. Had he hesitated to make her his wife, he must have sunk into the callousness of a ruffian, or that misery of miseries, the remorse of a poet.

Some months later he writes that his marriage "was not, perhaps, in consequence of the attachment of romance, but I have no cause to repent it. If I have not got polite tattle, modish manners, and fashionable dress, I am not sickened and disgusted with the multiform curse of boarding-school affectation; and I have got the handsomest figure, the sweetest temper, the soundest constitution, and the kindest heart in the country." It was during the honeymoon, as he calls it, that he wrote the beautiful "O a' the airts the wind can blaw." He used to say that the happiest period of his life was the first winter at Ellisland, with wife and children around him. It was then that he wrote, among other songs, "John Anderson, my Jo," "Tarn Glen," "My heart's in the Highlands," "Go fetch to me a pint of wine," and "Willie brewed a peck o' maut."

But the "golden days" of Ellisland were short. Burns's farming speculations once more failed, and he had to take up his excise commission. "I am now," says he, "a poor rascally gauger, condemned to gallop two hundred miles every week to inspect dirty ponds and yeasty barrels." Both in prose and verse he has recorded the feelings with which he first followed his new vocation, and his jests on the subject are uniformly bitter. It was a vocation which exposed him to temptations of the kind he was least likely to resist. His extraordinary conversational powers led him into peril wherever he went. If he entered an inn at midnight, after all the inmates were in bed, the news of his arrival circulated from the cellar to the garret; and ere ten minutes had elapsed, the landlord and all his guests were assembled round the ingle; the largest punch-bowl was produced; and "Be ours this night--who knows what comes to-morrow?" was the language of every eye in the circle that welcomed him.

At home, too, lion-gazers from all quarters beset him; they ate and drank at his cost, and often went away to criticise him and his fare, as if they had done Burns and his black bowl great honour in condescending to be entertained for a single evening with such company. Among others who called on him was Captain Grose, the antiquary, and it is to this acquaintance that we owe "Tam o' Shanter," which Burns believed to be the best of all his productions.

V.--Closing Years of the Poet's Life

Towards the close of 1791 he gave up his farm, and procuring an excise appointment to the Dumfries division, removed to the county town. His moral course from this time was downwards. "In Dumfries," says Heron, speaking from personal knowledge, "his dissipation became still more deeply habitual. He was here exposed more than in the country to be solicited to share the riot of the dissolute and idle." His intemperance was, as Heron says, in fits; his aberrations were occasional, not systematic; they were all to himself the sources of exquisite misery in the retrospect; they were the aberrations of a man whose moral sense was never deadened, of one who encountered more temptations from without and from within than the immense majority of mankind, far from having to contend against, are even able to imagine; of one, finally, who prayed for pardon, where alone effectual pardon could be found.

In how far the "thoughtless follies" of the poet did actually hasten his end, it is needless to conjecture. They had their share, unquestionably, along with other influences which it would be inhuman to characterise as mere follies. In these closing years of his life he had to struggle constantly with pecuniary difficulties, than which nothing could have been more likely to pour bitterness intolerable into the cup of his existence. His lively imagination exaggerated to itself every real evil; and this among, and perhaps above, all the rest; at least, in many of his letters we find him alluding to the probability of his being arrested for debts, which we now know to have been of very trivial amount.

In 1795 he was greatly upset by the death, in his absence, of his youngest child. Writing in January, 1796, he says: "I had scarcely begun to recover from that shock, when I became myself the victim of a most severe rheumatic fever, and long the die spun doubtful, until, after many weeks of a sick-bed, it seems to have turned up life, and I am beginning to crawl across my room, and once indeed have been before my own door in the street."

But a few days after this Burns was so imprudent as to join a festive circle at a tavern dinner, where he remained till about three in the morning. The weather was severe, and he, being too much intoxicated, took no precaution in thus exposing his debilitated frame to its influence. It has been said that he fell asleep upon the snow on his way home. The result was an acute return of his rheumatism, and his health gradually got worse. He went to the Solway for sea-bathing, but came back to Dumfries "visibly changed in his looks, being with difficulty able to stand upright and reach his own door."

It soon became known that he was dying, and the anxiety, not of the rich and the learned only, but of the mechanics and peasants, exceeded all belief. Wherever two or three people stood together their talk was solely of Burns. His good humour was unruffled, and his wit never forsook him; but he repressed with a smile the hopes of his friends, and told them he had lived long enough. The fever increased, and his strength diminished, and he died on July 21, 1796. His funeral, attended by ten or twelve thousand people, was an impressive and mournful sight. The grave was at first covered by a plain tombstone; but a costly mausoleum was subsequently erected on the most elevated site which the churchyard presented. Thither the remains of the poet were solemnly transferred on June 5, 1815.

It requires a graver audacity of hypocrisy than falls to the share of most men to declaim against Burns's sensibility to the tangible cares and toils of his earthly condition; there are more who venture on broad denunciations of his sympathy with the joys of sense and passion.

That some men in every age will comfort themselves in the practice of certain vices, by reference to particular passages both in the history and in the poetry of Burns, there is all reason to fear; but surely the general influence of both is calculated, and has been found, to produce far different effects. The universal popularity which his writings have all along enjoyed among one of the most virtuous of nations is of itself a decisive circumstance.

On one point there can be no controversy; the poetry of Burns has had most powerful influence in reviving and strengthening the national feelings of his countrymen. Amidst penury and labour his youth fed on the old minstrelsy and traditional glories of his nation, and his genius divined that what he felt so deeply must belong to a spirit that might lie smothered around him, but could not be extinguished. Burns "knew his own worth, and reverenced the lyre." But he ever announced himself, as a peasant, the representative of his class, the painter of their manners, inspired by the same influences which ruled their bosoms; and whosoever sympathised with his verse had his soul opened for the moment to the whole family of man.

Short and painful as were his years, Burns has left behind him a volume in which there is inspiration for every fancy and music for every mood; which lives, and will live in strength and vigour, "to soothe," as a generous lover of genius has said, "the sorrows of how many a lover, to inflame the patriotism of how many a soldier, to fan the fires of how many a genius, to disperse the gloom of solitude, appease the agonies of pain, encourage virtue, and show vice its ugliness." In this volume, centuries hence as now, wherever a Scotsman may wander he will find the dearest consolation of his exile.

MARTIN LUTHER

Table Talk

Martin Luther, "the monk who shook the world," was born Nov. 10, 1483, at Eisleben, in Germany. In 1507 he was ordained a priest, and became popular almost immediately as a preacher. A visit to Rome shocked him, and in revolt against the practice of raising money by the sale of indulgences, he began his career as a reformer. In 1518 he was summoned to Rome to answer for his opinions, which now included a total denial of the right of the Pope to forgive sins. He proceeded to attack the whole doctrinal system of the Roman Catholic Church. For this he was denounced in a papal bull and his writings were condemned to be burned. In 1525 he married an escaped nun. That Luther was a true child of his age may be seen in the selections made from his "Table Talk." His shrewdness, humour, plain bold speech, and his change of belief from an infallible Church to an infallible Bible there appear, as also do his narrowness of knowledge, asperity of temper, and susceptibility to superstition. He must be judged by the mind of his times, not by modern standards. We give some of his strong opinions that have not borne the wear and tear of later ages; but they are more than balanced by teaching what is beautiful, as well as true. Luther died on February 18, 1546.

God's Word and Book

That the Bible is God's word and book I prove thus. Infinite potentates have raged against it, and sought to destroy and uproot it--King Alexander the Great, the princes of Egypt and Babylon, the monarchs of Persia, of Greece, and of Rome, the Emperors Julius and Augustus--but they nothing prevailed; they are all gone and vanished, while the book remains and will remain. Who has thus helped it? Who has thus protected it against such mighty forces? No one, surely, but God Himself, who is the Master of all things.

The Holy Scriptures are full of divine gifts and virtues. The books of the heathen taught nothing of faith, hope, or charity; they present no idea of these things; they contemplate only the present, and that which man, with the use of his material reason, can grasp and comprehend. Look not therein for aught of hope and trust in God. But see how the Psalms and the Book of Job treat of faith, hope, resignation, and prayer; in a word, the Holy Scripture is the highest and best of books, abounding in comfort under all afflictions and trials. It teaches us to see, to feel, to grasp, and to comprehend faith, hope, and charity far otherwise than mere human reason can, and when evil oppresses us it teaches how these virtues throw light upon the darkness.

The multitude of books is a great evil. There is no measure or limit to the fever for writing. The Bible is now buried under so many commentaries that the text is nothing regarded. I could wish all my books were buried nine ells deep in the ground by reason of the ill example they will give. I would not have those who read my books, in these stormy times, devote one moment to them that they would otherwise have consecrated to the Bible itself.

God's Dealing with Us

How should God deal with us? Good days we cannot bear, evil we cannot endure. Gives He riches unto us--then we are proud, so that no man can live by us in peace; nay, we will be carried on heads and shoulders, and will be adored as gods. Gives He poverty to us--then are we dismayed, impatient, and murmur against Him.

God only, and not wealth, maintains the world; riches merely make people proud and lazy. Great wealth cannot still hunger, but rather occasions more dearth, for where rich people are there things are always dear. Moreover, money makes no man right merry, but much rather pensive and full of sorrow; for riches, says Christ, are thorns that prick people. Yet is the world so made that it sets therein all its joy and felicity, and we are such unthankful slovens that we give God not so much as a *Deo Gratias*, though we receive of Him overflowing benefits, merely out of His goodness and mercy. No man can estimate the great charge God is at only in maintaining birds and such creatures, comparatively nothing worth. I am persuaded that it costs Him yearly more to maintain only the sparrows than the revenue of the French king amounts to.

Points from "Popedom"

I much marvel that the pope extols his church at Rome as the chief, whereas the church at Jerusalem is the mother; for there Christian doctrine was first revealed. Next was the church at Antioch, whence the Christians have their name. Thirdly, was the church at Alexandria; and still before the Romish were the churches of the Galatians, of the Corinthians, Ephesians, Philippians. Is it so great a matter that St. Peter was at Rome? Which, however, has never yet been proved, nor ever will be, whereas our blessed Saviour Christ Himself was at Jerusalem, where all the articles of our Christian faith were made.

Prayer in popedom is mere tongue-threshing; not prayer but a work of obedience. Hence the confused sea of howling and babbling in cells and monasteries, where they read and sing the psalms and collects without any spiritual devotion. Though I had done no more but only freed people from that torment, they might well give me thanks for it.

Kings and princes coin money only out of metals, but the pope coins money out of everything--indulgences, ceremonials, dispensations, pardons; 'tis all fish comes to his net. 'Tis only baptism escapes him, for children come into the world without clothes to be stolen or teeth to be drawn.

Patristic Literature

I will not presume to criticise too closely the writings of the fathers, seeing they are received of the church and have great applause, but whoso reads Chrysostom will find he digresses from the chief points, and proceeds on other matters, saying nothing, or very little, of that which pertains to the business. St. Jerome wrote upon Matthew, upon the Epistles to the Galatians, and Titus, but, alas, very coldly. Ambrose wrote six books upon the first book of Moses, but they are very poor.

We must read the fathers cautiously, and lay them in the gold balance, for they often stumbled and went astray. Gregory expounds the five pounds mentioned in the Gospel, which the husbandman gave to his servant to put to use, to be the five senses, which the beasts also possess. The two pounds he construes to be the reason and understanding. Faithful Christians should heed only the embassy of our blessed Saviour Christ, and what He says.

None of the fathers of the church made mention of original sin until Augustine came, who made a difference between original and actual sin, namely, that original sin is to covet, to lust, and to desire, which is the root and cause of actual sin.

Hints for Preachers

The good preacher should know when to make an end. A preacher that will speak everything that comes into his mind is like a maid that goes to market, and, meeting another maid, makes a stand, and they hold together a goose-market.

I would not have preachers in their sermons use Hebrew, Greek, or foreign languages, for in the church we ought to speak as we use to do at home, the plain mother tongue, which everyone is acquainted with. It may be allowed in courtiers, lawyers, advocates, etc., to use quaint, curious words. St. Paul never used such high and stately words as Demosthenes and Cicero used.

Ambition is the rankest poison to the church when it possesses preachers. It is a consuming fire.

When I preach I sink myself deep down. I regard neither doctors nor magistrates, of whom are here in this church above forty; but I have an eye to the multitude of young people, children, and servants, of whom are more than two thousand. I preach to those. Will not the rest hear me?

Time's Forelock

It is said Occasion has a forelock, but it is bald behind. Our Lord has taught this by the course of nature. A farmer must sow his barley and oats about Easter; if he defer it till Michaelmas it were too late. When apples are ripe they must be plucked from the tree or they are spoiled. Procrastination is as bad as over-hastiness. There is my servant Wolf, when four or five birds fall upon the bird-net he will not draw it; but says, "Oh, I will stay until more come." Then they all fly away, and he gets none.

Occasion is a great matter. Terence says well, "I came in time, which is the chief thing of all." Julius Caesar understood Occasion; Pompey and Hannibal did not. Boys at school understand it not, therefore they must have fathers and masters, with the rod, to hold them thereto, that they neglect not time and lose it. Many a young fellow has a school stipend for six or seven years, during which he ought diligently to study, but he thinks, "Oh, I have time enough yet." But I say, "No, fellow; what little Jack learns not great John learns not." Occasion salutes thee, and reaches out her forelock to thee, saying, "Here I am, take hold of me." Thou thinkest she will come again. Then says she, "Well, seeing thou wilt not take hold of my top, take hold of my tail," and therewith she flings away.

Modern Luxury

Whereto serve or profit such superfluity, such show, such ostentation, such extraordinary luxurious kind of life as is now come upon us? If Adam were to return to earth, and see our mode of living, our food, drink, and dress, how would he marvel. He would say: "Surely this is not the world I was in?" For Adam drank water, ate fruit from the trees, and, if he had any house at all, 'twas a hut supported by four wooden forks; he had no knife or iron, and he wore simply a coat of skin. Now we spend immense sums in eating and drinking, now we raise sumptuous palaces, and decorate them with a luxury beyond all comparison. The ancient Israelites lived in great moderation and quiet. Boaz says: "Dip thy bread in vinegar and refresh thyself therewith."

Ministers and Matrimony

I advise in everything that ministers interfere not in matrimonial questions. First, because we have enough to do in our own office; secondly, because these affairs concern not the church, but are temporal things, pertaining to temporal magistrates; thirdly, because such cases are in a manner innumerable; they are very high, broad, and deep, and produce many offences, which may tend to the shame and dishonour of the Gospel. Moreover, we are therein ill dealt with--they draw us into the business, and then, if the issue is evil, the blame is laid altogether upon us. Therefore, we will leave them to the lawyers and magistrates.

Miscellaneous Topics

Philip Melancthon showing Luther a letter from Augsburg wherein he was informed that a very learned divine, a papist of that city, was converted, and had received the Gospel, Luther said, "I like best those that do not fall off suddenly, but ponder the case with considerate discretion, compare together the writing and arguments of both parties, and lay them on the gold balance, and in God's fear search after the upright truth; and of such fit people are made, able to stand in controversy. Such a man was St. Paul, who at first was a strict Pharisee and man of works, who stiffly and earnestly defended the law; but afterwards preached Christ in the best and purest manner against the whole nation of the Jews."

As all people feel they must die, each seeks immortality here on earth, that he may be had in everlasting remembrance. Some great princes and kings seek it by raising great columns of stone and high pyramids, great churches, costly and glorious palaces and castles. Soldiers hunt after praise and honour by obtaining famous victories. The learned seek an everlasting name by writing books. With these and such like things people think to be immortal. But as to the true everlasting and incorruptible honour and eternity of God, no man thinks or looks after these things.

When two goats meet on a narrow bridge over deep waters how do they behave? Neither of them can turn back again, and neither can pass the other because the bridge is too narrow. If they should thrust one another they might both fall into the water and be drowned. Nature, then, has taught them that if one lays himself down and permits the other to go over him both remain without hurt. Even so, people should endure to be trod upon rather than to fall into discord with one another.

Strong Opinions Outworn by Time

I should have no compassion on witches; I would burn all of them. We read in the old law that the priests threw the first stone at such malefactors. Our ordinary sins offend and anger God. What then must be His wrath against witchcraft, which we may justly designate high treason against divine majesty, a revolt against the infinite power of God. The maladies I suffer are not natural but devils' spells.

Luther, taking up a caterpillar, said: "'Tis an emblem of the devil in its crawling, and bears his colours in its changing hue."

The devil plagues and torments us in the place where we are most tender and weak. In Paradise he fell not upon Adam, but upon Eve. It commonly rains where it was wet enough before.

The anabaptists pretend that children, not as yet having reason, ought not to receive baptism. I answer: That reason in no way contributes to faith. Nay, in that children are destitute of reason they are all the more fit and proper recipients of baptism. For reason is the greatest enemy that faith has; it never comes to the aid of spiritual things.

I always loved music. A schoolmaster ought to have skill in music, or I would not regard him; neither should we ordain young men as preachers unless they have been well exercised in music.

Erasmus of Rotterdam is the vilest miscreant that ever disgraced the earth. He made several attempts to draw me into his snares, and I should have been in danger but that God lent me special aid. Erasmus was poisoned at Rome and at Venice with epicurean doctrines. His chief doctrine is that we must carry ourselves according to the time, or, as the proverb goes, hang the cloak according to the wind. I hold Erasmus to be Christ's most bitter enemy.

I never work better than when I am inspired by anger. When I am angry I can write, pray, and preach well, for then my whole temperament is quickened, my understanding sharpened, and all mundane vexations and temptations depart.

Characteristic Sayings

When the abbot throws the dice, the whole convent will play.

When men blaspheme we should pray and be silent, and not carry wood to the fire.

When Jesus Christ utters a word, He opens His mouth so wide that it embraces all heaven and earth, even though that word be but in a whisper.

When I lay sucking at my mother's breast I had no notion how I should afterwards eat, drink, and live. Even so we on the earth have no idea what the life to come will be.

The two sins, hatred and pride, deck and trim themselves out as the devil clothed himself in the Godhead. Hatred will be godlike; pride will be truth. These two are right deadly sins; hatred is killing, pride is lying.

A scorpion thinks that when his head lies hid under a leaf he cannot be seen; even so the hypocrites and false saints think, when they have hoisted up one or two good works, all their sins therewith are covered and hid.

Luther, holding a rose in his hand, said, "'Tis a magnificent work of God. Could a man make but one such rose as this he would be thought worthy of all honour, but the manifold gifts of God lose their value in our eyes from their very infinity."

MIRABEAU

Memoirs

Honoré Gabriel Riqueti, Comte de Mirabeau, was born at Bignon, near Nemours, on March 9, 1749, and died at Paris on April 2, 1791. His father was a most eccentric and tyrannical representative of the French aristocracy, and Honoré, a younger son, inherited something of his violent temperament, but was endowed with real genius. Entering the army, young Mirabeau soon displayed an erratic disposition by eloping with the young wife of an aged nobleman. He fled to Holland, but was captured and imprisoned. Being at length liberated, he turned to literature and politics, and soon gained celebrity in both. His magnificent oratorical powers brought him rapidly to the front in the period immediately anterior to the outbreak of the Revolution. Mirabeau's "Memoirs, by Himself, his Father, his Uncle, and his Adopted Son," published in eight volumes in 1834, contain no original writings by Mirabeau himself, except in the shape of extracts from his speeches, letters, and pamphlets. The following epitome has been prepared from the French text.

I.--"The Hurricane"

The Marquis of Mirabeau, father of Honoré Gabriel, the subject of these memoirs, was endowed with a mind of great power, rendered fruitful by the best education. He had, however, become independent at too early an age, and this had brought into play his natural inordinate vanity.

Honoré Gabriel, since so famous under the name of the Count of Mirabeau, was the fifth child of the marquis. Destined to be the most turbulent and active of youths, as well as the most eloquent of men and the greatest orator of his day, Gabriel was born with one foot twisted and his tongue tied, in addition to which his size and strength were extraordinary, and already two molars were formed in his jaw. At the age of three the boy nearly lost his life from small-pox, and was thus disfigured greatly for life; while the other children were, like the parents, gifted with wonderful beauty.

Young Gabriel was a most precocious child, and he received an excellent education. At the age of seven he was confirmed by a cardinal, but his childhood was difficult of control, and chastisement from his father and tutor was continual. His inquisitiveness was irrepressible. He relates that at the family supper after his confirmation, "they explained to me that God could not make contradictions--for instance, a stick with only one end. I asked whether a stick which had but one end was not a miracle. My grandmother never forgave me."

Placed under the kindly teaching of the Abbé Choquart in a military school of high repute in Paris, Gabriel made marvellously rapid progress, assiduously exercising his memory, which afterwards became a prodigious repository of the most diversified knowledge.

On July 10, 1767, Gabriel entered the army, joining the Marquis of Lambert's regiment. The young volunteer, who was now eighteen, behaved well, and speedily gave evidence of the military talents he afterwards displayed. But a quarrel arose over a love affair, which led to harsh punishment by his colonel. The incident was bitterly resented by his father, who condemned him without hearing his side of the matter, and actually procured his imprisonment in the fortress of the Isle of Rhé.

When the young soldier came out of prison he unwittingly offended an officer at Rochelle, who had been dismissed the service. The result was a duel, in which the aggressor was wounded. Gabriel was appointed to service in Corsica, with the rank of second-lieutenant, and here he distinguished himself by his zeal, his military talents, and his constant application.

Young Mirabeau was, in September, 1770, transferred to Limousin, in west Central France. Such was his energy that he was called "the hurricane." Now began a series of troubles caused by bitter quarrels between his parents, who were openly at variance. Each sought to gain an adherent in their son, who was condemned to witness the wickedness and folly of both in their ungovernable passion. The effect on the character of the young count was deplorable.

Then ensued a singular episode. The marquis had determined that Gabriel should marry before the age of twenty-three, and had fixed on Mary Emily de Covet, only daughter of the Marquis de Marignane, eighteen years of age, for his son's bride. She was plain, yet attractive, with a sweet smile, fine eyes, and beautiful hair, and was gay, lively, sensible, mild, and very amiable. Having been neglected by her father and ill-treated by her mother, she showed no disinclination to marriage, and in 1772 young Mirabeau obtained the hand of the wealthy heiress.

No sooner was the young count married than every attempt was made to ruin him. He received no property with his bride, and his avaricious father refused to advance him any money for necessary expenses. His father-in-law offered to lend him 60,000 livres, but his father's consent was indispensable, and this was sternly refused. Mirabeau, harassed by creditors, was dragged into lawsuits, and his embarrassments only set his father entirely against him. The marquis actually procured a *lettre de cachet*, obliging his son to leave the home he had set up, and to confine himself to the little town of Manosque.

Here domestic sorrow and the most painful circumstances assailed the young exile. But these did not prevent him from pursuing serious studies and composing his first work, the "Essay on Despotism." Misfortunes accumulated. Chastising with a horsewhip a baron who grossly insulted him, the count was again imprisoned, this time in the Château d'If, a gloomy citadel on a barren rock near Marseilles.

On May 25, 1770, Mirabeau was transferred to the Castle of Joux, near Pontarlier, where, on June 11, 1775, festivities were held, as at other places, to honour the coronation of Louis XVI. Here Mirabeau enjoyed a sort of half freedom, being allowed to visit in Pontarlier, and the event ensued which, it must sorrowfully be owned, tarnished his name. In a word, we see Mirabeau "ruin himself," by a fatal intimacy with the young wife of the aged Marquis of Monnier. The two fled to Dijon, where Mirabeau surrendered himself at the castle.

He was released after a short time and went on to Geneva, nearly perishing in a storm on the lake. Returning to Pontarlier, he was joined by Sophie Monnier, and the two left for Holland, and arrived at Amsterdam on October 7, 1776. Mirabeau was naturally obliged to draw his principal means of subsistence from his literary labours, and this, perhaps, had been his motive for choosing Holland as his residence, for at that period the Dutch booksellers entered largely into literary speculations.

Mirabeau and Sophie Monnier were arrested at Amsterdam on May 14, 1777. Both were brought to France. She was placed in a convent at Monilmontant, and Mirabeau was deposited on June 7 in the donjon of Vincennes, and was subjected to every sort of privation, remaining in confinement for forty-two months. His release marked the end of his private life; his public and political life was about to begin.

II.--Into Political Life

The "Essay on Despotism" had been the first sign of Mirabeau's political vocation, and the most singular instance, perhaps, of a war audaciously declared against despotism by a young man bearing its yoke. The keynote is that though the *natural* man may not be inclined to despotism, the *social* man assuredly is disposed to be a despot. This spirit, maintains Mirabeau, exists even in republics.

In 1784 Mirabeau visited England. One of his motives was to collect materials for his "Considerations on the Order of Cincinnatus," a treatise dealing with Washington and American independence. He was greatly delighted with English scenery. "It is here," he says, "that nature is improved, not forced. All tells me that here the people are something; that every man enjoys the development and free exercise of his faculties, and that I am in another order of things."

But he proceeds: "I am not an enthusiast in favour of England, and I now know sufficient of that country to tell you that if its constitution is the best known, the application of this constitution is the worst possible; and that if the Englishman is as a social man the most free in the world, the English people are the least free of any."

He resided in England from August to February, 1785. During that brief period he began to write his "History of Geneva," and he showed his versatility by composing for a young refugee clergyman a sermon on the immortality of the soul. By the gift of this sermon he drew the exiled preacher from poverty, for it was the means of obtaining for him a lucrative appointment.

Mirabeau sent forth from Paris several most able pamphlets on banking and on share companies. These were written with energy and often with violence. As they attacked many private interests they aroused against their author much hatred, insult, and calumny. He was accused of venality, though he was attacking and driving to despair powerful stock-jobbers, who would have paid him magnificently for silence, could he have been bought.

In July, 1785, Mirabeau went to Berlin. It is a singular fact that in his various journeys some accident always befel him. On the way to Berlin an attempt was made to assassinate him by some unknown enemies, but he safely reached the German capital. King Frederick the Great, now very aged, no longer received foreigners, yet he replied to a letter from Mirabeau and fixed a day for seeing him at Potsdam.

Mirabeau informed the king that he had come to seek permission to study the great military manoeuvres, and that he hoped to push on to Russia. During this period he worked like a labourer all day at his writings. Part of his time he spent at supper parties of the most tiresome etiquette. The same laborious habits attended him everywhere, in prison and in freedom, in his own country and in other lands. It was in Germany that he conceived the idea of his treatise on "The Reform of the Jews," which is acknowledged to be one of his best works.

Frederick the Great died on August 17, 1786. Feeling that he could do nothing useful, Mirabeau resolved at the close of 1786 to quit Berlin. He was urged also by a special motive in which he took pride, and which he thus described in a letter: "My heart has not grown old, and if my enthusiasm is damped, it is not extinguished. I have fully experienced this to-day. I consider one of the best days of my life that on which I received an account of the convocation of the notables, which no doubt will not long precede that of the National Assembly. In this I see a new order of things which may regenerate the monarchy. I should deem myself a thousand times honoured in being even the junior secretary of this assembly, of which I had the happiness of giving the first idea."

Mirabeau was prodigiously occupied at Berlin. He often did not retire to rest till one in the morning, but regularly rose at five, even in the midst of severe winter. Without anything on but a simple quilted dressing-gown, without stockings or waistcoat, he worked away without even calling up his servant to light a fire. Besides his correspondence in cypher, which occupied him much, he worked assiduously at his "Prussian Monarchy," which was published in 1788.

On departing from Berlin the count wrote a most eloquent letter of counsel to King Frederick William, appealing to him to cultivate peace, reminding him that his illustrious predecessor had conquered the admiration of mankind but never won their love, commending him not to extend the direct action of the royal power to matters which did not require it, advising him not to govern too much, and exhorting him to abolish military slavery; that is to say, the obligation then imposed on every Prussian to serve as a soldier from the age of eighteen to sixty or more, which forced men to go to the battle-field like cattle to the slaughterhouse.

In the same remarkable document Mirabeau raises his voice against the harsh laws which arbitrarily deprived Prussians of freedom to leave the country. The tyrannical prohibition of emigration excited his vehement protest, and he proceeded also to denounce to the new king the right of seizing the property of deceased foreigners, and demanded for burghers the freedom of purchasing the estates of nobles. He urged Frederick William to abolish the prerogatives claimed by nobles and the helotism of all who were not noble, and suggested that judges should be appointed for life and justice rendered free of expense.

III.--For King and People

It was chiefly the meeting of the notables which had hastened Mirabeau's return to Paris. He felt that his proper place was in the centre of the great events announced and begun by this convocation. After the undignified and inglorious prodigality of the previous reign, which had laid the foundation of serious financial vicissitudes, the young King Louis XVI. had brought with him to the throne the private virtues of a good and honest man, but not the qualities of a sovereign.

Though economic to excess himself, he nevertheless suffered to exist and even to increase around him those dilapidations which at last ruined the resources of the state. He had no confidence in himself, and Mirabeau respectfully reproached him with his fatal timidity. Nothing was done either to increase revenue or diminish expenditure.

The possessors of privilege and representatives of personal interest, the courtiers, the great lords, and the parliaments strenuously resisted all reforms and then drove from office the best intentioned, the most virtuous, and the ablest ministers whom the young king, in the sincerity of his patriotism, had chosen on his accession, in deference to public feeling. Among these ministers were Malesherbes, Turgot, Necker, and Calonne.

Mirabeau returned to Paris on January 27, 1787. He at once published that famous "Address to the Notables," in which he denounced the whole corrupt system of finance and in which he demanded local provincial administrations. This and his "Denunciation of Stock-jobbing" made great impression on the public mind.

Nevertheless, the "Denunciation" displeased the government, and the author was much persecuted. He learned that he was to be arrested and sent, not to the Bastille, but to a remote provincial fortress, where he would have been lost to public notice. So he escaped from Paris to Liège, whence he again attacked the administration of Calonne and the policy of Necker, declaring that loans should have been effected on methods less onerous for the state.

His exile from Paris was of brief duration, for friends intervened. But Mirabeau returned only to renew and intensify his attacks. He remained, however, only for a short time, for on May 24, 1787, he set out on a third journey to Prussia, in order to complete his great work on the "Prussian Monarchy." Returning to France, he reached Paris in September. Five months had elapsed since the assembling of the notables. The eloquent Leominie de Brienne, Archbishop of Toulouse, had been the most brilliant figure in the conclave. The first assembly broke up on July 27, 1787. Though gathered by the privileged orders, patriotism had raised its voice within it, and the archbishop, as prime minister, had failed to direct the new current aright.

Mirabeau disapproved of what had taken place in his absence, and declined to be employed by the administration, but he offered to undertake any foreign mission in the exercise of the king to which he might be appointed. The application was unsuccessful. The crisis approached nearer and nearer. Archbishop Brienne passed rapidly from violence to weakness. Mirabeau refused to countenance his plans for contracting a new loan of 420 millions. The king was resisted by an almost unanimous opposition, headed by the Duke of Orleans, and the loan was refused at a memorable sitting.

Mirabeau exhorted the government to announce in precise and solemn terms the convocation of the States-General in 1789, that bankruptcy might be averted and the national honour saved. Said he: "The year in which the king assembles the nation will be the finest in his life. Everybody knows that he has been deceived, and could not help being so, and everybody will do justice to his intentions. The assembled nation has a right to vote a tax. In future the nation alone will raise up its political fortunes."

Mirabeau saw that the nation ought to be trusted. He strenuously contended for a policy in accordance with this conviction. But he indefatigably continued his literary labours, sending forth pamphlet after pamphlet, one against the prison system in vogue, another demanding the liberty of the Press, in which he extolled the example of England. He became increasingly impatient with the ineptitude of the government, for the affairs of the state were lapsing into desperate disorder, and the public discontent was being steadily aggravated.

The aim of Mirabeau was at one and the same time to support the monarchy and to subvert the influences by which the throne was environed. He was solicitous of securing popular freedom, but regarded the monarchy as the only form of rule suitable for France in that age, and was led to adopt that peculiar statesmanship identifying the royal interest with the popular cause. Though ready to give his life for the people, he did not hesitate to risk his popularity by his fidelity to the throne.

IV.--President of the National Assembly

The immediate causes of the Revolution were now in full operation. Mirabeau, attempting to practise his own doctrine of the freedom of the Press, turned journalist and brought out a gazette. The famous National Assembly opened on May 5, 1789. He then entered on a career of immense political energy, beginning by issuing a stirring and eloquent "Address to the French People." This was especially a reply to a reactionary protest on the part of the clergy.

Soon there were disturbances everywhere. The Bastille was stormed by the furious Parisians and demolished. Just at this time Mirabeau lost his father, and the event overwhelmed him with grief. He refused to stand for election as mayor of Paris. But he brought about a constitutional organisation of the municipality, and delivered a splendid series of orations on various abuses, such as plural voting, iniquitous monopolies, etc. Yet he proved his studious moderation by strenuously declaiming against the famous "Declaration of the Rights of Man," pronouncing it inopportune and perilous. His heroic harangues provoked disorder in his audience dangerous to himself. But his courage was dauntless, for even when the king and his chief minister abandoned the royal prerogative, Mirabeau defended it.

Throughout the terrible events of 1789 Mirabeau was consistent as a loyalist and as a patriot. But disappointment awaited his generous illusions, for the vacillation of the king rendered the outlook hopeless.

At the end of January, 1791, he was appointed president of the National Assembly, which, during the stormy period of its existence during twenty-one months, had already had forty-two presidents.

He exercised his functions with consummate skill, but the end of his wonderful life was at hand. He had been in weak health from the very first sittings of the Assembly, his condition causing constant anxiety to his intimate friends and his admirers. He was depressed by sad presentiments, and was in constant apprehension of assassination, for it was well-known that there were plots against his life. After a brilliant oration, the great tribune went home exhausted, and, indeed, dying.

One of his last experiences was a pathetic interview with Talleyrand, with whom he had often crossed swords in debate. His weakness dated from February, 1788, when he was attacked with violent internal pains, and was bled to such an extent by a surgeon that he never recovered his wonderful natural vitality. After much suffering, endured with the most heroic fortitude, he passed away as if in sleep, with a sweet smile on his features. France mourned the loss of the greatest orator that had ever graced her tribune. His funeral was celebrated at St. Genevieve with splendid ceremonial. The verdict of those best qualified to judge was that Mirabeau was the most remarkable man of the eighteenth century, and that his premature death, soon after the outbreak of the Revolution, led to the overthrow of a monarchy which he alone could have saved.

THOMAS MOORE

Life of Byron

Thomas Moore, the Irish poet, was born in Dublin on May 28, 1779, was educated at Trinity College, and studied for the Bar at the Middle Temple. At twenty-one years of age he published a translation of Anacreon, and his reputation was further established by his love-poems, under the pseudonym of Thomas Little, in 1801. He received in 1803 an official post in Bermuda, but entrusted his duties there to a substitute, by whose defalcations he was later embarrassed. He was married at thirty-one to a beautiful and amiable actress, Bessy Dyke, and lived very happily for most of his life in Wiltshire, but with an interval of a few years in Paris. In 1835 he received a literary pension of £300, to which a Civil List pension of £100 was added in 1850. He died on February 25, 1852. Undoubtedly, Moore's most important contribution to prose literature was his "Letters and Journals of Lord Byron," published in 1830, six years after the poet's death; as payment he received £4,200. Although the work was frankly and even severely criticised in many quarters, it did a great deal to put Byron right with public opinion. Certainly no literary contemporary was better fitted to write the biography of his friend than Moore, who, moreover, had been marked for this work by a free gift of Byron's own memoirs.

I.--Ancestors and Early Days

It has been said of Lord Byron that he was prouder of being a descendant of those Byrons of Normandy, who accompanied William the Conqueror into England, than of having been the author of "Childe Harold." The remark is not altogether unfounded, for the pride of ancestry was a feature of his character; and justly so, for his line was honourably known on the fields of Cressy, Bosworth, and Marston Moor; and in the faithful royalist, Sir John Biron, afterwards Lord Biron, throughout the Civil Wars.

In 1784, the father of the poet, Captain John Byron, nephew of the fifth Lord Byron, with the sole object of relieving his debts, married, as his second wife, Miss Catherine Gordon, a wealthy lady of illustrious Scottish ancestry. Her fortune was swallowed up, and she was reduced to £150 a year, before she gave birth, on January 22, 1788, in Holles Street, London, to her first and only child, George Gordon Byron. The boy was somewhat deformed, one of his feet being twisted.

In 1790, we find the unhappy parents living in separate lodgings in Aberdeen; and this estrangement was followed by complete separation, the worthless Captain Byron proceeding to France, where he died in the following year. The mother, a woman of the most passionate extremes, sent the boy to day school and grammar school. His schoolmates remember him as lively, warm-hearted, and more ready to give a blow than to take one. To summer excursions with his mother in the Highlands the poet traces his love of scenery and especially of mountainous countries; and he refers many years after, still with keen feeling, to a little girl, Mary Duff, for whom, in his eighth year, he cherished a consuming attachment. So early were his sensibilities dominant.

On the death, in 1794, of the grandson of the old lord, little George stood in immediate succession to the peerage; in May, 1798, the fifth Lord Byron died at Newstead Abbey, and the boy's name was called in school with the title "Dominus." The Earl of Carlisle was appointed his guardian in chancery, and in the same summer, Lord Byron, in his eleventh year, took possession, with his mother, of the seat of his ancestors. The next year Mrs. Byron was placed on the Civil List for a pension of £300 a year. Removing to London, she placed George at school with Dr. Glennie at Dulwich, but thwarted the progress of his education with her fondness and self-will, until Lord Carlisle gave up all hope of ruling her. It was at this period that a boyish love for Margaret Parker, his cousin, who died shortly after, led Byron into the practice of verse.

From 1801 to 1805, from thirteen years of age to seventeen, George was at Harrow, where he sat beside Peel, the future statesman. This period of ardent friendship with his fellows includes also the romantic affection, in 1803, for Miss Chaworth, heiress of Annesley, near Newstead, who looked on her admirer as the mere schoolboy that he was. Leaving Harrow with the reputation of an idler who would never learn, Byron was entered at Trinity College, Cambridge, in October, 1805. His vacations were spent with his mother at Southwell, and her explosions of temper, in which she would throw poker and tongs, alienated him increasingly. In vacation and in term alike he read with extraordinary avidity and variety, wrote a great deal of verse, and in November, 1806, printed a small volume of poems for private circulation.

He was a frank and vivid correspondent; his letters to Miss Pigot, of Southwell, and others, are full of the liveliest descriptions of the Cambridge days. At this time Byron was painfully shy of new faces, and perpetually mortified on account of his poverty. He rose, and retired to rest, very late. He was very fond of the exercises of swimming, riding, shooting, fencing, and sparring; greatly devoted to his dogs, delighted in music, and was known as remarkably superstitious. Of his charity and kindheartedness there was no end. Always conscious of his deformity, and terribly afraid of becoming corpulent, he was sedulously careful of his person and dress.

"Hours of Idleness," Byron's first published volume, came out while he was at the university, and was received by the "Edinburgh Review" with a contempt which stung him to the quick. With intervals of dissipation in London and at Brighton, Byron threw himself, at Newstead, into the preparation of a satirical revenge, training himself for it by a deep study of the writings of Pope. After his coming of age, in 1809, he went up to London with his satire, and on March 13 took his seat in the House of Lords. A few days later "English Bards and Scotch Reviewers" was the talk of the town. Wild festivities at Newstead followed its publication, and on July 2 Byron sailed from Falmouth in the Lisbon packet.

II.--The Poet Finds Himself

Lord Byron was absent from England for two years, and in the solitude of his nights at sea and in his lone wanderings through Greece he had leisure and seclusion to look within himself, and there catch the first glimpses of his glorious mind. His deep passion for solitude grew to full power; the varied excitement of his travels invigorated his character and stored his imagination with impressions, and his inborn sadness rose from a querulous bitterness to the grandeur of his later melancholy.

His letters show him on Parnassus, where a flight of eagles seemed an omen of his destiny; at Athens, where he lodged with the mother of the "Maid of Athens"; standing among the ruins of Ephesus and the mounds of Troy; swimming the Hellespont in honour of Leander; at Constantinople, where the prospect of the Golden Horn seemed the fairest of all; at Patras, in the woeful debility of fever; and again at Athens, making acquaintance with Lady Hester Stanhope and "Abyssinian" Bruce. Through all these varied scenes his mind was brooding on the verses of the "Childe Harold."

On Byron's return to England, in July, 1811, that poem was placed in Mr. Murray's hands, and thus was laid the foundation of a long connection between author and publisher. Mrs. Byron died on August 1. With all her faults she had loved her son deeply, and he could at least look back upon dutiful and kindly behaviour to her. It was in November that I first had the pleasure of meeting the poet at dinner, and what I chiefly remarked was the nobleness of his air, his beauty, the gentleness of his voice and manner, and his marked kindness. From our first meeting our acquaintance quickly ripened into friendship.

On February 27, 1812, a day or two before the appearance of "Childe Harold," Byron made the first trial of his eloquence in the House of Lords, and it was on this occasion that he made the acquaintance of Lord Holland. The subject of debate was the Nottingham Frame-breaking Bill. Workmen were rioting and wrecking because their labour had been displaced by the introduction of machinery, and Byron's view was that "we must not allow mankind to be sacrificed to improvements in mechanism"--"the maintenance of the industrious poor is of greater consequence than the enrichment of monopolists"--"I have seen the state of these miserable men, and it is a disgrace to a civilised country." The speech was well received. The impression produced two days later by Byron's "Childe Harold" was as instantaneous as it has proved deep and lasting. Even the dashes of scepticism, with which he darkened his strain, served only to heighten its success. The Prince Regent had the poet presented to him, and the author of "Marmion" offered his praise. In the following May appeared the wild and beautiful fragment, "The Giaour." This new offspring of his genius was hailed with wonder and delight, and on my rejoining him in town this spring, I found an intense enthusiasm for Byron throughout the literary and social world. But his mind was already turning to freedom and solitude, and his third and last speech in the House of Lords was made in June.

III.--Byron's Unfortunate Marriage

Byron's restlessness is reflected throughout his "Journal," which he began at this time. He had dreams of living in the Grecian Islands and of adopting an Eastern manner of life; but in December, 1813, when "The Bride of Abydos" was published, he was still feverishly dissipating himself in England.

A significant entry in the "Journal" says: "A wife would be the salvation of me," and Lord Byron became a suitor for the hand of Miss Milbanke, a relative of Lady Melbourne. His proposal was not at first accepted, but a correspondence ensued between them, and in September, 1814, after the appearance of "The Corsair" and "Lara," they became formally affianced. I was much in his society at this time, and was filled with foreboding anxieties, which the unfortunate events that followed only too fully justified. At the end of December he set out for Seaham, the seat of Sir Ralph Milbanke, the lady's father, and on January 2, 1815, was married. On March 8, he wrote to me from Seaham: "Bell is in health, and unvaried good-humour and behaviour."

Lord Byron's pecuniary embarrassments now accumulated upon him, and just a year after his marriage, and shortly after the birth of their daughter, I received a letter which breathed a profound melancholy, due partly to his difficulties, but more, I thought, to a return of the restless and roving spirit. I replied: "Do tell me you are happier than that letter has led me to fear, and I shall be satisfied." It was only a few weeks later that Lady Byron adopted the resolution of parting from him. She had left London in January on a visit to her father, and Byron was to follow her. They had parted in the utmost kindness; she wrote him a letter, full of playfulness and affection, on the road; but immediately on her arrival her father wrote to acquaint Lord Byron that she would return to him no more. At the time when he had to stand this unexpected shock, his financial troubles, which had led to eight or nine executions in his house within the year, had arrived at their utmost; and at a moment when, to use his own expression, he was "standing alone on his hearth, with his household gods shivered around him," he was also doomed to receive the startling intelligence that the wife who had just parted with him in kindness, had parted with him for ever.

I must quote from a letter he wrote me in March: "The fault was not in my choice, unless in choosing at all; for I do not believe--and I must say it in the very dregs of all this bitter business--that there ever was a better, or even a brighter, a kinder, or a more amiable and agreeable being than Lady Byron. I never had any reproach to make her while with me. Where there is blame, it belongs to myself, and if I cannot redeem, I must bear it."

IV.--Wanderings and Work

On April 25, 1816, being now twenty-eight years of age, Byron took final leave of England, and sailed with two servants for Ostend. His route, by Flanders and the Rhine, may be traced in his matchless verses. He settled in Geneva, where he met Shelley and Mrs. Shelley; they boated on the lake and walked together, and Byron's susceptible mind was deeply influenced by his mystical companion. We may discover traces of that vague sublimity in the third canto of "Childe Harold," and traces also of Mr. Wordsworth's mood which Byron absorbed from Shelley's favourite author.

From November, 1816, his letters are dated from Venice. "This has always been, next to the East, the greenest island of my imagination, and it has not disappointed me." They are considerably taken up with love affairs of an irregular kind, and contain also many vivid pictures of Venetian society and manners. "Manfred" was completed in 1817, and was followed by the fourth canto of "Childe Harold." Margarita Cogni was the reigning favourite of Byron's unworthy harem at this time; and his poem of "Don Juan," now begun, most faithfully and lamentably reflects every whim and passion that, like the rack of autumn, swept across his mind.

But April, 1819, brought a revulsion against all this libertine way of living, and brought also the dawn of the only real love of his whole life. Lord Byron had first met the Countess Guiccioli in the autumn of 1818, when she made her appearance, three days after her marriage, at the house of the Countess Albrizzi, in all the gaiety of bridal array, and the first delight of exchanging a convent for the world. She has given her impressions of their meeting: "His noble and exquisitely beautiful countenance, the tone of his voice, his manners, the thousand enchantments that surrounded him, rendered him so superior a being to any whom I had hitherto seen, that it was impossible he should not have left the most profound impression upon me."

In June, Byron joined her at Ravenna, and for the next three years remained devotedly attached to her. She struck me, during our first interview, when I visited them at La Mira, as a lady not only of a style of beauty singular in an Italian, as being fair-complexioned and delicate, but also as being highly intelligent and amiable.

A letter to me from Pisa, dated August 27, 1822, has a mournful interest: "We have been burning the bodies of Shelley and Williams on the seashore. You can have no idea what an extraordinary effect such a funeral pile has, with mountains in the background and the sea before." Another, of November 17, to Lady Byron, shows that if the author of it had not right on his side, he had at least most of those good feelings which generally accompany it. "I have to acknowledge the receipt of Ada's [their daughter's] hair; this note will reach you about her birthday.... We both made a bitter mistake; but now it is over, and better so.... I assure you that I bear you now no resentment whatever.... Whether the offence has been solely on my side, or reciprocal, or on yours chiefly, I have ceased to reflect on any but two things--that you are the mother of my child, and that we shall never meet again."

Byron was thirty-five years old when from his exile at Genoa he turned his eyes to Greece, where a spirit was now rising such as he had imaged forth in dreams of song, but hardly could have dreamed that he should have lived to see it realised. He longed to witness, and very probably to share in, the present triumphs of liberty on those very fields where he had gathered for immortality such memorials of the liberty of the past. Lord Byron was in touch with the committee concerned with Grecian liberty in May, 1823, and two months later sailed with his party on July 14.

Arriving at Cephalonia he made a journey to Ithaca for a few days. His confidence in the Greek cause was soon clouded; the people were grossly degenerate, and he saw that the work of regeneration must be slow. To convince the government and the chiefs of the paralysing effect of their dissensions, to inculcate the spirit of union, to endeavour to humanise the feelings of the belligerents on both sides, so as to take from the war the character of barbarism--these, with the generous aid of his money, were the objects of his interference.

At length the time for action arrived, and, leaving Cephalonia, Byron landed at Missolonghi on January 4, 1824. He was welcomed with all honour, and at the end of the month received a formal commission from the government as commander of the expedition against Lepanto, a fortified town. This design was a failure, and Byron occupied himself with the fortification of Missolonghi, and with the formation of a brigade for the next campaign.

But his health had lately been giving way; he was living in little better than a swamp; and one day, after exposure to a heavy shower, he was seized with acute pains. On April 11, the illness, now recognised as rheumatic fever, increased, and on the 19th he was no more. The funeral took place in the Church of St. Nicholas, Missolonghi, on April 22, and the remains were carried to England on the brig Florida, and buried, close to those of his mother, in the village church of Hucknall.

V.--A Bewildering Personality

Can I clear away some of the mists that hang round my friend, and show him as worthy of love as he was of admiration? The task is not an easy one. In most minds some one influence governs, from which all secondary impulses are found to radiate, but this pivot of character was wanting to Lord Byron. Governed at different moments by totally different passions, and impelled sometimes, as in his excess of parsimony in Italy, by springs of action never before developed in his nature, he presents the strangest contradictions and inconsistencies, a bewildering complication of qualities.

So various, indeed, were his moral and intellectual attributes, that he may be pronounced to have been not one, but many. It was this multiform aspect that led the world to compare him with a medley host of personages: "within nine years," as he playfully records, "to Rousseau, Goethe, Young, Aretino, Timon of Athens, Dante, Petrarch, Satan, Shakespeare, Buonaparte, Tiberius, Æschylus, Sophocles, Euripides, Harlequin, Henry VIII., Mirabeau, Michael Angelo, Diogenes, Milton, Alfieri, and many others."

But this very versatility, which renders it so difficult to fix the fairy fabric of his character, is itself the clue to whatever was most dazzling in his might, or startling in his levity, or most attractive or most repellent in his life and genius. A variety of powers almost boundless, and a pride no less vast in displaying them; an unusual susceptibility and an uncontrolled impetuosity--such were the two great sources of all that varied spectacle of his life--unchecked feeling and dominant self-will.

Great versatility of power will hardly be found without a tendency to versatility of principle. Byron was fully aware, not only of this characteristic quality of his nature, but also of its danger to singleness of character; and this consciousness had the effect of keeping him in a general line of consistency, throughout life, on certain great subjects, and helped him to preserve unbroken the greater number of his personal attachments. But, except in some few respects, he gave way to his versatile humour without scruple or check; and it was impossible but that such a range of will and power should be abused. Is it to be wondered at that in the works of one thus gifted and carried away we should find, without any design of corrupting on his side, evil too often invested with a grandeur which belongs intrinsically but to good?

Nay, it will be found that even the strength and impressiveness of Byron's poetry is sometimes injured by a capricious and desultory quality due to this very pliancy of mind. It may be questioned whether a concentration of his powers would not have afforded a grander result. It may be that, if Lord Byron had not been so actively versatile, he would have been, not less wonderful, but more great.

Again, this love of variety was one of the most pervading weaknesses, not only to his poetry, but of his life. The pride of personating every kind of character, evil as well as good, influenced his ambition and his conduct; and to such a perverse length did he carry this fancy for self-defamation that, if there was any tendency to mental derangement, it was in this point that it manifested itself. I have known him more than once, as we have sat together, to throw out dark hints of his past life with an air of gloom and mystery designed to awaken interest; and I have little doubt that, to produce effect at the moment, there is hardly any crime so dark or so desperate of which, in the excitement of acting upon the imaginations of others, he would not have hinted that he had been guilty. It has sometimes occurred to me that the occult cause of his lady's separation from him may have been nothing more, after all, than some imposture of this kind, some dim confession of undefined horror.

But the over-frankness with which he uttered every chance impression of the moment was by itself enough to bring his character unfavourably before the world. Which of us could bear to be judged by the unnumbered thoughts that course like waves of the sea through our minds and pass away unuttered and even unowned by ourselves? To such a test was Byron's character, throughout his life, exposed.

Yet, to this readiness in reflecting all hues, whether of the shadows or lights of our variegated existence, Lord Byron owed his personal fascination. His social intercourse was perfectly charming, because whoever was with him occupied for the moment all his thoughts and feelings. Even with the casual acquaintance of the hour his heart was on his lips, ready to give away every secret of his life.

To my assertion that "at no time of his life was Lord Byron a confirmed unbeliever" it has been objected that his writings prove the direct contrary. But this is to confuse the words "unbeliever" and "sceptic," the former of which implies decision of opinion, and the latter only doubt. Many passages in his "Journal" show doubt strongly inclined to belief. "Of the immortality of the soul it appears to me there can be little doubt." "I have often been inclined to materialism in philosophy, but could never bear its introduction into Christianity, which appears to me essentially founded upon the soul." Here are doubt and unrest, but not unbelief.

And so I conclude my labours, undertaken at the wish of my friend, and leave his character to the judgement of the world. Let it be remembered that through life, with all his faults, he never lost a friend; that those about him in his youth, whether as companions, teachers, or servants, remained attached to him to the last; that the woman to whom he gave the love of his maturer years idolises his name; and that, with a single unhappy exception, those who were brought into relations of amity with him have felt towards him a kind regard in life, and retain a fondness for his memory.

JAMES COTTER MORISON

Life and Times of St. Bernard

James Augustus Cotter Morison, English essayist and historian, was born in London on April 20, 1832, and was the son of the inventor and proprietor of "Morison's Pills." His first years were spent in Paris, where he laid the foundation of his intimate knowledge of the French people. After graduating at Oxford, he wrote for the "Saturday Review" and other papers, and in 1863 brought out his "Life and Times of Saint Bernard." His other chief work is entitled "The Service of Man: an Essay towards the Religion of the Future," published in 1886. He had projected an historical study of France under Louis XIV., but never completed it. He died on February 26, 1888. Morison was a Positivist, and had many friends in that group, and his rich mind and genial temper endeared him to several of the leading literary men of his time, such as George Meredith, Mark Pattison and Matthew Arnold.

I.--The Early Days of a Useful Life

Saint Bernard was born in 1091, and died in 1153. His life thus almost coincides with the central portion of the Middle Ages. He saw the First and Second Crusades, the rising liberties of the communes, and the beginnings of scholasticism under Abelard. A large Church reformation and the noblest period of monasticism occurred in his day, and received deep marks of his genius.

He was the son of Tesselin, a wealthy feudal baron of Burgundy, remarkable for his courage, piety, justice and modesty. Alith, his mother, was earnest, loving and devout, and full of humility and charity. His earliest years were passed amid the European fervour of the First Crusade; and as he grew from boyhood into youth--at which time his mother died--he made choice of the monastic profession. His friends vainly tried to tempt him aside into the pursuit of philosophy; but his commanding personal ascendancy brought his brothers and friends to follow him instead into the religious life. Having assembled a company of about thirty chosen spirits, he retired into seclusion with them for six months, and then, in 1113, at the age of twenty-two, led them within the gates of Citeaux.

This community, founded fifteen years before, and now ruled by Stephen Harding, an Englishman from Dorsetshire, was exceedingly austere, keeping Saint Benedict's rule literally. Here Bernard's uncompromising self-mortification, and his love of, and communion with, Nature, showed themselves as the chief characteristics of his noble spirit. "Believe me," he said to a pupil, "you will find something far greater in the woods than you will in books; stones and trees will teach you that which you will never learn from masters." The arrival of Bernard and his companions was a turning-point in the history of Citeaux; and the monastery had to send out two colonies, to La Ferté and Pontigny, and in 1115 a third, under Bernard himself, to Clairvaux. Here, in a deep umbrageous valley, traversed by a limpid stream, the thirteen pioneers built a house little better than a barn. Their privations were great. Beech-nuts and roots were at first their main support; but soon the sympathy of the surrounding country brought sufficiency for their frugal needs. Bernard was consecrated Abbot of Clairvaux by the Bishop of Chalons, the renowned William of Champeaux, with whom he established a deep friendship.

His labours, anxieties and austerities had well-nigh brought Bernard to the grave, when the good bishop, finding him inflexible, went to Citeaux, and, prostrating himself before Stephen Harding, begged and obtained leave to direct and manage Bernard for one year only. The young abbot obeyed his new director absolutely, and lived in a cottage apart from the monastery "at leisure for himself and God, and exulting, as it were, in the delights of Paradise."

William of St. Thierry and other chroniclers, telling of Clairvaux at this time, are fervid in their reverence and praise. "Methought I saw a new heaven and a new earth" ... "the golden age seemed to have revisited the world" ... "as you descended the hill you could see it was a temple of God; the still, silent valley bespoke the unfeigned humility of Christ's poor. In this valley full of men, where one and all were occupied with their allotted tasks, a silence, deep as that of night, prevailed. The sounds of labour, or the chants of the brethren in the choral service, were the only exceptions. The order of this silence struck such a reverence even into secular persons that they dreaded breaking it even by pertinent remarks."

Saint Benedict's rule had reference only to a single religious house; but Abbot Stephen of Citeaux united in one compact whole all the monasteries which sprang from the parent stock of Citeaux, and established an organised system of mutual supervision and control. A general chapter was held annually in September, and every Cistercian abbot whose monastery was in France, Italy or Germany was bound to attend every year; those from Spain, every two years; those from Ireland, Scotland, Sicily and Portugal, every four years; those from Norway, every five years; and those from Syria and Palestine, every seven years. The "Charter of Charity," promulgated by this chapter for the guidance of the Cistercian Order, is a brief but pregnant document, which quite explains its success.

II.--A Great Preacher and Essayist

About 1119, Bernard, who had resumed the duties of abbot, began the career of literary and ecclesiastical activity--the wide and impassioned correspondence, the series of marvellous sermons--which have won for him the title of the Last of the Fathers. His early essays are vigorous, but lack judgement and skill; they are stiff and rhetorical, and far removed from the tender poetry of his later writings. Three years later we find Bernard credited with many miracles, narrated by William of St. Thierry, who afterwards retired to become a monk at Signy, where he wrote his record of the saint. It was then regarded as natural that a man of eminent piety should work miracles; and we ought to accept these stories, in their native crudity and simplicity, not as true, but as significant. Belonging to the time, as much as feudal castles and mail armour do, they form part of a picture of it.

With the exception of a visit to La Grande Chartreuse, and of another to Paris, where he preached the "true philosophy" of poverty and contempt of the world to the schools distracted by scholastic puzzles, Bernard remained a secluded monk of a new and humble Order. But already, in his thirty-fifth year, the foundations had been laid of that authority which enabled him to quell a widespread schism, to oppose a formidable heretic, and to give the strongest impulse to the Second Crusade. His power was growing, chiefly by his voluminous correspondence. He wrote to persons of all classes on all subjects; his letters afford to the historian a wide repertory of indubitable facts, and show what was the part played at that time by the spiritual power--that of a divine morality and superior culture coming into conflict with, and strong enough to withstand, a vigorous barbarism. These epistles are full of commonsense and clear, practical advice, and often give us a glimpse of the human, as distinct from the ascetic, element in monastic life. They show how men could pass pleasant and thoughtful days amid the barbarism of the time.

The feudal fighting, plundering and slaying seemed to spectators of that time, and doubtless to Bernard also, as fixed and unalterable, part of the nature of things. Louis VI., King of France, had spent his life in a succession of sieges, forays and devastations, as one feudal lord among others often more powerful than he. But generally he was in the right, and his enemies in the wrong; he generally fought for justice and mercy, and they for power and for plunder. The feudal aristocracy was now at the zenith of its power, and the peasant was oppressed by injustice, taxation and forced labour. Only the Church, and she only on grand occasions, could stand up for the poor; but now the royal power made common cause with Church and poor, and was rewarded by a gain in extent and in influence. Yet even Louis, whose whole life showed respect for the spiritual power, had some disagreement with the Bishop of Paris and with the Archbishop of Sens, so that the two ecclesiastics placed the kingdom under interdict, and fled to Cîteaux. Thence Bernard, with an astonishing tone of authority, called upon his king to do justice; and Louis was on the point of restoring the stolen property. Pope Honorius, however, sent letters to the king, raising the interdict, and thereupon Bernard turned his fearless indignation upon the supreme pontiff himself. "We speak with sadness; the honour of the Church has been not a little blemished in the time of Honorius."

The same intrepidity is shown in Bernard's controversy with the monks of Cluny, an abbey of pre-eminent power and moral authority, so that Louis had called it the "noblest member of his kingdom." Pontius, its abbot, having fallen into ways of pride and extortion, had been induced from Rome to resign his abbacy, and to promise a pilgrimage to the Holy Land; but soon afterwards he fell upon the monastery with an armed force, and ruled there like a robber chieftain. This scandalous outrage was soon reported at Rome, and the sacrilegious usurper was excommunicated and banished. Bernard seized the moment when laxity of observance of the rule had produced its bitterest fruit to break out in remonstrances and warnings, as well to his own Cistercians as to the Cluniacs, on the decline of the genuine monastic spirit. The invective of what he calls his "Apology" spares neither the softness, nor the ostentation, nor the avarice, of religious houses. It condemns even their stately sanctuaries. "The walls of your church are resplendent, but the poor are not there." It recalls the erring monasteries to real mortification. In another early treatise, "The Degrees of Humility and of Pride," the modes of pride are exhibited forcibly, and with not a little humour. Curiosity, thoughtless mirth, mock humility, and other symptoms of the protean vice are painted by a master.

But Bernard's period of retirement was drawing to a close; he was becoming indispensable to his contemporaries. In 1128 he was called to the Council of Troyes, at which the Order of Knights Templars was founded, and wrote a treatise in praise of the "new warfare," called the "Exhortation to the Knights of the Temple." He was brought, again, to the council convened by Louis VI. at Étampes to decide between the claims of the rival Popes in the Papal schism. The council opened by unanimous consent that Bernard's judgement should decide their views; and without hesitation he pronounced Innocent II. the lawful Pope, and Peter Leonis, or Anacletus II., a vain pretender. He bore the same testimony, in the presence of Innocent, before Henry I. of England, at Chartres, and before Lotharius, the German Emperor, at Liège. The Pope visited Clairvaux, where he was moved to tears at the sight of the tattered flock of "Christ's poor," then presided at the Council of Rheims, 1131, and continued his journey into Italy, still accompanied by the Abbot of Clairvaux. Bernard, convinced that the cause of Innocent was the cause of justice and religion, set no bounds to his advocacy of it in letters to kings, bishops and cities. Such was now the fame of his sanctity that on his approach to Milan the whole population came out to meet him.

He returned to Clairvaux in 1135, where he found the community all living in Christian amity, and again retired to a cottage in the neighbourhood for rest and reflection. "Bernard was in the heavens," says Arnold of Bonnevaux; "but they compelled him to come down and listen to their sublunary business." The buildings were too small for their constantly growing numbers, and a convenient site had been found in an open plain farther down the valley. Bishops, barons and merchants came to the help of the good work; and the new abbey and church rose quickly.

To Bernard's forty-fifth year belong the "Sermons on the Canticles." In the auditorium, or talking-room of the monastery, the abbot, surrounded by his white-cowled monks, delivered his spiritual discourses. A strange company it was: the old, stooping monk and the young beginner, the lord and the peasant, listening together to the man whose message they believed came from another world.

III.--St. Bernard and the Second Crusade

In the meanwhile, the affairs of the Papacy had not improved--Innocent was still an exile from his see. Worst of all, the monastery of Monte Casino, the head and type of Western monarchism, had declared for Anacletus, the anti-Pope; and in 1137 Bernard set out for Italy, visited Innocent at Viterbo, and proceeded to Rome. As he advanced, Anacletus was rapidly deserted by his supporters, and shortly afterwards solved the difficulty by his death. So ended the schism; and Bernard left Rome within five days after finishing his work. With broken health and depressed spirits he returned to

Clairvaux. His brother Gerard, who had shared his journey, died soon after they reached home; and Bernard's discourse on that event is one of the most remarkable funeral sermons on record. The monk had not ceased to be a loving and impassioned man.

Towards the end of 1139, the heresies of Peter Abelard, brought to his notice by William of St. Thierry, called the Abbot of Clairvaux again into public controversy. He implored Pope and cardinals to stay the progress of a second Arius. Abelard was at this time sixty-one years old, Bernard's senior by twelve years, and was without a rival in the schools. The two men were such that they could not but oppose one another; they looked at the shield from opposite sides; reconciliation, however desirable, could be only superficial. Bernard met Abelard, and "admonished him secretly." He well knew to what epoch this subtle mind, with its "human and philosophic reasons," was about to lead; his quick ear caught the distant thunder-roll of free inquiry. The heresies of Peter de Bruis and the rebellion of Arnold of Brescia had already marked the beginning of the great change. At last Bernard unwillingly yielded to Abelard's challenge to a public dispute at Sens; but his speech had hardly begun when Abelard rose in his place, refused to hear more, and appealed to Rome. He never reached Rome, but remained a penitent monk at Cluny, reconciled to his great antagonist.

Bernard was fifty-five years of age, and old for his years, when the Pope delegated to him the office of preaching the Second Crusade. Pale and attenuated to a degree which seemed almost supernatural, his contemporaries discovered something in the mere glance of his eyes which filled them with wonder and awe. When his words of love, aspiration and sublime self-sacrifice reached their ears, they were no longer masters of themselves or of their feelings. A great meeting had been convened by Pope and king at Vézelay, on Easter, 1146. Bernard, attended by the king, spoke from a platform erected on a hill; there was a shout of "Crosses! Crosses!" and the preacher scattered a sheaf of these badges among the people. The spiritual mind of Europe had spoken through Bernard, and now the military mind spoke through Louis VII. He called upon France to destroy the enemies of God. Then Bernard preached the Crusade through France and Germany, welcomed everywhere by almost unparalleled enthusiasm and attended by miraculous signs.

Bernard was shortly to die; but he had first to bear the trial of being reviled as the author of the calamities which had overtaken the Crusade. Why had he preached it and prophesied success if this was to be the event? A murmur of wrath against him was heard from the broad population of Europe. It was during this dark time that he began his largest literary work, the five books "De Consideratione," addressed to his disciple, Eugenius

III., a powerful and elaborate plea against the excessive centralization of all administration and decisions into the hands of the Papal Court. Bernard called this period "the season of calamities." He discovered that his secretary had been forging his name and used his authority to recommend men and causes most unworthy of his patronage. His health was such that he could take no solid food; sleep had left him; his debility was extreme. Pope Eugenius died in July, 1153; and Bernard had no wish to stay behind. "I am no longer of this world," he said; and on August 20 he passed away.

JOHN MORLEY

Life of Richard Cobden

In an age when many have gained the double distinction of eminence in statesmanship and in letters, the name of Lord Morley stands out as that of a man so illustrious in both provinces that it is hard to decide in which he has earned the greater fame. We are here concerned with him as a brilliant English man of letters. The "Life of Cobden" was published in 1881, when John Morley was in the height of his literary activity. Born at Blackburn on December 24, 1838, and educated at Cheltenham and Oxford, he had entered journalism, had edited the "Pall Mall Gazette" and the "Fortnightly Review," and had followed up his first book--a monograph on Burke--by a remarkable study of Voltaire, and by his work entitled "On Compromise." Political preoccupations drew him somewhat away from literature after 1881; but in 1901 he published his book on Cromwell, which was followed two years later by the monumental "Life of Gladstone."

I.--On the Road

Heyshott is a hamlet in a sequestered corner of West Sussex, not many miles from the Hampshire border. Here, in an old farmhouse, known as Dunford, Richard Cobden was born on June 3, 1804. His ancestors were yeomen of the soil, and, it is said, with every appearance of truth, that the name can be traced in the annals of the district as far back as the fourteenth century.

Cobden's father, a man of soft and affectionate disposition, but wholly without the energy of affairs, met with financial disaster in 1814, and relatives charged themselves with the maintenance of his dozen children. Richard was sent by his mother's brother-in-law, a merchant in London, to a school in Yorkshire. Here he remained for five years, a grim and desolate time, of which he could never afterwards endure to speak. In 1819 he was received as a clerk in his uncle's warehouse in Old Change; and at the age of twenty-one he was advanced from the drudgery of the warehouse to the glories of the road. What made the life of a traveller specially welcome to Cobden was the gratification that it offered to the master-passion of his life, an insatiable desire to know the affairs of the world.

In 1826, his employer failed, and for some months Cobden had to take unwelcome holiday. In September he found a situation, and again set out on the road with his samples of muslin and calico prints. Two years afterwards, in 1828, he and two friends determined to begin business on their own account. They arranged with a firm of Manchester calico-printers to sell goods on commission; and so profitable was the enterprise that in 1831 the partners determined to print their own goods, and took an old factory at Sabden in Lancashire.

Cobden's imagination was struck by the busy life of the county with which his name was destined to be so closely bound up. "Manchester," he writes with enthusiasm, "is the place for all men of bargain and business." His pen acquires a curiously exulting animation as he describes the bustle of its streets, the quaintness of its dialect, the abundance of its capital, and the sturdy veterans with a hundred thousand pounds in each pocket, who might be seen in the evening smoking clay pipes and calling for brandy-and-water in the bar-parlours of homely taverns. He prospered rapidly in this congenial atmosphere; but it is at Sabden, not at Manchester, that we see the first monument of his public spirit--a little stone school-house, built as the result of an agitation led by him with as much eager enthusiasm as he ever threw afterwards into great affairs of state.

Between 1833 and 1836 Cobden's character widened and ripened with surprising quickness. We pass at a single step from the natural and wholesome egotism of the young man who has his bread to win to the wide interests and generous public spirit of the good citizen. His first motion was towards his own intellectual improvement, and early in life he perceived that for his purposes no preparation could be so effective as that of travel. In 1833 and 1834 he visited the Continent; in 1835, the United States; and in 1836 and 1837 he travelled to Egypt, the Levant, and Turkey.

In the interval between the two latter journeys he made what was probably his first public speech, at a meeting to further the demand of a corporation for Manchester. The speech is described as a signal failure. "He was nervous," says the chronicler, "confused, and in fact practically broke down, and the chairman had to apologise for him."

He was much more successful in two pamphlets he published at this time, "England, Ireland, and America," and "Russia," in which he opened the long struggle he was to wage against the restriction of commerce, and the policy of intervention in European feuds. It is no strained pretension to say that already Richard Cobden, the Manchester manufacturer, was fully possessed of the philosophic gift of feeling about society as a whole, and thinking about the problems of society in an ordered connection.

II.--The Corn Laws

In 1837, Cobden was invited to become candidate for the borough of Stockport. Although he threw himself into the struggle with all his energy, on the day of election he was found to be at the bottom of the poll. Four years later he was returned for Stockport by a triumphant majority. But in 1841 he was no longer a rising young politician; he had become the leading spirit of a national agitation.

In October, 1838, a band of seven men met at an hotel in Manchester, and formed a new Anti-Corn-Law Association. They were speedily joined by others, including Cobden, who from this moment began to take a prominent part in all counsel and action. The abolition of the duties on corn was the single object of Cobden's political energy during the seven years that followed, and their destruction was the one finished triumph with which his name is associated.

After the rejection in the following year by a large majority of Mr. Villiers' motion that the House of Commons should consider the act regulating the importation of corn, the association developed into a League of Federated Anti-Corn-Law Associations in different towns and districts. The repealers began the work of propagandism by sending out a band of economic missionaries, who were not long in discovering how hardly an old class interest dies. In many districts neither law nor equity gave them protection. The members of the league were described in the London Press as unprincipled schemers, as commercial and political swindlers, and as revolutionary emissaries, whom all well-disposed persons ought to assist the authorities in putting down.

Before he entered Parliament, Cobden re-settled his business by entering into partnership with his brother Frederick, and married (May, 1840) a young Welsh lady, Miss Catherine Ann Williams. In Parliament Cobden was instantly successful. His early speeches produced that singular and profound effect which is perceived in English deliberative assemblies when a speaker leaves party recriminations, abstract argument, and commonplaces of sentiment, in order to inform his hearers of telling facts in the condition of the nation.

But Cobden's parliamentary work was at this time less important than his work as an agitator. If in one sense the Corn Laws did not seem a promising theme for a popular agitation, they were excellently fitted to bring out Cobden's peculiar strength. It was not passion, but persuasiveness, to which we must look for the secret of his oratorical success. Cobden made his way to men's hearts by the union which they saw in him of simplicity, earnestness, and conviction, with a singular facility of exposition. Then men were attracted by his mental alacrity, by the instant readiness with which he turned round to grapple with a new objection.

His patience in acquiring and shaping matter for argument was surpassed by his inexhaustible patience in dealing with the mental infirmities of those whom it was his business to persuade. He was wholly free from the unmeasured anger against human stupidity which is itself one of the most provoking forms of that stupidity.

III.--Cobden and Bright

In the autumn of 1841, Cobden and Bright made that solemn compact which was the beginning of an affectionate and noble friendship that lasted without a cloud or a jar until Cobden's death.

"On the day when Mr. Cobden called upon me," said Bright, "I was in the depths of grief, I might almost say of despair; for the light and sunshine of my house had been extinguished. All that was left on earth of my young wife, except the memory of a sainted life and of a too brief happiness, was lying still and cold in the chamber above us. Mr. Cobden called upon me as a friend, and addressed me, as you might suppose, with words of condolence. After a time he looked up, and said, 'There are thousands of houses in England at this moment where wives, mothers, and children are dying of hunger. Now,' he said, 'when the first paroxysm of your grief is past, I would advise you to come with me, and we will never rest till the Corn Law is repealed.' I accepted his invitation."

Although the agitation for repeal was in Cobden's mind only a part of the broad aims of peace and social and moral progress for which he strove, he was too practical to put forth his thoughts on too many subjects at once. He confined his enthusiasm to repeal until repeal was accomplished. But his efforts left him no time to attend to his own business, which was falling to pieces under the management of his brother Frederick. In the autumn of 1845 he felt compelled to give up his work as an agitator on account of his private affairs, but Bright and one or two friends procured the money that sufficed to tide over the emergency.

The cause was now on the eve of victory. The autumn of 1845 was the wettest in the memory of man. For long the downpour never ceased by night or by day; it was the rain that rained away the Corn Laws. The bad harvest and the Irish potato famine brought the long hesitation of Sir Robert Peel to an end. Soon after the opening of the session of 1846, he announced his proposals.

The repeal of the Corn Laws was to be total, but not immediate. For three years there was to be a lowered duty on a sliding scale, and then the ports were to be opened entirely. "Hurrah! Hurrah!" wrote Cobden to his wife on June 26, "the Corn Bill is law, and now my work is done!"

IV.--In the Cause of Peace

Cobden was now absent from England for fourteen months, travelling on the Continent. His reception was everywhere that of a great discoverer in a science which interests the bulk of mankind much more keenly than any other, the science of wealth. People looked on him as a man who had found out a momentous secret. He had interviews with the Pope, with three or four kings, with ambassadors, and with all the prominent statesmen. He never lost an opportunity of speaking a word in season. They were not all converted, but they all listened to him; and they all taught him something, whether they chose to learn anything from him in return or not.

On his return he joined with Bright in an agitation for financial and parliamentary reform. While he believed in an extension of the franchise as a means of attaining the objects he had in view, he was essentially an economical, a moral, and a social reformer. He was never an enthusiast for mere reform in the machinery. He made it his special mission to advocate financial reform, and left the advocacy for franchise extension very largely to his colleague.

Retrenchment was the keynote of the financial reform urged by Cobden; and retrenchment involved the furtherance of international peace and the reduction of British armaments by means of the abandonment of the policy of intervention in European disputes and the policy of "clinging to colonies," with the consequent expenditure upon colonial defence. From 1846 to 1851 Lord Palmerston was at the Foreign Office, and was incessantly active in the affairs of half the countries of Europe. To this policy of interference Cobden offered resolute opposition. He was especially energetic in protesting against the lending to Austria and Russia of money that was in effect borrowed to repay the cost of the oppressive war against Hungary. It is impossible not to admire the courage, the sound sense, and the elevation with which Cobden thus strove to diffuse the doctrine of moral responsibility in connection with the use of capital.

In 1852, a Protectionist Ministry under Lord Derby came into power, and the Anti-Corn Law League was revived. The danger, however, soon passed away; the Derby Ministry made no attempt to interfere with freedom of trade, and ere the year ended gave place to the Aberdeen Ministry. Cobden's policy of peace and retrenchment, however, became more and more unpopular. Cobden's urgent feeling about war was not in any degree sentimental. He opposed war because war and the preparation for it consumed the resources which were required for the improvement of the temporal condition of the population. But in the inflamed condition of public opinion his arguments were powerless.

The invasion panic of 1853 was followed in 1854 by the Crimean War, and in opposing that war Cobden and Bright found themselves absolutely alone.

"The British nation," said Lord Palmerston, "is unanimous in this matter. I say unanimous, for I cannot reckon Cobden, Bright, and Co. for anything." His estimate was perfectly correct; Cobden and Bright had the whole world against them. The moral fortitude, like the political wisdom, of these two strong men, stands out with a splendour that already recalls the great historic types of statesmanship and patriotism.

V.--Cobden as Treaty-Maker

In 1857, Cobden was compelled to retire for a time from politics. He vigorously opposed the Chinese War, and succeeded in defeating Lord Palmerston's Government in the House of Commons. Lord Palmerston, with his usual acuteness and courage, at once dissolved parliament, and in the General Election his victory was complete. The Manchester School was routed. Cobden, who contested Huddersfield, was heavily beaten; and at Manchester itself Bright was at the bottom of the poll. Cobden went to his home at Dunford, in Sussex, and remained there nearly two years. Once more he was afflicted with financial trouble. An unfortunate land speculation at Manchester, and certain investments in American railroads, had again brought him into difficulties, from which he was ultimately rescued by a munificent gift of £40,000 from subscribers whose names he never knew.

The General Election of 1859 was held while Cobden was absent in the United States, and on his return he found that he had been chosen member for Rochdale. To his surprise, he also received from his old enemy, Palmerston, an offer of the Presidency of the Board of Trade. Cobden, who had consistently refrained from accepting any office, courteously declined.

But he was none the less able to render a great service to the new Government. Mr. Bright, in a parliamentary speech, incidentally asked why, instead of lavishing the national substance in armaments, they did not go to the French Emperor and attempt to persuade him to allow his people to trade freely with ours. The idea of a commercial treaty occurred to M. Chevalier on reading the speech, and he wrote in this sense to Cobden, who was strongly impressed by the notion. He opened his mind to Gladstone, who was then Chancellor of the Exchequer; and, as the outcome, Cobden went to Paris in the autumn of 1859 as unofficial negotiator of a treaty.

The negotiation was long and tedious. Cobden had to convert the emperor to his views, and to await the reconciliation of the various French interests that were opposed to freedom of trade. It was not until November, 1860, that Cobden's labours were concluded. England cleared her tariff of protection, and reduced the duties which were retained for revenue on the two French staples of wine and brandy. France, on her part, replaced prohibition by a series of moderate duties.

Palmerston offered Cobden a choice between a baronetcy and a Privy Councillorship as a reward for his services. He replied begging permission most respectfully to deny himself the honour. "An indisposition to accept a title," he wrote, "being in my case rather an affair of feeling than of reason, I will not dwell further on the subject."

VI.--The Last Days of Cobden

When Cobden returned to England his public position had more than recovered the authority and renown which had been seriously impaired by his unpopular attitude on the Russian war. But he and Bright were soon involved in an almost angrier conflict than before with the upper and middle classes, on account of their championship of the North in the American Civil War.

The remaining years of his life were largely spent in systematic onslaughts upon the policy of Lord Palmerston, and in opposition to military expenditure. It was with the purpose of resisting a Canadian fortification scheme that he made his last journey to London in March, 1865. On his arrival he was seized by a sharp attack of asthma; bronchitis supervened, and it became evident that he would not recover. On the morning of Sunday, April 2, Bright took his place by the side of the dying man. As the bells were ringing for the morning service the mists of death began to settle heavily on his brow, and his ardent, courageous, and brotherly spirit soon passed tranquilly away.

He was buried by the side of his son in the little churchyard at Lavington, on the slope of the hill among the pine-woods. "Before we left the house," Bright has told us, "standing by me, and leaning on the coffin, was his sorrowing daughter, one whose attachment to her father seems to have been a passion scarcely equalled among daughters. She said, 'My father used to like me very much to read to him the Sermon on the Mount. His own life was, to a large, extent, a sermon based upon that best, that greatest of all sermons. His was a life of perpetual self-sacrifice.'"

SAMUEL PEPYS

Diary

Samuel Pepys, author of the incomparable "Diary," was born either in London or at Brampton, Huntingdonshire, on February 23, 1632-3, son of John Pepys, a London tailor. By the influence of the Earl of Sandwich, he was entered in the public service. Beginning as a clerk in the Exchequer, he was soon transferred to the Naval Department, and rose to the high office of secretary to the Admiralty. His services were interrupted for a time, on the baseless suspicion that he was a Catholic, during the panic about the supposed "Popish Plot," but he was returned to his charge, and held it until the accession of William and Mary. Pepys was a man of very wide interests. He was a member of parliament, and became president of the Royal Society. He was an accomplished musician and a keen critic of painting, architecture, and the drama. But it is as a connoisseur of human nature that Pepys is known to-day. The "Diary" extended over the ten years, January, 1659-60, to May, 1669; it closed when he was thirty-seven years old, and he lived thirty-four years afterwards. The manuscript, written in shorthand, fills six volumes, which repose at Magdalene College, Cambridge. It was deciphered in 1825, when it was published as "Memoirs of Samuel Pepys, comprising his Diary from 1659 to 1669, deciphered by the Rev. J. Smith, and a Selection of his Private Correspondence, edited by Lord Braybrooke." Pepys died on May 26, 1703.

I.--"God Bless King Charles"

January 1, 1659-60. Blessed be God, at the end of last year I was in very good health, without any sense of my old pain, but upon taking of cold. I lived in Axe Yard, having my wife and servant, Jane, and no other in family than us three.

The condition of the state was thus: the Rump, after being disturbed by my Lord Lambert, was lately returned to sit again. The officers of the army all forced to yield. Lawson still lies in the river, and Monk is with his army in Scotland. The New Common Council of the City do speak very high; and had sent to Monk their sword-bearer, to acquaint him with their desires for a free and full parliament, which is at present the desires, and the hopes, and the expectations of all. My own private condition very handsome, and esteemed rich, but indeed very poor; besides my goods of my house, and my office, which at present is somewhat certain.

March 9, 1660. To my lord at his lodging, and came to Westminster with him in the coach; and I telling him that I was willing and ready to go with him to sea, he agreed that I should. I hear that it is resolved privately that a treaty be offered with the king.

May 1. To-day I hear they were very merry at Deal, setting up the king's flag upon one of their maypoles, and drinking his health upon their knees in the streets, and firing the guns, which the soldiers of the castle threatened, but durst not oppose.

May 2. Welcome news of the parliament's votes yesterday, which will be remembered for the happiest May-day that hath been many a year to England. The king's letter was read in the house, wherein he submits himself and all things to them. The house, upon reading the letter, ordered £50,000 to be forthwith provided to send to his majesty for his present supply. The City of London have put out a declaration, wherein they do disclaim their owning any other government but that of a king, lords, and commons.

May 3. This morning my lord showed me the king's declaration to be communicated to the fleet. I went up to the quarter-deck with my lord and the commanders, and there read the papers; which done, the seamen did all of them cry out, "God bless King Charles!" with the greatest joy imaginable. After dinner to the rest of the ships quite through the fleet.

May 11. This morning we began to pull down all the state's arms in the fleet, having first sent to Dover for painters to come and set up the king's. After dinner we set sail from the Downs, but dropped anchor again over against Dover Castle.

May 12. My lord gave order for weighing anchor, which we did, and sailed all day.

May 14. In the morning the Hague was clearly to be seen by us. The weather bad; we were sadly washed when we come near the shore, it being very hard to land there.

May 23. Come infinity of people on board from the king to go along with him. The king, with the two dukes and Queen of Bohemia, Princess Royal, and Prince of Orange, come on board, where I, in their coming in, kissed the king's, queen's, and princess's hands, having done the other before. Infinite shooting of the runs, and that in a disorder on purpose, which was better than if it had been otherwise. We weighed anchor, and with a fresh gale and most happy weather we set sail for England.

May 24. Up, and made myself as fine as I could, with the stockings on and wide canons that I bought at Hague. Extraordinary press of noble company, and great mirth all day.

May 25. By the morning we were come close to the land, and everybody made ready to get on shore. I spoke to the Duke of York about business, who called me Pepys by name, and upon my desire did promise me his future favour. The king went in my lord's barge with the two dukes, and was received by General Monk with all love and respect at his entrance upon the land of Dover. The shouting and joy expressed by all is past imagination.

1660-1661. At the end of the last and the beginning of this year, I do live in one of the houses belonging to the Navy Office, as one of the principal officers; my family being myself, my wife, Jane, Will Hewer, and Wayneman, my girl's brother. Myself in constant good health, and in a most handsome and thriving condition. Blessed be God for it. The king settled, and loved of all.

II.--The Plague

July 31, 1665. I ended this month with the greatest joy that I ever did any in my life, because I have spent the greatest part of it with abundance of joy, and honour, and pleasant journeys, and brave entertainments, and without cost of money. We end this month after the greatest glut of content that ever I had, only under some difficulty because of the plague, which grows mightily upon us, the last week being about 1,700 or 1,800 of the plague. My Lord Sandwich at sea with a fleet of about one hundred sail, to the northward, expecting De Ruyter, or the Dutch East India fleet.

August 8. To my office a little, and then to the Duke of Albemarle's about some business. The streets empty all the way now, even in London, which is a sad sight. To Westminster Hall, where talking, hearing very sad stories. So home through the City again, wishing I may have taken no ill in going; but I will go, I think, no more thither. The news of De Ruyter's coming home is certain, and told to the great disadvantage of our fleet; but it cannot be helped.

August 10. To the office, where we sat all morning; in great trouble to see the bill this week rise so high, to above 4,000 in all, and of them above 3,000 of the plague. Home to draw over anew my will, which I had bound myself by oath to dispatch by to-morrow night; the town growing so unhealthy that a man cannot depend upon living two days.

August 12. The people die so that now it seems they are fain to carry the dead to be buried by daylight, the nights not sufficing to do it in. And my lord mayor commands people to be within at nine at night, that the sick may have liberty to go abroad for air. There is one also dead out of one of our ships at Deptford, which troubles us mightily. I am told, too, that a wife of one of the grooms at court is dead at Salisbury, so that the king and queen are speedily to be all gone to Milton. So God preserve us!

August 16. To the Exchange, where I have not been in a great while. But, Lord! how sad a sight it is to see the streets empty of people, and very few upon the 'Change. Jealous of every door that one sees shut up lest it should be the plague; and about two shops in three, if not more, generally shut up.

August 22. I walked to Greenwich, in my way seeing a coffin with a dead body therein, dead of the plague, which was carried out last night, and the parish have not appointed anybody to bury it; but only set a watch there all day and night, that nobody should go thither or come thence, this disease making us more cruel to one another than we are to dogs.

August 25. This day I am told that Dr. Burnett, my physician, is this morning dead of the plague, which is strange, his man dying so long ago, and his house this month open again. Now himself dead. Poor, unfortunate man!

August 30. I went forth and walked towards Moorfields to see (God forgive my presumption!) whether I could see any dead corpse going to the grave. But, Lord! how everybody looks, and discourse in the street is of death and nothing else, and few people going up and down, that the town is like a place distressed and forsaken.

September 3 (Lord's Day). Up; and put on my coloured silk suit very fine, and my new periwig, bought a good while since, but durst not wear, because the plague was in Westminster when I bought it; and it is a wonder what will be the fashion after the plague is done as to periwigs, for nobody will dare to buy any hair, for fear of the infection, that it has been cut off the heads of people dead of the plague. My Lord Brouncker, Sir J. Minnes, and I up to the vestry at the desire of the justices of the peace, in order to the doing something for the keeping of the plague from growing; but, Lord! to consider the madness of the people of the town, who will, because they are forbid, come in crowds along with the dead corpses to see them buried.

September 6. To London, to pack up more things; and there I saw fires burning in the streets, as it is through the whole city, by the lord mayor's order.

September 14. To the Duke of Albemarle, where I find a letter from my Lord Sandwich, of the fleet's meeting with about eighteen more of the Dutch fleet, and his taking of most of them; and the messenger says they had taken three after the letter was sealed, which being twenty-one, and those took the other day, is forty-five sail, some of which are good, and others rich ships. Having taken a copy of my lord's letter, I away toward the 'Change, the plague being all thereabouts. Here my news was highly welcome, and I did wonder to see the 'Change so full--I believe two hundred people. And, Lord! to see how I did endeavour to talk with as few as I could, there being now no shutting up of houses infected, that to be sure we do converse and meet with people that have the plague upon them. I spent some thought on the occurrences of this day, giving matter for as much content on one hand and melancholy on another, as any day in all my life. For the first, the finding of my money and plate all safe at London; the hearing of this good news after so great a despair of my lord's doing anything this year; and the decrease of 500 and more, which is the first decrease we have yet had in the sickness since it begun. Then, on the other side, my finding that though the bill in general is abated, yet in the City within the walls it is increased; my meeting dead corpses, carried close to me at noonday in Fenchurch Street.

One of my own watermen, that carried me daily, fell sick as soon as he had landed me on Friday last, when I had been all night upon the water, and is now dead of the plague. And, lastly, that both my servants, W. Hewer and Tom Edwards, have lost their fathers of the plague this week, do put me into great apprehension of melancholy, and with good reason.

November 15. The plague, blessed be God! is decreased 400, making the whole this week but 1,300 and odd, for which the Lord be praised!

December 25 (Christmas Day). To church in the morning, and there saw a wedding in the church, which I have not seen many a day, and the young people so merry with one another, and strange to see what delight we married people have to see these poor fools decoyed into our condition, every man and woman gazing and smiling at them.

December 31. Thus ends this year, to my great joy, in this manner. I have raised my estate from £1,300 in this year to £4,400. I have got myself greater interest, I think, by my diligence, and my employments increased by that of treasurer for Tangier and surveyor of the victuals. It is true we have gone through great melancholy because of the plague, and I put to great charges by it, by keeping my family long at Woolwich, and myself and my clerks at Greenwich, and a maid at London; but I hope the king will give us some satisfaction for that. But now the plague is abated almost to nothing, and I intending to get to London as fast as I can. To our great joy the town fills apace, and shops begin to be open again.

III.--The Great Fire

September 2, 1666. Some of our maids sitting up late last night to get things ready against our feast to-day, Jane called us up about three in the morning to tell us of a great fire they saw in the City. So I rose, and slipped on my nightgown, and went to her window, and thought it to be on the back side of Mark Lane at the farthest, and so went to bed again. About seven rose again to dress myself, and there looked out at the window, and saw the fire not so much as it was, and further off. By-and-by Jane comes and tells me that above 300 houses have been burned down, and that it is now burning down all Fish Street, by London Bridge. So I made myself ready, and walked to the Tower, and there got up upon one of the high places; and there I did see the houses at that end of the bridge all on fire, and an infinite great fire on this and the other side of the bridge. So down with my heart full of trouble to the lieutenant of the Tower, who tells me that it begun this morning in the king's baker's house in Pudding Lane.

So I down to the waterside, and there got a boat, and through bridge, and there saw a lamentable fire. Everybody endeavouring to remove their goods, and flinging into the river, or bringing them into lighters that lay off; poor people staying in their houses till the very fire touched them, and then running into boats or clambering from one pair of stairs by the waterside to another. And among other things, the poor pigeons, I perceive, were loth to leave their houses, but hovered about the windows and balconies till they burned their wings and fell down. Having staid, and in an hour's time seen the fire rage every way, and nobody, to my sight, endeavouring to quench it, I to White Hall, and there up to the king's closet in the chapel, where people come about me, and I did give them an account which dismayed them all, and word was carried in to the king.

So I was called for, and did tell the king and Duke of York what I saw, and that unless his majesty did command houses to be pulled down, nothing could stop the fire. They seemed much troubled, and the king commanded me to go to my lord mayor from him and command him to spare no houses, but to pull down before the fire every way. Meeting with Captain Cocke, I in his coach, which he lent me, to Paul's, and there walked along Watling Street, as well as I could, every creature coming away loaded with goods to save, and here and there sick people carried away in beds. At last met my lord mayor in Canning Street, like a man spent. To the king's message, he cried, like a fainting woman, "Lord! what can I do? I am spent; people will not obey me. I have been pulling down houses; but the fire overtakes us faster than we can do it." So I walked home, seeing people almost all distracted, and no manner of means used to quench the fire. The houses, too, so very thick thereabouts, and full of matter for burning, as pitch and tar in Thames Street, and warehouses of oil and wines and brandy.

Soon as I dined, I away, and walked through the City, the streets full of people, and horses and carts loaden with goods. To Paul's Wharf, where I took boat, and saw the fire was now got further, both below and above bridge, and no likelihood of stopping it. Met with the king and Duke of York in their barge. Their order was only to pull down houses apace; but little was or could be done, the fire coming so fast. Having seen as much as I could, I away to White Hall by appointment, and there walked to St. James's Park, and there met my wife, and Creed and Wood and his wife, and walked to my boat; and upon the water again, and to the fire, still increasing, and the wind great. So near the fire as we could for smoke, and all over the Thames you were almost burned with a shower of fire-drops.

When you could endure no more upon the water, we to a little ale-house on the Bankside, and there stayed till it was dark almost, and saw the fire grow; and as it grew darker, appeared more and more, and in corners and upon steeples, and between churches and houses, as far as we could see up the hill of the City, in a most horrid, malicious, bloody flame, not like the fine flame of an ordinary fire. We stayed till, it being darkish, we saw the fire as only one entire arch of fire from this to the other side of the bridge, and in a bow up the hill for an arch of above a mile long; it made me weep to see it. The churches, houses, and all on fire and flaming at once; and a horrid noise the flames made, and the cracking of houses at their ruin. So home with a sad heart.

IV.--Of the Badness of the Government

April 26, 1667. To White Hall, and there saw the Duke of Albemarle, who is not well, and do grow crazy. Then I took a turn with Mr. Evelyn, with whom I walked two hours; talking of the badness of the government, where nothing but wickedness, and wicked men and women command the king; that it is not in his nature to gainsay anything that relates to his pleasures; that much of it arises from the sickliness of our ministers of state, who cannot be about him as the idle companions are, and therefore he gives way to the young rogues; and then from the negligence of the clergy, that a bishop shall never be seen about him, as the King of France hath always; that the king would fain have some of the same gang to be lord treasurer, which would be yet worse.

And Mr. Evelyn tells me of several of the menial servants of the court lacking bread, that have not received a farthing wages since the king's coming in. He tells me that now the Countess Castlemaine do carry all before her. He did tell me of the ridiculous humour of our king and knights of the Garter the other day, who, whereas heretofore their robes were only to be worn during their ceremonies, these, as proud of their coats, did wear them all day till night, and then rode in the park with them on. Nay, he tells me he did see my Lord Oxford and Duke of Monmouth in a hackney coach with two footmen in the park, with their robes on, which is a most scandalous thing, so as all gravity may be said to be lost among us.

V.--The End of the Diary

November 30, 1668. My wife after dinner went the first time abroad in her coach, calling on Roger Pepys, and visiting Mrs. Creed and my cousin Turner. Thus endeth this month with very good content, but most expenseful to my purse on things of pleasure, having furnished my wife's closet and the best chamber, and a coach and horses that ever I knew in the world; and I am put into the greatest condition of outward state that ever I was in, or hoped ever to be. But my eyes are come to that condition that I am not able to work. God do His will in it!

December 2. Abroad with my wife, the first time that ever I rode in my own coach, which do make my heart rejoice and praise God. So she and I to the king's playhouse, and there saw "The Usurper," a pretty good play. Then we to White Hall; where my wife stayed while I up to the duchess, to speak with the Duke of York; and here saw all the ladies, and heard the silly discourse of the king with his people about him.

December 21. To the Duke's playhouse, and saw "Macbeth." The king and court there, and we sat just under them and my Lady Castlemaine. And my wife, by my troth, appeared, I think, as pretty as any of them; I never thought so much before, and so did Talbot and W. Hewer. The king and Duke of York minded me, and smiled upon me; but it vexed me to see Moll Davis in the box over the king and my Lady Castlemaine, look down upon the king, and he up to her. And so did my Lady Castlemaine once; but when she saw Moll Davis she looked like fire, which troubled me.

May 31, 1669. Up very betimes, and continued all the morning examining my accounts, in order to the fitting myself to go abroad beyond sea, which the ill-condition of my eyes and my neglect hath kept me behindhand in. Had another meeting with the Duke of York at White Hall on yesterday's work, and made a good advance; and so being called by my wife, we to the park, Mary Batelier and a Dutch gentleman, a friend of hers, being with us. Thence to "The World's End," a drinking house by the park; and there merry, and so home late.

And thus ends all that I doubt I shall ever be able to do with my own eyes in the keeping of my journal, having done now so long as to undo my eyes almost every time that I take a pen in my hand; and therefore resolve, from this time forward to have it kept by my people in longhand, and must be contented to set down no more than is fit for them and all the world to know. And so I betake myself to that course, which is almost as much as to see myself go into my grave; for which, and all the discomforts that will accompany my being blind, the good God prepare me! S. P.

PLINY THE YOUNGER

Letters

Gaius Plinius Caecilius Secundus, or Pliny the Younger, was born in 62 A.D. at Novum Comum, in the neighbourhood of Lake Como, in the north of Italy. His family was honourable, wealthy, and able, and his uncle, Pliny the Elder, was the encyclopaedic student and author of the famous "Natural History." On his father's death, young Pliny, a boy of nine, was adopted by the elder Pliny, educated in literary studies and as an advocate, and was a notable pleader before his twentieth year. Through a succession of offices he rose to the consulship in the year 100, and afterwards continued to hold important appointments. He was twice married, but left no children. The date of his death is unknown. The "Letters of Pliny the Younger" are valuable as throwing light upon the life of the Roman people; but they are also models of Latin style, and have all the charm of their author's upright, urbane, and tolerant character. His epistle to the Emperor Trajan with regard to the Christians is of peculiar interest.

To Cornelius Tacitus

You will certainly laugh, and well may you laugh, when I tell you that your old friend has turned sportsman, and has captured three magnificent boars. "What," you say, "Pliny?" Yes, I myself, though without giving up my much loved inactivity. While I sat at the nets, you might have found me holding, not a spear, but my pen. I was resolved, if I returned with my hands empty, at least to bring home my tablets full. This open-air way of studying is not at all to be despised. The activity and the scene stimulate the imagination; and there is something in the solemnity and solitude of the woods, and in the expectant silence of the chase, that greatly promotes meditation. I advise you whenever you hunt in future to take your tablets with you as well as your basket and flask. You will find that Minerva, as well as Diana, haunts these hills.

To Minucius Fundanus

When I consider how the days pass with us at Rome, I am surprised to find that any single day taken by itself is spent reasonably enough, or at least seems to be so, and yet when I add up many days together the impression is quite otherwise. If you ask anyone what he has been doing to-day, he will tell you perhaps that he has been attending the ceremony of a youth's coming of age; he has assisted at a wedding, been present at the hearing of a lawsuit, witnessed a will, or taken part in a consultation. These occupations seem very necessary while one is engaged in them; and yet, looking back at leisure upon the many hours we have thus employed, we cannot but consider them mere frivolities. Looking back especially on town life from a country retreat, one is inclined to regret how much of life has been spent in these wretched trifles.

This reflection is one which often occurs to me at my place at Laurentum, when I am immersed in studies or invigorating my bodily health. In that peaceful home I neither hear nor say anything which needs to be repented of. There is no one there who speaks evil of anyone; and I have not to complain of any man, except sometimes of myself when I am dissatisfied with my work. There I live undisturbed by rumours, free from the vicissitudes of hope and fear, conversing only with myself and my books. What a true and genuine life it is; what a delightful and honest repose--surely more to be desired than the highest employments. O sea and solitary shore, secret haunt of the Muses, with how many noble thoughts have you inspired me! Do you then, my friend, take the first opportunity of leaving the noisy town with all its empty pursuits, and devote your days to study or leisure. For, as Attilius well says, it is better to have nothing to do than to be doing of nothing.

To Septicius Clarus

How did it happen, my friend, that you failed to keep your engagement to dine with me? I shall expect you to repay me what I spent on the festival--no small sum, I can assure you. I had prepared for each of us, you must know, a lettuce, three snails, two eggs, and a barley cake served with sweet wine and snow; the snow most certainly I shall charge to your account, as it melted away. There were olives, beetroots, gourds, onions, and a hundred other dainties. You would also have heard a comedian, or the reading of a poem or a lute-player, or even if you had liked, all three, such was my liberality. But luxurious delicacies and Spanish dancing girls at some other house were more to your taste. I shall have my revenge of you, depend upon it, but I won't say how. Indeed, it was not kind thus to mortify your friend--I had almost said yourself; for how delightfully we should have passed the evening in jests and laughter, and in deeper talk! It is true you may dine at many houses more sumptuously than at mine but nowhere will you find more unconstrained gaiety, simplicity and freedom. Only make the experiment, and if you do not ever afterwards prefer my table to any other, never favour me with your company again.

To Avitus

It would be a long story, and of no great importance, if I were to tell you by what accident I dined lately with a man who, in his own opinion, entertained us with great splendour and economy, but in my opinion with meanness combined with extravagance. He and a few of his guests enjoyed some very excellent dishes indeed, but the fare placed before the rest of the company was of the most inferior kind. There were three kinds of wine in small bottles, but it was not intended that the guests should take their choice at all. The best was for himself and for us; another vintage was for his friends of a lower order--for you must know he divides his friends into classes--and the third kind was for his own and his guests freed-men. My neighbor noticed this, and asked me if I approved of it. "Not at all," I said.

"What then," said he, "is your custom in entertaining?"

"Mine," said I, "is to offer the same fare to everybody. I invite my friends to dinner without separating them into classes. Everyone who comes to my table is equal, and even my freed-men are then my guests just as much as anyone else."

He asked me if I did not find this very expensive. I assured him that it was not so at all, and that the whole secret lay in drinking no better wine myself that I gave to others. If a man is wise enough to moderate his own luxury, he will not find it very expensive to entertain all his visitors on equal terms. Restrain your own tastes if you would really economise. This is a better way of saving expense than making these insulting distinctions between guests.

It would be a pity if a man of your excellent disposition should be imposed upon by the immoderate ostentation which prevails at some tables under the guise of frugality. I tell you of this as an example of what you ought to shun. Nothing is to be more avoided than this preposterous association of extravagance and meanness--defects which are unpleasant enough when found separately, but are particularly detestable when combined.

To Baebius Macer

I am glad to hear that you are so great an admirer of my Uncle Pliny's works as to wish to have a complete collection of them. You will wonder how a man so much occupied as he was could find time to write so many books, some of them upon very difficult subjects. You will be still more surprised when you hear that for a considerable time he practised at the bar, that he died in his fifty-sixth year, and that from the time of his retirement from the bar to his death he was employed in some of the highest offices of state, and in the immediate service of the emperors. But he had a very quick intelligence, an incredible power of application, and an unusual faculty of doing without sleep. In summer he used to begin to work at midnight; in winter, generally at one in the morning, or two at the latest, and often at midnight. But he would often, without leaving his studies, refresh himself by a short sleep. Before daybreak he used to wait upon the Emperor Vespasian, who also was a night worker, and after that attended to his official duties. Having taken a light meal at noon, after the custom of our ancestors, he would in summer, if unoccupied, lie down in the sun, while a book was read to him from which he made extracts and notes. Indeed he never read without making extracts; he used to say that no book was so bad as not to teach one at least something. After this reading he usually took a cold bath, then a light refreshment, and went to sleep for a little while. Then, as if beginning a new day, he resumed his studies until dinner, when a book was again read to him, upon which he would make passing comments. I remember once, when his reader had pronounced a word wrongly, someone at the table made him repeat it again; upon which my uncle asked his friend if he had not understood it. He admitted that the word was clear enough. "Why did you stop him then?" asked my uncle; "we have lost more than ten lines by this interruption of yours." Even so parsimonious was he of every moment of time! In summer he always rose from dinner by daylight, and in winter as soon as it was dark; this was an invariable law with him.

Such was his life amidst the noise and bustle of the city; but when he was in the country his whole time, without exception, was given to study except when he bathed. And by this exception I mean only the time when he was actually in the bath, for all the time when he was being rubbed and dried he was read to, or was himself dictating. Again, when travelling he gave his whole time to study; a secretary constantly attended him with books and tablets, and in winter wore very warm gloves so that the cold weather might not interrupt my uncle's work; and, for the same reason, when in Rome, he was always carried in a chair. I remember he once reproved me for going for a walk, saying that I might have used the hours to greater advantage; for he thought all time was lost which was not given to study. It was by this extraordinary application that he found time to write so many volumes, besides a hundred and sixty books of extracts which he left me, written on both sides in an extremely small hand, so that their number might be reckoned considerably greater.

To Cornelius Tacitus

I understand you wish to hear about the earthquake at Misenum. After my uncle had left us on that day, I went on with my studies until it was time to bathe; then I had supper and went to bed. But my sleep was broken and disturbed. There had been many slight shocks, which were very frequent in Campania, but on this night they were so violent that it seemed as though everything must be overthrown. My mother ran into my room, and we went out into a small court which separated our house from the sea. I do not know whether to call it courage or rashness on my part, as I was only eighteen years old; but I took up Livy and read and made extracts from him. When morning came the light was faint and sickly; the buildings around us were tottering to their fall, and there was great and unavoidable danger in remaining where we were. We resolved to leave the town. The people followed us in consternation, and pressed in great crowds about us on our way out. Having gone a good distance from the house, we stood still in the midst of a dreadful scene. The carriages for which we had sent, though standing upon level ground, were being thrown from side to side, and could not be kept still even when supported by large stones. The sea appeared to roll back upon itself, driven from its shores by the convulsive movements of the earth; a large portion of the sea-bottom was uncovered, and many marine animals were left exposed. Landward, a black and dreadful cloud was rolling down, broken by great flashes of forked lightning, and divided by long trains of flame which resembled lightning but were much larger.

Soon afterwards the clouds seemed to descend and cover the whole surface of the ocean, hiding the island of Capri altogether and blotting out the promontory of Misenum. My mother implored me earnestly to make my escape, saying that her age and frame made it impossible for her to get away, but that she would willingly meet her death if she could know that she had not been the cause of mine. But I absolutely refused to forsake her, and seizing her hand I led her on. The ashes now began to fall upon us, though as yet in no great quantity. I looked back and saw behind us a dense cloud which came rolling after us like a torrent. I proposed that while we still had life we should turn out of the high road, lest she should be trampled to death in the dark by the crowd.

We had scarcely sat down when darkness closed in upon us, not like the darkness of a moonless night, or of a night obscured by clouds, but the darkness of a closed room where all the lights have been put out. We heard the shrieks of women, the cries of children, and the shouts of men; some were calling for their children, others for their parents, others for their husbands or wives, and recognising one another through the darkness by their voices. Some were calling for death through very fear of death; others raised their hands to the gods; but most imagined that the last eternal night had come, and that the gods and the world were being destroyed together. Among these were some who added imaginary terrors to the real danger, and persuaded the terror-stricken multitude that Misenum was in flames. At last a glimmer of light appeared which we imagined to be a sign of approaching flames, as in truth it was; but the fire fell at a considerable distance from us, and again we were immersed in darkness. A heavy shower of ashes now rained upon us, so that we were obliged from time to time to shake them off, or we should have been crushed and buried in the heap. I might congratulate myself that during all this horror not a sigh or expression of fear escaped me, if it had not been that I then believed myself to be perishing with the world itself, and that all mankind were involved in the same calamity--a miserable consolation indeed, but a powerful one.

At last this dreadful darkness was dissipated by degrees like a cloud of smoke; real day returned, and even the sun appeared, though very faintly as he appears during an eclipse. Everything before our trembling eyes was changed, being covered over with white ashes as with deep snow. We returned to Misenum, where we refreshed ourselves as well as we could and passed an anxious night between hope and fear. There was more fear than hope, however; for the earthquake still continued and many crazy people were running about predicting awful horrors.

You must read my story without any view of writing about it in your history, of which it is quite unworthy; indeed, my only excuse for writing it in a letter is that you have asked for it.

To Calpurnia, His Wife

It is incredible how impatiently I wish for your return, such is the tenderness of my love for you, and so unaccustomed are we to separation. I lie awake great part of the nights thinking of you; and in the day my feet carry me of their own accord to your room at the hours when I used to see you, but not finding you there I go away as sorrowful and disappointed as an excluded lover. The only time when I am free from this distress is when I am in the forum busy with the lawsuits of my friends. You may judge how wretched my life is when I find my repose only in labour and my consolation in miseries and cares.

To Germinius

You must very well know the kind of people who, though themselves slaves to every passion, are mightily indignant at the vices of others, and most severe against those whom they most closely resemble. Surely leniency is the most becoming of all virtues, even in persons who have least need of anyone's indulgence. The highest of all characters, in my estimation, is that of a man who is as ready to pardon human errors as though he were every day himself guilty of them, and who yet abstains from faults as though he never forgave them. Let us observe this rule, both in our public and in our private relations--to be inexorable to ourselves, but to treat the rest of the world with tenderness, including even those who forgive only themselves. Let us always remember the saying of that most humane and therefore very great Thrasea: "He who hates vices, hates mankind."

Perhaps you will ask who it is that has moved me to these reflections? There was a certain person lately--But I will tell you of that when we meet. No; on second thoughts I will not tell you even then, lest by condemning him and exposing his conduct I should be violating the principle which I have just condemned. So, whoever he is, and whatever he may be, the matter shall remain unspoken; since to expose him would be of no advantage for the purpose of example; but to hide his fault will be of great advantage to good nature.

To the Emperor Trajan

It is my rule, to refer to you all matters about which I have any doubt. For who can be more capable of removing my scruples or of instructing my ignorance?

I have never been present at any trials of Christians, and am, therefore, ignorant of the reasons for which punishment is inflicted, as well as of the examinations which it is proper to make of their guilt. As to whether any difference is usually made with respect to the ages of the guilty, or whether no distinction is to be observed between the young and the old; whether repentance entitles them to a pardon, or whether it is of no advantage to a man who has once been a Christian that he has ceased to be one; whether the very profession of Christianity unattended by any criminal act, or only the crimes that are inherent in the profession are punishable--in all these points I am very doubtful.

In the meantime, the method which I have observed towards those who have been brought before me as Christians is this. I have interrogated them as to whether they were Christians; if they confessed I repeated the question twice again, adding threats at the same time; and if they still persevered I ordered them to execution. For I was persuaded that whatever the nature of their opinions might be, their pertinacity and inflexible obstinacy ought certainly to be punished. Others also were brought before me possessed by the same madness, but as they were Roman citizens I ordered them to be sent to Rome. As this crime spread while it was actually under prosecution, many fresh cases were brought up. An anonymous paper was given me containing a charge against many persons. Those who denied that they were Christians, or that they had ever been so, repeated after me an invocation to the gods, offered wine and incense before your statue, which for this purpose I had ordered to be placed among the statues of the gods, and even reviled the name of Christ; and so, as it is impossible to force those who are really Christians to do any of these things, I thought it proper to dismiss them. Others who had been accused confessed themselves at first to be Christians, but immediately afterwards denied it; and others owned that they had formerly been of that number, but had now forsaken their error. All these worshipped your statue and the images of the gods, at the same time reviling the name of Christ.

They affirmed that the whole of their guilt, or their error, had been as follows. They met on a stated day before sunrise and addressed a form of invocation to Christ as to a God; they also bound themselves by an oath, not for any wicked purpose but never to commit thefts, robberies, or adulteries, never to break their word, nor to deny a trust when they should be called upon to deliver it up. After this had been done they used to separate, and then reassemble to partake in common of an innocent meal. They had desisted, however, from this custom, after the publication of my edict, by which, in accordance with your orders, I had forbidden fraternities to exist. Having received this account I thought it all the more necessary to make sure of the real truth by putting two slave-girls, who were said to have taken part in their religious functions, to the torture; but I could discover nothing more than an absurd and extravagant superstition.

I have, therefore, adjourned all further proceedings in the affair in order to consult with you. It appears to be a matter highly deserving your consideration, especially as very many persons are involved in the danger of these prosecutions; for the inquiry has already extended and is likely further to extend to persons of all ranks and ages, and of both sexes. This contagious superstition is not confined to the cities only, but has spread its infection among the villages and country districts as well; and it seems impossible to cure this evil or to restrain its progress. It is true that the temples which were once almost deserted have lately been frequented, and that the religious rites which had been interrupted are again revived; and there is a general demand for animals for sacrificial victims, which for some time past have met with few purchasers. From all this it is easy to imagine what numbers might be reclaimed from this error if pardon were granted to those who may repent of it.

CARDINAL RICHELIEU

Political Testament

Armand Jean du Plessis, Duc de Richelieu, the great French cardinal-statesman, was born in Paris on September 5, 1585, of a noble family, and was at first educated for the profession of arms, but entered the Church in order to become Bishop of Luçon in 1606. Having come up to Paris to make his way in the world, he was appointed almoner to the young queen Anne of Austria, and rose in 1616 to be Secretary of State for War and for Foreign Affairs. He received the cardinal's hat in 1622, and for a period of eighteen years, from 1624 to 1642, he was, in everything but name, the Majesty of France. His mind was bold, unscrupulous, remorseless, and inscrutable. Yet it was always noble--the minister who sent so many to the scaffold could truly say that in his vast labours he had but one pleasure, to know that so many honest folk slept in security while he watched night after night. He was a friend to literature, was founder of the Academy, and was himself a considerable author in history and theology. His greatest work, "Testament Politique du Cardinal de Richelieu," which was published in 1764, and in which is embodied his counsel in statecraft, is a literary achievement of no small importance, exhibiting as it does not only a political acumen of a very high order but an acute faculty for literary expression. Richelieu died on December 4, 1642.

Retrospect

At the time when your majesty admitted me to your counsels and confided to me the direction of public affairs I may say with truth that the Huguenots divided the state with your majesty, the great families behaved as though they had no sovereign, and the governor of provinces as if they had been sovereigns themselves. Every man took his own audacity to be the measure of his merit, so that the most presumptious were considered the wisest, and proved often the most fortunate. Abroad the friendship of France was despised. At home private interests were preferred to the general advantage. The dignity of the throne had so far declined, through the fault of my predecessors in office, that it was almost unrecognisable. To have continued to entrust to their hands the helm of the state would have led to irremediable disaster; yet, on the other hand, too swift and too great a change would have been fraught with dangers of its own. In that emergency the wisest considered that it was hardly possible to pass without shipwreck through the reefs and shoals, and there were many who had foretold my fall even before your majesty had raised me to power.

Yet, knowing what kings may do when they make good use of their power, I was able to promise your majesty that your prudence and firmness, with the blessing of God, would give new health to this kingdom. I promised to devote all my labours, and all the authority with which I might be clothed, to procuring the ruin of the Huguenot party, to humbling the pride of the great, to reducing all your subjects to their duty, and to elevating your majesty's name among foreign nations to its rightful reputation.

I asked, to that end, your majesty's entire confidence, and assured you that my policy would be the direct contrary of that of my predecessors, inasmuch as, instead of removing the queen, your mother, from your majesty's counsels, I would leave nothing undone to promote the closest union between you, to the great advantage and honour of the kingdom.

The success which has followed the good intentions which it has pleased God to give me for the administration of this state will justify, to the ages to come, the constancy with which I have pursued this design--that the union which exists between your majesties in nature, may be completed also between you in grace. And if, after many years, this purpose by the malice of your enemies, has been defeated, it is my consolation to remember how often your majesty has been heard to say that when I was working most for the honour of the queen, your mother, she was conspiring for my ruin.

Of Education

Letters are one of the greatest ornaments of states, and their cultivation is necessary to the commonwealth. Yet it is certain that they should not be taught indiscriminately to every one. A nation whose every subject should be educated would be as monstrous as a body having eyes in every part; pride and presumption would be general, and obedience almost disappear.

Unrestrained trade in knowledge must banish that trade in merchandise to which states owe their wealth; ruin husbandry, the true mother and nurse of peoples; and destroy our source of soldiery, which springs up in rustic ignorance rather than from the forcing-ground of culture and the sciences. It would fill France with half-taught fellows, minds formed only to *chicane*, men who might ruin families and trouble public peace, but could not be of any service to the state. There would be more people capable of doubts than capable of resolving them; more intelligences fitted to oppose than to defend the truth.

Indeed, when I consider the great number who make a profession of teaching, and the crowds of children who are taught, I seem to see an infinite multitude of weaklings and diseased, who, having no other desire than to drink pure water for their healing, are urged by an inordinate thirst to drink all that is offered them, though it is mostly impure and often poisoned, whereby their thirst and their malady are equally aggravated.

Two principal evils arise from the great number of colleges established in every district: there are not sufficient worthy teachers to supply them; and many children of little aptitude are compelled by their parents to study. In the result, almost all the pupils leave with but a smattering of learning, some because they have been badly taught, others because they have been incapable of more. The remedy that I propose is this. Let the colleges in all towns which are not of metropolitan rank be reduced to two or three classes, sufficient to raise the young out of gross ignorance, such as is harmful even to those who are destined for military service or for trade. Then, before the children are determined to any special line of life, two are three years will reveal their dispositions and their capacities; and the more promising children, who will then be sent on to the metropolitan colleges, will succeed far better; for they will have minds suited for education and will be placed in the hands of the best teachers.

Finally, let care be taken that the colleges shall not all come under the same hands. The universities, on the one hand, the Jesuits on the other, tend towards a monopoly of education. Let their emulation increase their virtues and efficiency; but let neither party be deprived of the instruction of youth; let neither secure a monopoly.

Of the Nobility

The nobility, which is one of the principal nerves of the state, may contribute much to its consolidation and power, but it has been for some time past greatly depreciated by the large number of officials whom the misfortunes of our age have raised up to its prejudice. It must be supported against the enterprises of people of that kind, whose wealth and pride overwhelmed the nobles, who are rich only in courage.

But as the nobility must be defended from their oppressors, so also must they be strictly prevented from oppressing those who are below them, whom God has armed to labour but not to self-defence. Uncompromisingly justice must ensure security, under shelter of your laws, to the least and feeblest of your subjects.

Those nobles who do not serve the state are a charge upon it; and, like a paralysed limb, are a burden where they should be a defence and a comfort. As men of gentle birth should be well treated so long as they deserve it, so they should be checked severely when they are found wanting to the obligations of their birth; and I have no hesitation in advising that those who have so degenerated from the virtues of their fathers as to avoid the service of the crown with their swords and with their lives, deserve to be degraded from their hereditary honours and advantages, and should be reduced to take part in bearing the burdens of the people.

Of the Disorders of Justice

It is much easier to recognise the defects of justice than to prescribe the remedy. Certain it is that they have arrived at such a point that they could hardly be graver; yet I know that it is your majesty's desire that the administration of justice should be as pure as the imperfections and corruptions of mankind will permit.

In the opinion of the great majority of the people, the sovereign remedy consists in suppressing venality, in doing away with the hereditary principle in judicial offices, and in giving their positions gratuitously to men of such well-known probity and capacity that not even envy itself can contest their merit. But as it would be difficult to follow this counsel at any time, and is quite impossible to follow it here and now, it is useless to propose means calculated to secure that end.

Although it is always dangerous to hold a view which others do not share, I must boldly say that in my opinion, in the present state of affairs and in any that one can foresee, it is better to suffer venality and hereditary offices to continue than to change, from top to bottom, your majesty's judicial establishment. The present abuses are great; but I believe that a system under which the offices of justice should be appointed by nomination by the king would lead to even greater abuses. The distribution of these important charges would, in effect, depend on the favour and intrigue of the courtiers who might at the time have most power with the king, or on whose reports he must base his nominations.

Certainly venality and heredity in this matter are evils, but they are evils of long standing. We have only to look back to the reigns of St. Louis, when offices were already paid for, and of the great Francis, who erected the principle into a regular traffic, to see that so inveterate a custom is not easily to be eradicated. Our aim should be to turn the minds of men gently and continuously to better ways, and not to pass suddenly from one extreme to the other. The architect whose skill is able to correct the weakness of an ancient building, and to bring it into some degree of symmetry without first pulling it down, deserves far greater praise than the man who must throw it into ruins in order to construct something entirely new. It is difficult to change the established order without changing the hearts of those who possess it, and it is often prudent to weaken one's remedies in order that they may have the greater effect.

To the Officers of Finance

These form a class of men who are prejudicial to the state, yet are necessary to and we can only hope to reduce their power within tolerable limits. At present, their excesses and irregularities are intolerable; and it is impossible that they should further increase their wealth and their power without ruining the state, and themselves with it.

I do not advise the general confiscation of their gains, although the excessive wealth which they amass in a short time, easily proved by the difference between their possessions on entering office and what they own at present, must often be the result of thefts and extortions. Confiscation may be made, in its turn, the greatest of injustice and violence. Yet I do not think that anyone could complain if the more flagrant offenders were chastised. Otherwise, they will, as I have said, ruin the kingdom, which bears on its face the marks of their frauds.

The gold with which they have gorged themselves has opened to them alliances with the most ancient families, whose blood and character are thereby so far debased that their representatives resemble their ancestors no more in the generosity of their motives than they do in the purity of their features.

I can advise nothing but a great reduction in the number of these officials, a reform which might be easily accomplished; and the appointment, in times to come, only of substantial men, of character and position suitable to this responsibility. As for the plan of squeezing these financiers like a sponge, or of making treaties and compositions with them, it is a remedy worse than the disorder; it is as much as to teach them that peculation is their business and their right.

Of the People

All statesmen agree that if the people were in too easy a condition it would be impossible to restrain them within the limits of their duty. Having less knowledge and cultivation than those in other ranks of the state, they would not easily follow the rules prescribed by reason and by law, unless bound thereto by a certain degree of necessity.

Reason does not permit us to exempt them from all taxation, lest, having lost the symbol of their subjection, they should forget their legitimate condition, and, being free from tribute, should think themselves free from obedience also.

Mules accustomed to a load suffer more from a long rest than they do from work; but, on the other hand, their work must be moderate and the load proportionate to their strength. So it is with the taxation of the people, which becomes unjust if it is not moderated at the point at which it is useful to the public.

There is a sense in which the tribute which kings draw from the people returns to the people again, in the enjoyment of peace and in the security of their life and possessions; for these cannot be safeguarded unless contribution be made to the state. I know of several princes who have lost their kingdoms and their subjects by letting their strength decay through fear of taxing them; and subjects have before now fallen into servitude to their enemies, through wishing too much liberty under their natural sovereign. The proportion between the burden and the strength of those who have to support it ought to be even religiously observed; a prince cannot be considered good if he draws more than he ought from his subjects; yet the best princes are not always those who never levy more than is necessary.

Reason and Government

Man, having been made a rational creature, ought to do nothing except by reason; for, otherwise he acts against nature, and so against the Author of nature. Again, the greater a man is, and the higher his position, the more strictly is he bound to follow reason. It follows that if he is sovereignly rational, he is bound to make reason reign; that is to say, it is his duty to make all those who are under his authority revere and obey reason religiously. Love is the most potent motive for obedience; and it is impossible that subjects should not love their prince if they know that reason is the guide of all his actions.

Since reason should be the guide of princes, passion, which is of all things the most incompatible with reason, should be allowed no influence on their actions. Passion can only blind them; make them take the shadow for the substance; and win for them odium in the place of affection.

Government requires a masculine virtue and an immovable firmness; for softness exposes those in whom it is found to the machinations of their enemies. Though there have been notable exceptions, their softness and their passions have generally made women unfit for rule.

Public Interests First

The public advantage should be the single object of the king and his counsellors, or should at least be preferred to every private interest. It is impossible to estimate the good which a prince and his ministers may do if they religiously follow this principle, or to estimate the disasters which must fall upon the state whose public interests are ruled by private considerations. True philosophy, the Christian law, and the art of statesmanship, unite to teach this truth.

The prosperity which Spain has enjoyed for several centuries has been due to no other cause than that her council has consistently preferred the interests of the state to all others, and most of the calamities which have visited France have been due to the preference of private advantage.

It is easy for princes to consent to the general regulations of their state, because in making them they have only reason and justice before their eyes, and men willingly embrace reason and justice when there are no obstacles to turn them from the right path. But when occasions arise for putting these regulations into practice, we do not find that princes always show the same firmness, for then the interests of factions and of minorities are pressed upon them; pity, sympathy, favour, and importunities solicit them and oppose their just designs; and they have not always strength enough to conquer themselves and to despise these partial considerations, which ought to have no weight at all in the affairs of the commonwealth.

It is on these occasions that they must gather up all their strength against their weakness, and remember that God has placed them there to safeguard the public interest.

The Power of Kingship

Power is one of the most necessary conditions of the greatness of kings and of the happiness of their government, and those who have to do with the conduct of a state should omit nothing which may enhance the authority of their master and the respect in which he is held by all the world.

As goodness is the object of love, power is the cause of fear; and fear, founded in esteem and reverence, makes dutiful conduct the interest of every subject, and warns all foreigners not to offend a prince who can harm them if he will.

I have said that the power of which I speak must be founded on esteem, and I will add that if it be otherwise founded it is dangerous in the extreme. Princes are never in a more perilous position than when they are the objects of hatred or aversion rather than of a reasonable fear.

That kingly power which causes princes to be feared with esteem and love, includes within it different elements of power; it is a tree with several branches, which draw their nourishment from common Stock. Thus, the prince must be powerful by his reputation. Secondly, by a reasonable number of soldiers, continually maintained. Thirdly, by a notable reserve, in gold, in his coffers, ready for the unforeseen occasions which arise when least expected. And, lastly, by the possession of the hearts of his people. If the finances be considerately adjusted on the principles which I have advised the people will find entire relief, and the king will base his power on the possession of the hearts of his subjects. They will know that they are his care, and their own interests will lead them to love him.

The kings of old thought so highly of this foundation of kingship that some of them held it worthier to be King of the French than King of France. Indeed, this nation was in old time illustrious for passionate attachment to its princes; and under the earlier kings, until Philip the Fair, the treasure of hearts was the sole public treasure that was maintained in this kingdom.

I know that we cannot judge of the present altogether by the past, and that what was good in one century is not always possible in another. Yet, though the treasure of hearts may not suffice to-day, it is quite certain that without it the treasure of gold is almost worthless; without that treasure of hearts we shall be bankrupt in the midst of abundance.

The Whole Duty of Princes

In conclusion, as kings are obliged to do many more things as sovereigns than they do in their private capacity, they are liable to be guilty of far more faults by omission than those of which a private person could be guilty by commission. Considered as men, they are subject to the same faults as all other men; but considered as charged with the welfare of the public, they are subject also to many duties which they cannot omit without sin.

If princes neglect to do all that they can to rule the various orders of their state; if they are careless in the choice of good advisers, or despise their salutary counsels; if they fail to make their own example a speaking voice; if they are idle in the establishment of the reign of God, and of reason, and of justice; if they fail to protect the innocent, to reward public services, and to chastise the guilty and disobedient; if they are not solicitous to foresee and to provide for the troubles which may arise, or to turn aside, by careful diplomacy, the storms which darken the horizon; if favour rather than merit dictates their choice of ministers for the high offices of the kingdom; if they do not immovably establish the state in its rightful power; if they do not on all occasions prefer public interests to private interests; then, however upright their life may otherwise be, they will be found far more guilty than those who actively transgress the commandments and the laws of God. And if kings or magistrates make use of their power to commit any injustice or violence which they cannot commit as private persons, they commit a king's or a magistrate's sin, which has its source in their authority, and one for which the King of Kings will doubtless demand a searching account on the day of judgement.

JEAN JACQUES ROUSSEAU

Confessions

Rousseau's "Confessions" were written in England at Wootton, in Staffordshire, where he had taken refuge after his revolutionary ideas incurred the displeasure of the authorities in France. They were first published in 1782. From this refuge he was pursued from place to place by his delusions through miserable years, until he died, near Paris, on July 2, 1778. In no circumstances or relation of his life was Rousseau a pleasant spectacle. The "Confessions," unexpurgated, are often revolting to any sane mind, and have been proved to be untrustworthy even as a record of fact. But almost incredible baseness was coupled with extraordinary gifts, and it is impossible to overestimate Rousseau's influence upon the modern world, and upon its literature and its whole point of view and way of thinking. (Rousseau, biography: see FICTION.)

I am undertaking a task for which there is no example, and one which will find no imitator. It is to exhibit a man in the whole truth of nature; and the man whom I shall reveal is myself. Myself alone; for I verily believe I am like no other living man. In this book I have hidden nothing evil and added nothing good; and I challenge any man to say, having unveiled his heart with equal sincerity, "I am better than he."

I was born at Geneva in 1712, son of Isaac Rousseau, watchmaker, and of Susanne, his wife. My birth, the first of my misfortunes, cost my mother her life, and I came into the world so weakly that I was not expected to live. My father's sister lavished on me the tenderest care, and he, disconsolate, loved me with extreme affection.

Like all children, but even more than others, I felt before I thought; and my consciousness was first awakened by reading stories with my father. Sometimes we read together until the birds were singing in the morning light. These tales gave me a most precocious insight into human passions, and the confused emotions which swept through me brought with them the queerest and most romantic views of life. But when I was seven we came to the end of my mother's old stock of romances, and we fell back on Bossuet, Molière, Plutarch, Ovid, and the like. Plutarch went far to cure me of novels; indeed, his "Lives" were the means of forming that free and republican spirit, intolerant of servitude, which has been my torment. To my aunt, who knew endless songs, and used to chant them with a sweet, tiny thread of a voice, I owe my passion for music.

These, then, were my first affections. These formed that heart of mine, so proud yet so tender; they fashioned that effeminate yet untamable character, which has ever drifted between weakness and virtue. For I have been in contradiction with myself, in such a way that abstinence and fruition, pleasure and wisdom, have escaped me equally.

My father having left Geneva, I remained under the care of my uncle Bernard, and was placed, with his son of my own age, in the house of M. Lambercier, protestant minister at Bossey, to learn all the trivialities that are called education. Here I gained my keen love of country pleasures, and tasted, with my cousin, the delights of simple friendship. But a cruel punishment for a fault which I had not committed, put an end to my childish simplicity, and soon I left Bossey without regret. There followed two or three years of indolence at Geneva.

After a brief and luckless trial of a notary's office I was apprenticed to an engraver, a petty tyrant, whose injustice taught me to lie and to steal. Restless, dissatisfied, and in perpetual terror of my master's savagery, I here reached my sixteenth year. But one day, finding the city gates closed on my return from a country excursion, I determined, rather than face the inevitable thrashing, to seek my fortune in the unknown world.

Madame de Warens

How fair were the illusions of freedom and of the future! I asked little- -only a manor where I should be the favourite of the lord of the land, his daughter's lover, her brother's friend, and protector of the neighbourhood. I roamed the countryside, sleeping at nights in hospitable cottages, and on arriving at Confignon I called, out of curiosity, on M. de Ponteverre, the parish priest. He gave me a dinner which convinced me, even more than his arguments, of the advantages of the catholic faith; and I was willing enough to set off, with his introduction, to Annecy. Here I was to seek Mme. de Warens, a recent convert, who was in receipt of a pension from the King of Sardinia. I was assured that her benevolence would support me for the present. Three days later I was at Annecy.

This introduction fixed my character and destiny. I was now in my sixteenth year, doubtless of engaging though not striking appearance; I had the timidity of a loving nature, always afraid of giving offence; and I was quite without knowledge of the world or of manners. I arrived on Palm Sunday, 1728. Mme. de Warens had left the house for church; I ran after her, saw her, spoke to her--how well do I remember the place, so often in later days wet with my tears and covered with kisses!

I saw an enchanting form, a countenance full of graciousness, a dazzling colour, blue eyes beaming kindness; you may imagine that my conversion was from that moment decided. Smiling, she read the good priest's letter, and sent me back to the house for breakfast.

Louise Éléonore de Warens, daughter of a noble family of Vevai, in the Vaud country, had early married M. de Warens, of Lausanne. The marriage was childless and otherwise unfortunate; and the young wife, exasperated by some domestic difficulty, had abandoned her husband and her country, and crossing the lake, had thrown herself at the feet of the king. He took her under his protection, gave her a moderate pension, and for fear of scandal sent her to Annecy, where she renounced her errors at the Convent of the Visitation.

She had been six years at Annecy when I met her, and was now twenty-eight years of age. Her beauty was still in its first radiance, and her smile was angelic. She was short of stature, but it was impossible to imagine more beautiful features or hands. Her education had been very desultory; she had learned more from lovers than from teachers. She had a strong taste for empirical medicine and for alchemy, and was always compounding elixirs, tinctures and balms, some of which she regarded as valuable secrets. So it was that charlatans, trading on her weakness, made her consume, amid drugs and furnaces, a talent and a spirit which might have distinguished her in the highest societies. Yet her loving and sweet character, her compassion for the unhappy, her inexhaustible goodness and her open and gay humour never changed; and even when old age was coming on, in the midst of poverty and varied misfortunes, her inward serenity preserved to the end the charming gaiety of her youth. All her mistakes arose from a restless activity which demanded incessant occupation. She thirsted, not for intrigues, but for enterprises.

Well, the first sight of Mme. de Warens inspired me not only with the liveliest attachment, but with an entire trust which was never disappointed. Her presence filled my whole being with peace and confidence.

Three Years in Turin

My situation was discussed with the Bishop, and it was decided that I should go to Turin and remain for a time at an institution devoted to the instruction of catechumens. Thither I went, regarding myself as the pupil, the friend, and almost the lover, of Mme. de Warens. The great doors closed upon me, and here I was instructed for several weeks in very indifferent company. At length, having been received into the church, I found myself in the street with twenty francs in my pocket, and the counsel that I should be a good Christian.

I took a lodging in Turin, and was presently introduced, by the kindness of my hostess, to the service of a countess. But this lady died shortly afterwards, and I left her house bearing with me lasting remorse for an atrocious action: I had accused a fellow-servant of a theft which I had myself committed, and thus may very well have caused the poor child's ruin.

Returning to my old lodging, I spent my days in wandering about town, often offending the public by my depravities. But I had kept certain acquaintances made during my situation with the countess, and one of these, a M. Gaime, whom I sometimes visited, gave me most valuable instructions in the principles of morals. He was a priest, and one of the most honest men I have known. I had cherished false ideas of life; he gave me a true picture of it, and showed me that happiness depends only on wisdom, and that wisdom is to be found in every rank. He used to say that if everyone could read the hearts of others, most would wish to descend in the social scale. This M. Gaime is the original, in large part, of my vicar of Savoy.

Then followed a new situation in the house of the Count de Gouvon, where, nominally a footman, I was soon treated more as a pupil or even as a favourite. His son, a priest, did his best to teach me Latin, and I have since realised that it was the purpose of this noble family, who had considerable political ambition, to train a talented dependent who might serve them in offices of great responsibility. But my fatal inconstancy frustrated this good fortune, my flagrant disobediences led to my dismissal, and presently I was on the road to Geneva with a gay lad from thence who had found me out in Turin.

I happened to own a mechanical toy, a little fountain, and our mad project was nothing less than to pay our way throughout the world by showing its performances in every village. We started in the highest spirits, but the fountain was never remunerative, and soon its works went wrong. This threw no gloom over our merry, fantastic journey, and it was only when Annecy was near that I became a little thoughtful, for my benefactress supposed that my last place had established me for life.

We entered the little town and parted, and I came trembling to her door. The adorable woman showed little surprise, and no sorrow. I told her my story, and was forgiven. Henceforth her home was mine.

Seeking a Career

The house was an old one, but spacious and comfortable, and the window of my room looked out, over garden and stream, to the open country. The ménage was by no means magnificent, but was abundant in a patriarchal way; Madame de Warens had no idea of economy, and with her hospitalities and speculations was ever running more deeply into debt. The household, besides herself and me, consisted of housemaid, cook, and a footman named Claude Anet.

From the first day, the sweetest familiarity reigned our intercourse. She called me "Little one," I called her my little mother, and these names express the relation of our hearts. She sought always my good, never her own pleasure; she was deeply attached to me, and lavished on me her maternal caresses. I was now about nineteen years old, but was only occupied about the house in writing for her, or in helping her in her pharmaceutical experiments.

But madame was thinking of my future, and sent me on some pretext to see M. d'Aubonne, a relative of hers, to find out what might be made of me. His report of me was, that I was a poor-spirited creature, narrow, ignorant, and clownish, and that the career of village priest was the best that could be hoped for. Once more, therefore, I was set to Latin at the seminary; but after some months I was returned by the bishop and the rector as incapable of learning, though a passably well-conducted youth. In the meantime I had been taken with a strong taste for music, and it was arranged that I should spend the winter at the house of M. le Maitre, director of music at the cathedral; he was a young man of great talent and of high spirits, and lived only twenty paces from my little mother. There I spent one of the most pleasant times of my life. But it was cut short by a quarrel between Le Maitre and the cathedral chapter, who had, as he thought, put a slight upon him. His revenge was to desert his post on the eve of the elaborate Easter services, and madame desired me to assist him in his flight. I was to attend him to Lyons, and remain with him as long as he should need me. Her purpose was, as I have since learned, to detach me from a plausible adventurer, M. Venture, a man of great musical talent who had turned up at Annecy, and had engaged my fancy. Our flight was successful. But on the second day after our arrival at Lyons Le Maitre fell ill with a sudden seizure in the street, and I, after telling the bystanders the name of his inn, and begging them to carry him thither, slipped round the nearest corner and disappeared. Le Maitre was deserted at his worst need by the only friend on whom he had to count. I returned at once to Annecy, only to find that madame had left for Paris.

M. Venture, however, was still there, and had turned the heads of all the ladies in the place, and for a time I shared his lodging. Then, after travelling with Merceret, the housemaid, as far as her home at Fribourg--for she had to return thither and could find no other attendant--I turned aside to Lausanne, with the idea of seeing the lake. I arrived here without a penny, and it occurred to me to play Venture's game on my own account. I took a false name, called myself a Parisian, and having secured a lodging, set up as a teacher of music, though I knew next to nothing of the art. There was a professor of law in the town who was an amateur of music, and held concert parties in his house; to this man I had the effrontry to propose a symphony of my own. I worked a fortnight at this production, wrote out the instrumental parts, and on the appointed evening stood up before the orchestra and audience, tapped my desk, raised by baton, and--never since music began has there been such an orgy of discords. The musicians could hardly sit in their chairs for laughing, yet played even louder and louder as the fun took hold of them; the audience sought to stop their ears; and I, sweat pouring down my face, conducted this atrocity to the end. But the end was a little minuet which Venture had taught me; I had appended it to my symphony, calling it my own work. Its magic put the whole room in good humour, and I was feliciated on my taste in melody. Next day one of my orchestra came to see me, and in my despair and broken spirit I told him my whole story. By nightfall it was known to all Lausanne. But at Neufchâtel, through the next winter, I gradually learned music by teaching it.

My next occupation was that of interpreter to a Greek prelate and archimandrite of Jerusalem, whom I met when dining in a little restaurant. He was collecting money throughout Europe for the restoration of the Holy Sepulchre; and accompanying him from city to city, I was of much service to him, even addressing the Senate at Berne on behalf of his project. Unfortunately for my employer, he addressed himself to the Marquis de Bonac, who had been ambassador to the Porte, and knew all about the Holy Sepulchre. I don't know what passed at their interview, but the archimandrite disappeared and I was detained. In my desolation I told the marquis the history of my life, and by him was sent to Paris, with plenty of money in my pocket, to enter the service of a young friend of his in the army. My first sight of the city was a disappointment which I have never got over, and the proposed engagement fell through. Coming to the end of my resources, I set out by way of Lyons, where I suffered the extremity of poverty, to find Mme. de Warens, who was now, as I learned, at Chambéri. I came to her house and found the intendant-general with her. Without addressing me, she said, "Here, sir, he is; protect him as long as he deserves it, and his future is assured." And to me, "My child, you belong to the king." And thus I became a secretary in the ordnance survey. After five years of follies and sufferings since I had left Geneva, I began to earn an honest living.

Our Little Circle

It was in 1732, and I was nearly twenty-one years old, when I began the life of the office. I lived with the little mother in a dismal house, which she rented because it belonged to the financial secretary who controlled her pension. The faithful Claude Anet was still with her, and shortly after my return I learned accidentally that their relation was closer than I had ever dreamed of. In a fit of temper his mistress had taunted him outrageously. The poor fellow, in despair, had taken laudanum; and madame, in her terror and distress, told me the whole story. We brought him round, and things went on as before, but it was hard to me to know that anyone was more intimate with her than myself.

My passion for music increased this year until I could hardly take interest in anything else, and at last the work at the office grew so intolerable to me that I determined to resign my place. I extorted an unwilling permission from madame, said good-bye to my chief, and threw myself into the teaching of music.

I soon had as many pupils as I needed, and the constant intercourse with these ladies was very pleasant to me. But from the stories which I carried home of our interviews the little mother apprehended dangers of which I was not at that time conscious. The course which she took was a singular one. She had rented a little garden outside the town, and here she invited me to spend the day with her. Thither we went, and from the drift of her conversation, which was full of good sense and kindliest warnings, I gradually perceived the degree of her goodness towards me. The compact involved conditions, and my answer was to be given on that day week.

Thus was established among the three of us a society to which there is perhaps no parallel. All our wishes, our cares, our interests were in common. If one of us was missing from the dinner-table, or a fourth was present, all seemed out of order. But our little circle was broken all too soon. Claude Anet, on a botanical excursion, fell a victim to pleurisy, and died, notwithstanding all her care. He had been a most watchful economist of her pension and a restraint on her enterprises, and his loss was felt not only in our diminished party, but also in the wasting of her resources. For the next three years these went from bad to worse. Unfortunately, the life to which I had taken, of drifting from one interest to another--now literature, now chess, now a journey, now music--brought in nothing and cost a good deal; and to complete our anxieties, I fell ill nearly to death. Her care and utter devotion saved me, and from that time our very existence was in common.

Les Charmettes

I was ordered to the country. We found near Chambéri a little house, Les Charmettes, set in a garden among trees, as retired and solitary a home as if it had been a hundred miles from the town. There we took up a new life towards the autumn of 1736; there began the brief happiness of my existence. We were all in all to one another; together we roamed the country, worked in the garden, gathered fruit and flowers, lay under the trees and listened to the birds. Golden hours, your memory is my only treasure!

Even a sudden illness, which affected my heart so that its pulse has from that time incessantly throbbed like a drum in my ears, and has made me a constant sufferer from insomnia, turned out to be a heavenly blessing. Thinking myself a dead man, I only then began to live, and applied myself very eagerly to learning. With my little mother as my teacher, I turned to the study of religion. I sought books, and philosophy, the sciences, and Latin followed in their turn. Nature, learning, leisure, and our ineffably sweet companionship--I thought, poor fool, that these joys would be with me to the end. It was otherwise decreed.

My bodily condition has become pitiable, and it was determined that I should go to Montpellier to consult a physician. I fell in, on the way thither, with the Marquis de Torignan and his party, who were travelling in the same direction. We struck up acquaintance, and I joined them, taking an assumed name, and giving myself out for an Englishman. Becoming intimate with a Madame de Larnage, who was among them, I continued to travel with her day by day, after the others had reached their destination. She was a woman of infinite charm. Mme. de Warens was forgotten utterly, and I willingly agreed to settle down in her vicinity, after fulfilling the purpose of my journey to Montpellier. However, after two pleasurable months in that city, when I found myself at the stage where the road divided--one road going to Mme. de Larnage, the other to Les Charmettes--I balanced love against pleasure, and finding an equipoise, I decided by reason.

The little mother knew by my letter at what hour I should arrive. I came to the garden; no one came out to meet me. I entered; the servants seemed surprised to see me. I ran upstairs and found her; her welcome was restrained and cold. The truth burst upon me. My place was taken!

Darkness flooded my soul, and from that moment onward my sensibilities have been but half-alive. I took a situation as tutor in a private family, but all my thoughts were of Charmettes and of our innocent life together, now gone for ever. O dreadful illusion of human destiny!

The Gathering Gloom

I take up my pen again, after an interval of two years, to add a sequel to my confessions. How different is the picture now! For thirty years fate had favoured my inclinations, but for the second thirty, which I must try to sketch, she has ground me in the mortar of the most appalling afflictions.

This second part must inevitably be inferior, in every respect, to the first. For I wrote, before, with pleasure and at ease; but now my decaying memory and enfeebled brain have made me almost incapable of work, and I have nothing to tell of but treacheries, perfidies, and torturing memories. The walls around me have ears; I am encompassed by spies and vigilant enemies. Racked with anxiety and fear, I scribble page after page without revising them. An immense conspiracy surrounds me....

[These delusions of suspicion are perhaps the most characteristic symptoms of insanity. They colour so deeply the entire texture of Rousseau's prolix second part as to make it not only unreliable, but almost unreadable. Only its human interest gives value to the first part; from the second part human interest is totally absent. The unhappy creature, besotted with intellectual pride, was already insane, inhuman; and this morbid condition had been aggravated by years of brooding rancour before he wrote this miserable indictment of men who had done their best to befriend him.--ED.]

LA ROCHEFOUCAULD

Memoirs

Francois, Duc de la Rochefoucauld, was born in Paris on September 15, 1613. Sprung from one of the noblest families of France, handsome, winning, and brave to recklessness, he intrigued and fought against Richelieu and Mazarin, and was one of the leaders in the civil war of La Fronde. But though marked by birth and talent for a high position in the state, he failed in nearly everything he undertook, owing to his extraordinary indolence of mind, and in the prime of his life he became a rather embittered spectator of a world in which he was not able to make his way. The "Memoirs," with their studied tone of historical coldness, present a striking contrast to the brilliant vivacity of the "Maxims." This, in all probability, is due to the fact that while the latter were frequently added to and edited during their author's lifetime, no such fate befell the "Memoirs," of which the first edition, published without La Rochefoucauld's authority, appeared in 1662. Barely a third of them could be attributed to their reputed author, the work being compiled mainly from various commonplace books. In spite of La Rochefoucauld's protests, the pirated "Memoirs" continued to be printed, and it was not until very many years after his death, in 1817, that an authentic edition made its appearance. The "Memoirs" are of great literary value, yielding in interest to no memoirs of the time. La Rochefoucauld died in Paris on March 17, 1680.

Court Intrigues

King Louis XIII. was of feeble constitution, further impaired by over-exertion in hunting. His temperament was severe and solitary; he wished to be governed, but was sometimes impatient of government. His mind took note only of details, and his knowledge of war was fit rather for a subordinate officer than for a king. Cardinal Richelieu, who owed all his elevation to the queen-mother, Marie de Médicis, was ruler of the state. His vast and penetrating mind formed projects as bold as he was personally timid. His policy was to establish the king's authority and his own, by the ruin of the Huguenots and of the great houses of the kingdom, and then to attack the house of Austria, a power most redoubtable to France. He stuck at nothing, either to advance his satellites or to destroy his enemies. The passion which he had long cherished for the queen had changed to dislike, and she had an aversion for Richelieu. The king was embittered against her by jealousy and by the sterility of their marriage. The queen was an amiable woman, without falsity of any kind, and with many virtues; her intimate friend was Madame de Chevreuse, who was of her own age and of kindred sentiments.

But Madame de Chevreuse almost always brought misfortune to those whom she interested in her projects. She had much spirit, ambition, and beauty, and made full use of her charms to forward these enterprises of hers. Already Cardinal Richelieu had accused the queen and her of complicity in Chalais's plot against the king's life--for Chalais had been her warm admirer--and the king believed in their guilt to the end of his days. Again, when the young and handsome Lord Holland came to France to arrange the marriage of the King of England to the sister of the King of France, and quickly won the affection of Madame de Chevreuse, the two lovers thought fit to celebrate their attachment by inspiring a similar intrigue between the French queen and the Duke of Buckingham, who had not so much as met one another. This astonishing undertaking was successful. Buckingham came over to wed madame in the name of his master, and his ardent love for the queen, which she fully returned, deeply wounded both the king and Richelieu. The cardinal sought his revenge through Lady Carlisle. That haughty and jealous woman, to whom Buckingham had long been attached, noticed one night at a ball in England that he was wearing diamonds which she had not seen before, and contrived, unobserved, to detach them, in order that she might send them to Richelieu. These diamonds had been the gift of the King of France to his queen, and it was intended that the cardinal, by showing them to the king, should prove the queen's weakness. But the Duke of Buckingham discovered his loss the same night, and at once suspected Lady Carlisle's design. He issued an immediate order that the English ports should be closed, and that no one should be permitted, under whatever pretext, to leave the country; and then, having had exactly similar jewels prepared, he sent them to the Queen of France, with an account of the whole matter.

It was at this time that the cardinal formed the project of the destruction of the Huguenot party, and of laying siege to La Rochelle. The Duke of Buckingham came with a powerful fleet to aid La Rochelle, but in vain; the fortress was taken, and the duke was assassinated in England. This murder gave the cardinal an inhuman joy; he jested at the queen's sorrows, and began to hope again.

After the ruin of the Huguenots I returned from the army to court, being now seventeen years old, and began to notice the state of affairs. The queen-mother and the cardinal were at enmity, and though everyone saw that something would come of it, no one could foretell what would happen. The cardinal's situation was precarious, the king had learned of his love for the queen, and was quite ready to disgrace him, and even asked the queen-mother to nominate someone to replace him. She hesitated, and that hesitation was her ruin and saved the cardinal.

The reversal of the situation took place on the famous "day of dupes," on which the queen-mother, presuming too much on her power, challenged the cardinal, in the king's presence, with his ingratitude and treacheries. No one doubted but that Richelieu's day was over, and the whole court crowded to the queen-mother to share her imaginary triumph. But the king went the same day to Versailles, and the cardinal followed him; the queen, fearing that she would find Versailles dull and uncomfortable, remained behind; and the wily statesman made such good use of his opportunity that the king's consent was won to the downfall of his mother. She was soon arrested, and her sorrows lasted as long as her life.

Many were implicated in her ruin, and were exiled or thrown into the Bastille, or brought to the scaffold; and so much bloodshed and so many fortunes reversed brought odium on the name of Richelieu. The mild regency of Marie de Médicis was remembered, and all the great families lamented that liberty was a thing of the past.

For my part, I thought that the queen's cause was the only one, which an honourable man could follow. She was unhappy; the cardinal was rather her tyrant than her lover; she had been good to me, and had trusted me; Mademoiselle d'Hautefort, with whom I had great friendship, was her friend, too--sufficient reasons, these, to dazzle a youth who had seen almost nothing of the world, and to turn his steps in a direction quite contrary to his interests. King and cardinal alike soon came to detest me, and my life thenceforth was troubled by the visitations of their displeasure. In recording the scenes in which I have had a part, I have no intention of writing history, but only of touching on a few personal episodes.

Richelieu's Death

War was declared in 1635 against the King of Spain, and I accompanied the French army of twenty thousand men which marched to the support of the Prince of Orange in Flanders. During neither this nor the following winter was I allowed at court. Madame de Chevreuse, who had been sent to Tours on the occasion of Richelieu's triumph had heard a good account of me from the queen, and invited me to see her; we soon struck up a very great friendship, and I came to be a confidential intermediary between the queen and her, and was often entrusted by one or other of them with most perilous commissions.

When I was at last readmitted to court in 1637, I found the queen in great trouble. She had been accused of a crime against the state, a treasonable understanding with the Spanish minister; some of her servants were arrested; the chancellor examined her like a criminal; it was even proposed to seclude her at Havre, annul her marriage, and repudiate her altogether. In this extremity, abandoned by all the world, she proposed that I should kidnap her and Mademoiselle d'Hautefort and carry them off to Brussels. Difficult and dangerous as this project was, it gave me greater joy than any I had known, for I was at an age when a man likes to engage in dashing and heroic feats. Happily, however, the chancellor's investigations proved her majesty not guilty.

But an unfortunate series of accidents led to my imprisonment for a week in the Bastille. A signal had been agreed upon between the queen and Madame de Chevreuse during the recent trouble. If all went well, Madame de Chevreuse was to receive a prayer-book bound in green, but a red binding was to indicate disaster. I never knew which of the two ladies made the mistake, but when the queen was acquitted Madame de Chevreuse received what she took to be the signal of misfortune; concluded that both she and the queen were undone, and disguising herself as a man, she fled to Spain. This escapade, so surprising at the very moment when the Queen's troubles had come to an end, inspired the king and the cardinal with the gravest suspicions that they had not, after all, fathomed her majesty's treachery. The cardinal summoned me to Paris, and hinted at unpleasant consequences if I did not reveal all I knew. I knew nothing; and as my manner seemed more reserved and dry than he was accustomed to, I was sent to the Bastille.

The little time that I spent there showed me more vividly than anything I had yet seen the picture of vengeance. I saw there men of great names and of great merits, an infinite number of men and women of all ranks in life, all unhappy in the affliction of long and cruel incarceration. The sight of so many pitiable creatures did much to increase my natural hatred for Cardinal

Richelieu's administration. I was released in eight days, and thought myself very fortunate to escape at a period when none others were set at liberty.

But my disgrace was well repaid. The queen showed herself gratefully aware of all that I had suffered in her service; Mademoiselle d'Hautefort gave full expression to her esteem and friendship; and Madame de Chevreuse was not less gracious. I enjoyed not only the favour of those to whom I was attached, but also a certain approval which the world is not slow to give to the unfortunate whose conduct has not really been disgraceful. Under these conditions an exile of two or three years from court was not intolerable. I was young; the king and the cardinal were failing in health; I had everything to hope for from a change. I was happy in my family, and enjoyed all the pleasures of country life, and the neighbouring provinces were full of other exiles.

Cardinal Richelieu died on December 4, 1642. Although his enemies could only rejoice at finding themselves free at last from so many persecutions, the event has shown that the state could ill spare him. He had made so many changes in public affairs that he alone was able to direct them safely. No one before Richelieu had known all the power of the kingdom, or had been able to gather it all up into the hands of the sovereign. The severity of his adminstration had cost many lives; the nobility had been humbled, and the common people had been loaded with taxes; but the grandeur of his political designs, such as the taking of La Rochelle, the destruction of the Huguenot party, and the weakening of the house of Austria, no less than his intrepidity in carrying them out, have secured for his memory a justly-merited fame.

Under Mazarin's Rule

I returned to Paris immediately after the death of Richelieu, thinking that I might have occasion to serve the queen. In accordance with the late cardinal's will, Cardinal Mazarin succeeded to his powers. The king's state of health went from bad to worse, and the court was filled with intrigues with regard to the regency which must so soon be appointed. His death took place on May 14, 1643. The queen at once brought her little son, Louis XIV., to Paris; two days later she was declared regent in parliament; and the same evening, to the amazement of his enemies, she appointed Cardinal Mazarin chief of the council.

Mazarin's mind was great, industrious, insinuating, and artful, and his character was so supple that he could become as many different men as he had occasion to personate. But he was shortsighted even in his grandest projects; and, unlike his predecessor, whose mind was bold but his temperature timid, Mazarin was bolder in temper than in conception. A pretended moderation veiled his ambition and his avarice; he said he wanted nothing for himself.

The court was now divided between the Duke of Beaufort and the cardinal, and it was expected that the return of Madame de Chevreuse would incline the queen to the former party. But the queen was in no hurry for that lady's return, knowing well what turmoils she was apt to bring in her train. Perhaps I urged her recall more boldly than was wise; at any rate, I won my point, and her majesty sent me to form Madame de Chevreuse for her appearance at court under the new conditions.

I represented to her how indispensable Cardinal Mazarin was to the state; that he was accused of no crime, and was guiltless of Richelieu's oppressions; and that the most fatal course she could take would be to attempt to govern the queen. Madame de Chevreuse promised to follow my advice, and came up to court, but her old instincts of domination were too much for her, and she soon declared herself openly against the minister who enjoyed all the queen's confidence. She even attempted his overthrow, and for that purpose united herself to the party known as the "*Importans*," which was led by the Duke of Beaufort.

After various manoeuvres on the part of the cardinal and of Madame de Chevreuse to get the upper hand, Mazarin discovered a plot against his life, in which the Duke of Beaufort was implicated, and had the duke arrested and imprisoned. At the same time Madame de Chevreuse was sent away to Tours, and as I was unwilling to promise that I would have no more to do with her, I lost the favour of the queen, provoked the cardinal's displeasure, and soon found that Madame de Chevreuse herself was forgetful of all I had done for her.

Kept in idleness, tantalised by promises of office which were never fulfilled, and forbidden even to follow the wars, my wretched position led me at last to seek some way of showing my resentment at the treatment I had received from the queen and cardinal. The means were at hand. Like many others, I had come under the spell of the beauty and charm of Madame de Longueville, and thus come gradually into association with the party of the Fronde. I followed the Duke of Enghien, her brother, to the attack on Courtray, then to Mardick, where I was wounded; and this time of military service united me more closely to his later interests.

By the year 1647 everyone was weary of Mazarin's rule. His bad faith, his weakness, and his trickiness were becoming known, provinces and towns alike were groaning under taxation, and the citizens of Paris were reduced to mere despair. Parliament tried respectful remonstrances in vain;

the cardinal thought himself safe in the servility of the nation. But the great majority in France desired a change, and then smouldering discontent soon burst into a flame.

The Duke of Enghien, who had become, by the death of his father, Prince of Condé, had gained in 1648 a great victory in Flanders, and a solemn thanksgiving was held in Notre Dame to celebrate it. Mazarin chose this moment for the arrest of Broussel and other members of parliament who had voiced most urgently the public distress. The action roused Paris to a fury which astonished him; the people sought him to tear him to pieces; barricades were erected in the streets, and the king and queen were besieged in the royal palace. Resistance to the parliament's demands were at the moment impossible; the prisoners had to be released.

I was at this time absent from Paris, having been sent down by the queen to my government at Poitou, which I had purchased; the province was almost in insurrection and I had to pacify it. I happened to be deeply wounded by a new slight which Cardinal Mazarin had put upon me, when Madame de Longueville sent for me to come to Paris, informing me that the whole plan for a civil war had been drawn up, and asking for my counsel in the matter. The news delighted me, and I arrived at the capital eager for my revenge on the queen and the cardinal.

Mazarin, on the other hand, had formed his plan. Realising that Paris was unsafe, he determined to leave it, to place the king at Saint-Germain, and to lay siege to the city, which would soon be reduced to famine and dissensions. Their escape was made at midnight on the eve of Epiphany, 1649, all the court following in great disorder.

The city was for a time in much perplexity, but the arrival of the Duke of Beaufort, who had broken prison at Vincennes, put heart into the people, who took him for their liberator. Other great personages threw in their lot with the popular cause; a large war-chest was quickly raised and troops were levied, and the parliament of Paris put itself into communication with the other parliaments of the kingdom. All preparations were made for a civil war, the real basis of which was a general hatred of Cardinal Mazarin, which was common to both parties. In an early engagement outside the city I was so gravely wounded as to see no more of this war, the events of which are hardly worth narrating. On April 1, 1649, the Parliament received an amnesty from the king. Neither party had vanquished the other; the cardinal and the parliament were each as strong as before, but everyone was glad to be rid, for the time, of the horrors of civil war.

Wars of the Fronde

The Prince of Condé, who had great influence in the council, showed himself so contemptuous to Mazarin, and became so inconvenient to the queen by his arrogance that she decided to arrest him, and to involve Madame de Longueville, the duke, her husband, and the Prince of Conti in the same disgrace. Accordingly, on January 18, 1650, the Prince of Condé, the Duke of Longueville, and the Prince of Conti were seized and imprisoned at Vincennes, and the order was given at the same time to arrest Madame de Longueville and myself. But we succeeded in escaping together to Dieppe, where we were forced to separate; Madame de Longueville found refuge at Stenay, where she met with Turenne, and I returned to my government of Poitou and formed an alliance there with the Duke of Bouillon, Turenne's brother. Together the duke and I matured designs which led to the civil war in the south.

My father having died at Verteuil in March, 1650, I succeeded to the title of Duke of La Rochefoucauld. I invited a large number of nobles and gentlemen of that region to the funeral ceremonies; our plans were put before them; though some of them held back, most were favourable; and I soon found myself at the head of a force of two thousand horse and eight hundred foot. The Duke of Bouillon and I were joined by the young Princess of Condé, with her son the Duke of Enghien; we gathered more troops at Turenne, and marched upon Bordeaux. After overcoming some opposition, the princess entered that city in triumph on May 31, 1650, and we joined her a few days later.

The grievance of the princess and the presence of her son excited the liveliest enthusiasm, and the party opposed to Mazarin had entire mastery of the town. The revolt of Bordeaux carried with it almost all Guienne, and Mazarin determined to crush it before it should extend to the neighbouring provinces. A royal army of veterans was sent down, Bordeaux was closely invested, an obstinate defence was made, but the town had to capitulate on September 28, on the condition of an amnesty to the princess and her adherents.

Meanwhile Turenne, with a Spanish force, had made a vain attempt to rescue the captive princes, and Mazarin had removed them to Havre, where the government was devoted to him. There was now such general dread and hatred of the cardinal, that people were willing to unite with those whom they had considered their mortal enemies in order to secure his ruin. In the early days of 1651 I was summoned to Paris by the Princess Palatine, who united a taste for gallantry with a remarkable talent for intrigue, and remained for some time hidden in her house, where I was witness to many consultations for the removal of Mazarin from power. I even made a last attempt to persuade the cardinal himself to release the princes; in four nocturnal interviews I tried to show him how all parties were uniting to compass his ruin, but was unable to convince him without betraying secrets which were not my own. Mazarin gave me no hope of their liberation.

Then arose a general storm against the minister, and he made his escape on the night of February 7. The queen would have followed him with her son, but the Frondeurs and the partisans of the princes kept her prisoner in her palace. Without any hope of assistance, and daunted day and night by an infuriated populate, she sent for me and gave me an order to the governor of Havre to release the princes immediately. I warned the leaders of the Fronde that her sincerity was not above suspicion, and that all depended upon her close imprisonment, and so set out along the northern road upon my mission. But the cardinal had been beforehand with me, the princes were at liberty, and on February 16 they entered Paris in triumph.

Mazarin, who had fled to Cologne, whence he continued to direct the queen's cabinet, returned to France at the head of a small army in January, 1652, and arrived at Poitiers without meeting any resistance. The party opposed to him was rent by faction and strife, but the Prince of Condé united it, and fought an indecisive engagement with the royal troops on April 8. On the 11th the prince and I were well received in Paris, but it was evident that the citizens were weary of all these troubles, desired nothing so much as the king's return, and detested the ambition of the leaders of faction. Indeed, the magistrates were negotiating with Mazarin, and declared the city neutral. On July 2 the Prince of Condé was marching his force from Saint-Cloud to Charenton when he was attacked by Turenne; and in the sanguinary combat which followed, and in which I was fighting beside the prince, I received a wound in the head which prevented my taking any further part in these disturbances.

Shortly afterwards, the Prince of Condé, his popularity wholly gone, took service under the King of Spain; King Louis XIV., amid general acclamations, returned to Paris on October 21; and Cardinal Mazarin, having overcome all his enemies, entered the capital in a veritable triumph, in February, 1653.

MADAME DE SÉVIGNÉ

Letters

Marie de Rabutin-Chantal, who became Madame de
Sévigné, was born at Paris on February 6, 1626. Her father
and mother died during her childhood and Marie was left
to the care of her uncle, priest of Coulanges; she received
an admirable education and became a great lover of history
and of classical literature. At eighteen years of age she
married the Marquis Henri de Sévigné, who was killed in
a duel in 1651, and thenceforth Madame de Sévigné gave
herself up altogether to the care of her two children. Her
wit, her kindliness, and happiness, her charity and fidelity,
and especially a certain rare genius for friendship, won for
her the warm devotion of many great people of that brilliant
age. Her daughter was married in 1669 to the Comte de
Grignan, a great official, lieutenant-general of Languedoc
and then of Provence, a man of honour, but accustomed
to the most lavish expenditure, which burdened his life
with enormous debts. The famous "Letters" of Madame de
Sévigné numbering over 1,000 were written over a period
of twenty-five years, chiefly to this daughter, Madame de
Grignan. They are valued for their vivacious and graceful
style, the light which they throw upon the thoughts and
movements of her time, but especially for their revelation of
a wonderfully sweet and gracious personality. Madame de
Sévigné died on April 18, 169696.

Love for her Daughter

My dear child: I have been here but three hours, and already take my
pen to talk to you. I left Paris with the Abbé, Hélène, Hébert and Marphise,
so that I might get away from the noise and bustle of the town until Thursday
evening. I want to have perfect quietness, in which to reflect. I intend to fast
for many good reasons, and to walk much to make up for the long time I
have spent in my room; and above all, I want to discipline myself for the
love of God.

But, my dear daughter, what I shall do more than all this, will be to think of you. I have not ceased to do so since I arrived here; and being quite unable to restrain my feelings, I have betaken myself to the little shady walk you so loved, to write to you, and am sitting on the mossy bank where you so often used to lie. But, my dear, where in this place have I not seen you? Do not thoughts of you haunt my heart everywhere I turn?--in the house, in the church, in the field, in the garden--every spot speaks to me of you. You are in my thoughts all the time, and my heart cries out for you again and again. I search in vain for the dear, dear child I love so passionately; but she is 600 miles away, and I cannot call her to my side. My tears fall, and I cannot stop them. I know it is weak, but this tenderness for you is right and natural and I cannot be strong.

I wonder what your mood will be when you receive this letter; perhaps at that moment you will not be touched with the emotions I now feel so poignantly, and then you may not read it in the spirit in which it was written. But against that I cannot guard, and the act of writing relieves my feelings at the moment--that is at least what I ask of it. You would not believe the condition into which this place has thrown me.

Do not refer to my weakness, I beg of you; but you must love me, and have respect for my tears, since they flow from a heart which is full of you.

The Brinvilliers Affair

The Brinvilliers affair is still the only thing talked of in Paris. The Marquise confessed to having poisoned her father, her brothers, and one of her children. The Chevalier Duget had been one of those who had partaken of a poisoned dish of pigeon-pie; and when the Brinvilliers was told three years later that he was still alive, her only remark was "that man surely has an excellent constitution." It seems she fell deeply in love with Sainte Croix, an officer in the regiment of her husband, the Marquis, who lived in their house. Believing that Sainte Croix would marry her if she were free, she attempted to poison her husband. Sainte Croix, not reciprocating her desire, administered an antidote, and thus saved the poor Marquis's life.

And now, all is over. The Brinvilliers is no more. Judgment was given yesterday and this morning her sentence was read to her--she was to make a public confession in front of Notre Dame, after which she was to be executed, her body burnt and her ashes scattered to the winds. She was threatened with torture, but said it was unnecessary and that she would tell all. Accordingly she recounted the history of her whole life, which was even more horrible than anyone had imagined, and I could not hear of it without shuddering.

At six in the morning she was led out, barefoot, and clad only in one loose garment, with a halter round her neck. From Notre Dame she was carried back in the same Tumbril, in which I saw her lying on straw, with the Doctor on one side of her and the executioner on the other; the sight of her struck me with horror. I am told that she mounted the scaffold with a firm step, and died as she had lived, resolutely, and without fear or emotion.

She asked her confessor to place the executioner so that she need not gaze on Degrais, who, you *will remember*, tracked her to England, and ultimately arrested her at Liège. After she had mounted the ladder to the scaffold she was exposed to the public for a quarter of an hour, while the executioner arranged her for execution. This raised a murmur of disapproval among the people, and it was a great cruelty. It seems that some say she was a saint; and after her body had been burned, the people crowded near to search for bones as relics, but little was to be found, as her ashes were thrown into the fire. And, it may be supposed, that we now inhale what remains of her. It is to be hoped that we shall not inhale her murderous instincts also.

She had two confessors, of whom one counselled her to tell everything, the other nothing. She laughed, and said, "I may in conscience do what pleases me best."

I was pleased to hear what you think of this horrible woman; it is not possible that she should be in Paradise; her vile soul must be separated from others.

Devotion

You ask me if I am devout. Alas! No, which is a sorrow to me; but I am in a way detached from what is called the world. Old age, and a little sickness give one time to reflect. But, my dear child, what I do not give to the world, I give to you; so that I hardly advance in the region of detachment; and you know the true way towards a devout life lies in some degree of effacement, first of all, of that which our heart holds dearest.

One of my great desires is to become devout. Every day I am tormented by this idea. I do not belong to God, neither do I belong to the Devil; this indecision is a perpetual torment to me, although between ourselves, I believe this state to be a most natural one. One does not belong to the Devil, because one fears God: also, one does not belong to God, because His law is hard, and one does not like to renounce oneself. These are the luke-warm, and their great number does not surprise me at all; I can enter into their reasonings; but God hates them; therefore we must cease to serve in this state--and there is the difficulty.

I am overwhelmed by the death of M. du Mans; I had never thought of death in connection with him. Yet he has died of a trifling fever, without having had time to think either of heaven or of earth. Providence sometimes shows its authority by sudden visitations, from which we should profit.

What you say as to the anxieties which we so often and so naturally feel about the future, and as to how our inclinations are insensibly changed by necessity, is a subject worthy of a book like Pascal's; nothing is so satisfying, nothing so useful as meditations of this kind. But how many people of your age think this? I know of none; and I honour your sound reasoning and courage. With me it is not so, especially when my heart afflicts me; my words are indifferently good; I write as those who speak well; but the depth of my feeling kills me. This I feel when I write to you of the pain of separation. I have not myself found the proverb true, "To cloak oneself according to the cold." I have no cloak against cold like this. Yet I manage to find occupation, and the time passes somehow. But in general it is true that our thoughts and inclinations turn into other channels, and our sorrows cease to be such.

Love of Life

You ask me, dear child, if I am still in love with life. I must confess that I find its sorrows grievous, but my distaste for death is even stronger. It is sad to think I must finish my life with death, and if it were possible I would retrace my steps. I find myself embarked on life without my consent, and am in a perplexing situation. I shall have to take leave of life, and the fact overwhelms me: for how, or by what gate, shall I pass away? When will death come, and in what disposition will it find me? Shall I suffer a thousand pains which will make me die in despair? Shall I die in a transport of joy? Shall I die of an accident? How shall I stand before God? What shall I have to offer Him? Shall I return to Him in fear and necessity, and be conscious of no other feeling but terror? What can I hope for? Am I worthy of Paradise? Or worthy only of Hell? What an alternative! What perplexity! Nothing is so mad as to leave one's safety thus in uncertainty; but nothing is more natural; and the foolish life I lead is perfectly easy to understand. I plunge myself into these thoughts; and I find death so terrible, that I hate life more because it leads to death, than because it leads me through troublesome places. You will say I wish to live for ever. Not at all; but if I had been asked, I would willingly have died in my nurse's arms, for I should thus have avoided many sorrows and would have secured heaven with certainty and ease.

The Order of God

Providence wills order; but if order is nothing other than the will of God, almost all that occurs is done against His will: all the persecutions, for instance, against St. Athanasius; all the prosperity of ill-doers and tyrants--all this is against order and therefore against the will of God. We must surely hold to what St. Augustine says, that God permits all these things so that he may manifest His glory by means that are unknown to us. St. Augustine knows no rule nor order but the will of God. If we did not follow this doctrine, we should be forced to conclude that almost everything is contrary to the will of Him who made it, and this seems to me a dreadful conclusion.

I should like to complain to Father Malebranche about the mice which eat everything here; is that in order? Sugar, fruit, preserves, everything is devoured by them. And was it order last year, that miserable caterpillars destroyed the leaves of our forest-trees and gardens, and all the fruit in the country-side? Father Payen, most peaceable of men, has his head broken; is that order? Yes, Father, all that is doubtless good. God knows how to dispose of it to His glory, though we know not how. We must take it as true, for if we do not regard the will of God as equivalent to all law and order, we fall into great difficulties.

You are such a philosopher, my very dear child, that there is no way of being happy with you. Your mind runs on beyond our hopes to picture to itself the loss of all we hope for; and you see, in our meetings, the inevitable separation that is to follow. Surely that is not the way to deal with the good things Providence prepares for us; we should rather husband and enjoy them. But after having made this little reproach, I must confess in all honesty that I deserve it just as much as you. No one can be more daunted than I am by the flight of time, nor feel more keenly beforehand the griefs which ordinarily follow pleasures. Indeed, my daughter, life mingles its good and ill: when one has what one desires, one is all the nearer to losing it; when it is further from us, we dream of finding it. So we must just take things as God sends them. For my part, I would cherish the hope of seeing you without mixing in with other feelings; and look forward to holding you in my arms next month. I wish to believe God will allow us this perfect joy, although it would be the easiest thing in the world to mix it with bitterness, if we so desired. All that remains, my very dear one, is to breathe and to live.

The Prince of Orange and England

The Prince of Orange has declared himself protector of the religion of England, and has asked to have charge of the education of the young Prince. It is a bold step, and several of the English nobility have joined him. We are all hoping that the Prince of Orange has made a mistake, and that

King James II. will give him a good beating. He has received the Milords, confirmed the attachment of those most devoted to him, and has declared entire liberty of conscience. But we understand that the King of England has united all his people round him, by affording a greater degree of religious liberty.

What shall we say of this English nation? Its customs and manners go from bad to worse. The King of England has escaped from London, apparently by kind permission of the Prince of Orange; the Queen will arrive at St. Germain in a day or two. It is quite certain that war will be declared against us soon, if indeed we are not the first to declare it. We are sending the Abbé Testu to St. Germain to help in establishing there the King and Queen of England and the Prince of Wales. Our King of France has behaved quite divinely to these Majesties of England; for to comfort and sustain, as he has done, a betrayed and abandoned king, is to act in the image of the Almighty.

It is good news that the King of England has left this morning for Ireland, where they are anxiously awaiting him. He will be better there than here. He is travelling through Brittany like lightning, and at Brest he will find Marshall d'Estrée with transport and frigates ready. He carries large treasure, and the King has given him arms for ten thousand men; as his Majesty of England was saying good-bye, he said, laughing, that he had forgotten arms for himself, and our King gave him his own. Our heroes of romance have done nothing more gallant. What will not this brave and unfortunate King accomplish with these ever victorious weapons? He goes forth with the helmet and cuirass of Renaud, Amadis, and our most illustrious paladins, supported by unexampled generosity and magnanimity.

Old Age

So you have been struck by Madame de la Fayette's words, inspired by so much friendliness. I never let myself forget the fact that I am growing old; but I must confess that I was simply astonished at what she said, because I do not yet feel any infirmity to keep me in mind of my advancing years. I think of them, however, and find that life offers us hard conditions: here have I been led, in spite of myself, to the fatal period at which one must die--old age. I see it; old age has stolen upon me; and my only desire is to go no further. I do not want to travel along that road of infirmities, pains, the loss of memory, the disfigurements to which I look forward as an outrage; yet I hear a voice saying in my ear--"You must pass down that road, whether you like it or not, or else you must die"; and this second alternative is as repugnant to nature as the first. This is the inevitable lot of whoever advances too far along the course of life. Yet, a return to God's will, and submission to that universal law which has condemned us all to death, is enough to seat reason again on her throne, and to give us patience. Do you too have patience, my darling; don't let your love, too tender, cause you tears which your reason must condemn.

Your brother has come under the Empire of Ninon de Lenclos; I fear it will bring evil; she ruined his father. We must recommend him to God. Christian women, or at least who wish to be so, cannot see disorder like his without sorrow.

But what a dangerous person this Ninon is! She finds that your brother has the simplicity of a dove, and is like his mother; it is Madame de Grignan who has all the salt of the family, and is not so simple as to be ruled. Someone, meaning to take your part, tried to correct her notion of you, but Ninon contradicted him and said she knew you better. What a corrupt creature! Because you are beautiful and spirited she must needs add to you another quality without which, on her principles, you cannot be perfect. I have been deeply troubled by the harm she is doing to my son. But do not speak of the matter to him; Madame de la Fayette and I are doing our best to extricate him from his perilous attachment.

We have been reading for our amusement those little Provincial Letters. Heavens, what charm they have! How eagerly my son reads them! I always think of my daughter, and how worthy of her is the incomparable justice of their reasoning; but your brother says that you complain that the writer is always saying the same thing. Well, well; all the better! Is it possible that there should be a more perfect style, or a finer, more delicate or more natural raillery? Could anything be more worthy of comparison with Plato's "Dialogues"? But after the first ten letters, what earnestness, solidity, force and eloquence! What love for God and for truth, what exquisite skill in maintaining it and making it understood, characterise these eight last letters with their so different tone! I understand that you have read them only hurriedly, enjoying the more amusing passages; but that is not how one reads them at leisure.

ROBERT SOUTHEY

The Life of Nelson

Robert Southey, man of letters and poet-laureate, was born at Bristol on August 12, 1774, and received at various schools a desultory education, which he completed by an idle year at Oxford. Here he became acquainted with Coleridge; and Southey, who had practised verse from early boyhood, and acquired a strong taste for the drama, being also an ardent republican and romanticist, was easily enlisted by the elder poet in his scheme for a model republic, or "Pantisocracy," in the wilds of America. They married two sisters, the Misses Fricker, and a third sister married Robert Lovel, also a poet. The experiment of pantisocracy was fortunately never carried out, and Southey's career for the next eight years was exceedingly fragmentary; but in 1803 there was a reunion of the three sisters at Keswick, though one of the husbands, Lovel, was dead. Here Southey entered steadily and industriously on the life of an author for livelihood; it was by no means unremunerative. Southey's output of work, both prose and verse, was very voluminous, and its quality could not but suffer. He was appointed poet-laureate in 1813; and received a government pension of £160 a year from 1807, which was increased by £300 a year in 1835. He died on March 21, 1843. In a prefatory note to that peerless model of short biographies, the "Life of Nelson," which appeared in 1813, and is considered his most important work, Southey describes it as "clear and concise enough to become a manual for the young sailor, which he may carry about with him till he has treasured up the example in his memory and in his heart."

I.--A Captain at Twenty

Horatio, son of Edmund and Catherine Nelson, was born on September 29, 1758, in the parsonage of Burnham Thorpe, a Norfolk village, where his father was rector. His mother's maiden name was Suckling; her grandmother was an elder sister of Sir Robert Walpole, and this child was named after his godfather, the first Lord Walpole. Mrs. Nelson died in 1767, leaving eight children, and her brother, Captain Maurice Suckling, R.N., visited the widower, and promised to take care of one of the boys.

Three years later, when Horatio was twelve years old, he read in the newspaper that his uncle was appointed to the Raisonnable, and urged his father to let him go to sea with his Uncle Maurice.

The boy was never strong, but he had already given proofs of a resolute heart and a noble mind. Captain Suckling took an interest in him, and sent him on a first voyage in a merchant ship to the West Indies, and then, as coxswain, with the Arctic expedition of 1773, when Horatio showed his courage by attacking a Polar bear.

A voyage to the East Indies followed, and gave him the rank of midshipman. But the tropical climate reduced him almost to a skeleton; he lost for a time the use of his limbs, and was sent home as his only chance of life. He returned under great depression of spirits. In later years he related how the despair was cleared away by a glow of patriotism, in which his king and country came vividly before his mind. "Well, then," he exclaimed, "I will be a hero, and, confiding in Providence, I will brave every danger!"

On April 8, 1777, he passed his examination for a lieutenancy, and was appointed to the Lowestoft frigate, Captain Locker, then fitting out for Jamaica. Privateers under American colours were harassing British trade in the West Indies, and Nelson saw much active service. He was removed to the Bristol flagship, then to the command of the Badger, then to the Hinchinbrook, and before the age of twenty-one he had gained a rank which brought all the honours of the service within his reach.

An expedition was at this time projected to seize the region of Lake Nicaragua, and thus to cut the communication of the Spaniards between their northern and southern possessions; and in pursuit of this policy Nelson was sent with a small force, early in 1780, to Honduras. Here, after deeds of great gallantry, his command was almost annihilated by the deadly climate, and he himself was so reduced by dysentery that he was compelled to return to England.

His next ship was the Albemarle, twenty-eight guns, in which he was kept, to his great annoyance, in the North Sea for the whole winter of 1781-2, and was sent in the spring to Quebec. The Albemarle then served on the West Indian station until tidings came that the preliminaries of peace had been signed, and she returned to England, and was paid off in 1783.

"I have closed the war," said Nelson, in one of his letters, "without a fortune; but there is not a speck on my character. True honour, I hope, predominated in my mind far above riches." He did not apply for a ship, because he was not wealthy enough to live on board in the manner which was then customary.

But, after living for a time in lodgings in St. Omer's in France, he was appointed to the Boreas, going to the Leeward Islands, and on his arrival in the West Indies in 1784, found himself senior captain, and therefore second in command on that station.

The Americans were at this time trading with our islands, taking advantage of the register of their ships, which had been issued while they were British subjects. Nelson knew that, by the Navigation Act, no foreigners, directly or indirectly, were permitted to carry on any trade with these possessions; and also that the Americans had made themselves foreigners with regard to England.

Contrary to the orders both of the admiral and of the governor, he insisted that our ships of war were not sent abroad to make a show of, and seized four American vessels at Nevis; and when the matter was brought into court at that place he pleaded his own cause, and the ships were condemned.

While the lawsuit was proceeding, Nelson formed an attachment to a young widow, Mrs. Nisbet, niece of the President of Nevis, and was married to her on March 11, 1787. She was then in her eighteenth year, and had one child, a son, Josiah, who was three years old. They returned together to England and took up their abode at the old parsonage, where Nelson amused himself with farming and country sports, and continued a relentless campaign against the speculators and fraudulent contractors attached to the naval service in the West Indies. After many vain attempts to secure a ship, he was at last appointed, on January 30, 1793, to the Agamemnon, sixty-four guns.

II.--In the Mediterranean

The Agamemnon was ordered to the Mediterranean under Lord Hood, and Nelson was sent with despatches to Sir William Hamilton, our envoy to the court of Naples. Sir William, after his first interview with him, told Lady Hamilton that he was about to introduce a little man to her who could not boast of being very handsome, but who would one day astonish the world. Thus that acquaintance began which ended in the destruction of Nelson's domestic happiness, though it threatened no such consequences then. Here also began that acquaintance with the Neapolitan court which led to the only blot on Nelson's public character.

Having accomplished this mission, Nelson was sent to join Commodore Linzee at Tunis, and shortly afterwards to co-operate with General Paoli and the Anti-Gallican party in Corsica. At this time, 1794, Nelson was able to say, "My seamen are now what British seamen ought to be, almost invincible.

They really mind shot no more than peas." And again, after capturing Bastia, "I am all astonishment when I reflect on what we have achieved! I was always of opinion, have ever acted up to it, and never had any reason to repent it, that one Englishman was equal to three Frenchmen." The Agamemnon was then dispatched to co-operate in the siege of Calvi with General Sir Charles Stuart, at which Nelson lost the sight of one eye; and later played a glorious part in the attack by Admiral Hotham's squadron on the French fleet. This action saved Corsica for the time.

Nelson was made colonel of marines in 1795, a mark of approbation which he had long wished for; and the Agamemnon was ordered to Genoa, to co-operate with the Austrian and Sardinian forces. The incapacity and misconduct of the Austrian General de Vins, however, gave the enemy possession of the Genoese coast. The Agamemnon, therefore, could no longer be useful on this station, and Nelson sailed for Leghorn to refit, and then joined the Mediterranean fleet under Sir John Jervis.

England at that time depended too much on the rotten governments of the Continent, and too little upon itself. Corsica was therefore abandoned by Britain, and Nelson, after superintending the evacuation of Corsica, was ordered to hoist his broad pennant on board the Minerva frigate. He then sailed for Gibraltar, and proceeded westward in search of the admiral.

III.--St. Vincent and the Nile

Off the mouth of the Straits of Gilbraltar he fell in with the Spanish fleet; and on February 13, 1797, reaching the station off Cape St. Vincent, he communicated this intelligence to Sir John Jervis, and was directed to shift his broad pennant on board the Captain. On the following morning was fought the battle of Cape St. Vincent. The British had only fifteen ships of the line against twenty-seven Spanish ships, but Britain, largely through Nelson's intrepidity, secured an overwhelming victory. The commander-in-chief was rewarded with the title of Earl St. Vincent, and Nelson was advanced to the rank of rear-admiral and received the Order of the Bath.

Admiral Sir Horatio Nelson was now removed to the Theseus, and was employed in the blockade of Cadiz, where he went through the most perilous action in which he was ever engaged. Making a night attack upon the Spanish gunboats, his barge, carrying twelve men, was attacked by an armed launch carrying twenty-six men; the admiral was only saved by the heroic devotion of his coxswain; but eighteen of the enemy were killed, the rest wounded, and their launch taken.

Twelve days later Nelson sailed at the head of an expedition against Teneriffe, and on the night of July 24, 1797, made a boat attack on the port of Santa Cruz. On this occasion he was wounded in the right elbow, and the arm had to be amputated. The small force, which had made its way into the town, capitulated on honourable terms, and the Spanish governor distinguished himself by the most humane and generous conduct to his enemies. There is no doubt that Nelson's life was saved by the careful attentions of his stepson, Nisbet, who was with him in the boat.

Nisbet was immediately promoted, and honours awaited Nelson in England. The freedom of the cities of Bristol and London were conferred on him, and he received a pension of £1,000 a year. He had performed an extraordinary series of services during the war; including four actions with the fleets of the enemy, three actions with boats employed in cutting out of harbour, and in taking three towns; he had commanded the batteries at the sieges of Bastia and Calvi, he had assisted at the capture of twenty-eight ships of war, and had taken and destroyed nearly fifty merchant vessels; and had been engaged against the enemy upwards of a hundred and twenty times, in which service he had lost his right eye and right arm.

Early in 1789, Sir Horatio Nelson hoisted his flag in the Vanguard, and left England to rejoin Earl St. Vincent. He was dispatched to the Mediterranean, to ascertain the object of Bonaparte's great expedition, then fitting out at Toulon; and sailed from Gibraltar on May 9 with three ships of the line, four frigates, and a sloop. The Vanguard was dismantled in a storm, but was refitted in the Sardinian harbour of St. Pietro, and was joined by a reinforcement of eleven ships from Earl St. Vincent.

The first news of the enemy's armament was that it had surprised Malta, but Nelson soon heard that they had left that island on June 16, and judged that Egypt was their destination. He arrived off Alexandria on the 28th, but did not find them; returned by a circuitous course to Sicily, then sailed to the Morea, where he gained news of the French, and on August I came in sight of Alexandria and the French fleet. "Before this time to-morrow," he said to his officers, "I shall have gained a peerage or Westminster Abbey."

Bonaparte's ships of war, under Admiral Brueys, were moored in Aboukir Bay in a strong line of battle; and the advantage of numbers, both in ships, guns, and men, was in favour of the French. Yet only four French ships out of seventeen escaped, and the victory was the most complete and glorious in the annals of naval history.

Nelson was now at the summit of his glory; and congratulations, rewards, and honours were showered upon him by all the states, princes, and powers to whom his victory had given respite. He was created Baron Nelson of the Nile and of Burnham Thorpe, with a pension of £2,000 a year for his own life, and those of his successors; a grant of £10,000 was voted to him by the East India Company; and the King of Naples made him Duke of Bronte.

IV.--Lady Hamilton

As soon as his shattered frame had sufficiently recovered, Nelson was called to services of greater importance than any one in which he had been hitherto employed.

The kindest attentions and warmest affection were awaiting him at Naples; the king, the queen, and Lady Hamilton, who was the queen's constant favourite, welcomed their hero and deliverer with the most splendid festivities. General Mack, with whom Nelson was to co-operate, was at the head of the Neapolitan troops; and while he marched with 32,000 men into the Roman state, 5,000 Neapolitans were embarked on the British and Portuguese squadron to take possession of Leghorn.

Nelson's fears of the result were soon verified. "The Neapolitan officers," he said, "did not lose much honour, for God knows they had not much to lose--but they lost all they had." The French in the Roman State routed the cowardly Neapolitans. There was a strong revolutionary party in Naples itself; and it was agreed that the royal family must seek safety in flight. Their secret escape, with much treasure, on board the Vanguard, was conducted with the greatest address by Lady Hamilton, and Nelson conveyed them through a wild storm to Palermo.

He had by this time formed an infatuated attachment for Lady Hamilton, which totally weaned his affections from his wife. He was dissatisfied with himself and weary of the world. But, in accordance with his principle of duty "to assist in driving the French to the devil and in restoring peace and happiness to mankind," he at length expelled the French from Naples and restored Ferdinand to his throne. Weak in health, dispirited, and smarting under a censure from the Admiralty for a disobedience to orders, Nelson resigned his command, and reached England in November 1800, having travelled with Sir William and Lady Hamilton.

The great admiral was welcomed to England with every mark of popular honour; but he had forfeited domestic happiness for ever. Before he had been three months at home, he separated from Lady Nelson, vowing that there was nothing in her or in her conduct that he could have wished otherwise.

In January 1801 he was sent to the Baltic as second in command under Sir Hyde Parker. Russia, Denmark, and Sweden had founded a confederacy for making England resign her naval rights, and the British Cabinet decided instantly to crush it. The fleet sailed on March 12; Nelson represented to Sir Hyde Parker the necessity of attacking Copenhagen; and on April 2 the British vessels opened fire on the Danish fleet and land batteries. The Danes, in return, fought their guns manfully, and at one o'clock, after three hours' endurance, Sir Hyde Parker gave the signal for discontinuing action. Nelson ordered that signal to be acknowledged, but continued to fly the signal for close action. "You know, Foley," he said, turning to the captain of the ship, "I have only one eye; I have a right to be blind sometimes!" Then, putting the glass to his blind eye, in the mood that sports with bitterness, he exclaimed, "I really do not see the signal. Keep mine for closer battle flying! That's the way I answer such signals. Nail mine to that mast!" Admiral Graves disobeyed in like manner, and the other ships of the line also continued the action. The victory was soon complete, and Sir Hyde Parker heartily expressed his satisfaction and gratitude.

For the battle of Copenhagen, Nelson was raised to the rank of viscount. Had he lived long enough, he would have fought his way up to a dukedom.

After holding a command in the English Channel, to watch the preparations which were being made at Boulogne for an invasion of England, Nelson retired on the conclusion of the Peace of Amiens to his estate at Merton, in Surrey, meaning to pass his days there in the society of Sir William and Lady Hamilton. Sir William died early in 1803, and, as the government would do nothing for her, Nelson settled on Lady Hamilton a sum equal to the pension of £1,200 a year which her husband had enjoyed. A few weeks after this event the war was renewed, and the day after his majesty's message to parliament, Nelson departed to take command of the Mediterranean fleet.

He took his station immediately off Toulon, and there, with incessant vigilance, waited for the coming out of the enemy. From May 1803 to August 1805 he left the Victory only three times, each time upon the king's service, and on no occasion for more than an hour.

War having been declared between England and Spain, the Toulon fleet, having the Spaniards to co-operate with them, put to sea on January 18, 1804. Nelson, who was off Sardinia when he heard the news the next day, sought them in vain through the Mediterranean, until he heard that they had been dispersed by a gale, and had returned to Toulon. On March 31 they emerged again, and passed out of the Straits of Gibraltar, but the British fleet was kept by adverse winds from reaching the Atlantic till April 5.

The enemy had thirty-five days start on their run to the West Indies, and Nelson, misled by false information, sought them among the islands, until he learned at Antigua on June 9 that they had sailed again for Europe. He made all speed across the Atlantic, and again sought the enemy vainly, until he joined Admiral Cornwallis off Ushant on August 15. The same evening he was ordered to proceed with the Victory and Superb to Portsmouth.

V.--Trafalgar

Here, at last, he heard news of the combined fleets; Sir Robert Calder had fallen in with them near Finisterre and had fought an indecisive engagement.

On September 14, 1805, he passed through the crowds at Portsmouth, many of whom were in tears, many kneeling and blessing him as he passed. He arrived off Cadiz on September 29 with twenty-three ships, and on October 9 he sent Collingwood his plan of attack--what he called "the Nelson-touch." These tactics consisted in cutting through the line of the enemy in three places.

On the morning of the 19th the enemy came out of the port of Cadiz, and all that day and night, and the next day, the British pursued them. At daybreak of the 21st, the combined fleets were distinctly seen from the Victory, about twelve miles to leeward. Signal was made to bear down on the enemy in two lines, and all sail was set, the Victory leading.

Nelson now retired to his cabin and wrote in his diary a prayer committing himself and the British cause to Heaven, and then wrote a memorial setting forth Lady Hamilton's services to Britain, and leaving her and her daughter Horatia as a legacy to his country.

Villeneuve, commanding the enemy, was a skilful seaman, and his plan of defence was as original as the plan of attack. He formed the fleet in a double line, every alternate ship being a cable's length to windward of her second ahead and astern. Nelson, certain of triumph, issued his last signal: "England expects every man to do his duty," which was received throughout the fleet with acclamations.

The English lines, led by Nelson and by Collingwood, swept down upon the hostile fleet, the Victory steering for the bow of the Santissima Trinidad. At four minutes after twelve she opened fire, and almost immediately ran against the Redoubtable. Four ships, two British and two French, formed as compact a tier as if they had been moored together, their heads all lying the same way.

At a quarter past one, a ball fired from the mizzen-top of the Redoubtable struck Nelson on the left shoulder, and he fell on his face. "They have done for me at last, Hardy," he said; "my backbone is shot through." He was carried below, laid on a pallet in the midshipmen's berth, and insisted that the surgeon should leave him--"for you can do nothing for me." He was in great pain, and expressed much anxiety for the event of the action, until Captain Hardy was able to tell him that fifteen of the enemy had been taken. Repeating that he left Lady Hamilton and Horatia as a legacy to his country, and exclaiming, "Thank God, I have done my duty!" Nelson expired.

He cannot be said to have fallen prematurely whose work was done.

MADAME DE STAAL

Memoirs

Marguerite Jeanne de Launay, Baronne de Staal, was born in Paris on May 30, 1684. Her father was a painter of the name of Cordier who was in England when his daughter was born; and the name by which she was known, de Launay, was that of her mother's family. Her story is told by herself, with admirable sincerity, in these Memoirs, which follow her life until the year 1735, when, at the age of fifty-one, she married Baron de Staal, a widower and an officer in the Guard. Her death took place in Paris on June 16, 1750. Her Memoirs, first published in 1755, are among the most interesting records of that period, and though their historical accuracy has been doubted, her portraits of persons are vivid and convincing. Her style has been highly commended by Sainte-Beuve and other French literary critics.

A Convent Child

If I write the record of my life, it is not because it deserves attention, but in order to amuse myself by my recollections. My story is just the opposite of the ordinary romance, wherein a girl brought up as a peasant becomes an illustrious princess; for I was treated in childhood as a person of distinction, and had to find out later that I was a nobody and owned nothing in the world. And so, not having been trained from the first to ill fortune, my spirit has always rebelled against the servitude in which I have had to live.

My father, for some reason that I never knew, had to leave France and live in England; and my mother, alone in Paris and without resources, took me with her as an infant to find a refuge in the abbey of Saint-Sauveur d'Evreux in Normandy, where Madame de La Rochefoucauld, the abbess, received us free of charge.

There was at that time a lengthy disagreement between King Louis XIV. and the Pope with regard to the nomination of abbesses, in consequence of which two ladies Mesdames de Grieu, having been disappointed of an expected establishment, retired to Saint-Sauveur, where they formed a great friendship with my mother, and became devoted to her two-year-old child. I was naturally very popular in the convent, and having a bright disposition I was educated with the utmost care.

Chiefly with a view to giving me greater advantage, the elder Madame de Grieu sought and at length obtained the Priory of Saint-Louis at Rouen, and took me thither with the consent of my mother. Saint-Louis was like a little kingdom, where I reigned as a sovereign; the abbess and her sister had no thought but to satisfy my every fancy, and the whole convent was forced to pay court to me. All that was done for me cost me so little that it seemed a matter of course that I should be flattered and served, and at an early age I had contracted all the defects which I have since had to allow for in the great.

This extreme indulgence would have turned my defects into vices, if devotion had not ruled my passions from the first. Religion was the one great object before my eyes; I had been well instructed in it; I read continually the devotional books in the convent library, and passed much of my time in prayer and meditation. Yet my early desire to become a nun passed gradually away, until I thought of it no more.

Mademoiselle de Silly, an amiable and cultivated young lady whose actions were ruled by principles rather than by feelings, came to live at Saint-Louis, and I was soon attached to her with all the ardour of a girl's affection; her tastes became mine, and I used to read all day beside her. She was then studying the philosophy of Descartes, and I became absorbed in questions of that kind to the neglect of everything else, until, fearing lest they might disturb my faith, I resolutely banished them from my mind.

I was about fourteen years old when the convent of Saint-Louis fell into great poverty owing to a famine which was desolating France, and the disaffection of the nuns was centred on me as a chief cause of unnecessary expense. Their complaints came to the archbishop of Rouen, and abbess had difficulty in keeping me with her. My helpless condition began to force itself on my attention; and I realised that if the abbess were to die I was alone and without support in the world.

An unexpected event now drew me closer to Mademoiselle de Silly. Her mother, having come to Rouen, took her home to Silly, and invited me to accompany her. I accepted joyfully, and spent several months in the solitary and melancholy old castle. The Marquis was extremely economical, the Marquise very devout, and we saw few people. One visitor from the neighborhood, however, attracted me strongly; and as he came often and stayed long, my friend and I agreed that one of us had pleased him. When he had declared his affection, and it was not for me, I learned what jealousy is--a kind of horror like that of falling down through a fathomless abyss.

During the next visit to Silly in the following year the son of the house arrived, and at first kept very much to himself and to his books. But having heard his sister and myself complaining of these unsociable ways, he frankly confessed his fault and amended it, and from that day we spent every hour together. His mind and his manner was infinitely agreeable; and in my successive visits to Silly we formed a delightful friendship which was never interrupted by more ardent feelings.

Thrown on the World

At length my dear abbess fell so dangerously ill that I saw I was about to lose her; and I became desolately aware that I owed her all, and that her death would not only leave me absolutely helpless, but would also deprive me of my best friend. I never knew anyone else so abundant in goodness, with so much sweetness, attention for others and forgetfulness of self, nor with such exact regard for every duty. Her death came soon, and it was evident that neither her sister nor I could remain at the convent. Several generous helpers came forward with offers of support, but in my uncertain position I judged it better to refuse them all. I was resolved to suffer any misery and servitude rather than sacrifice my independence, and only accepted a small loan sufficient to take me to Paris.

I was soon in the great city, looking out for a situation as children's governess; fortunately, I had a taste for that occupation, and imagined that taste for it meant talent. I had a sister, in the household of the Duchess de La Ferté, and found her very amiable and helpful. With her assistance I went to board at a cheap rate in the convent of the Presentation, and she succeeded in inspiring her mistress with so elevated an idea of my attainments that the Duchess soon afterwards sent for me. After showing me off as a prodigy of learning to all her friends, the Duchess de La Ferté, a voluble and enthusiastic woman, conceived a violent affection for me, and projected innumerable schemes for my advancement, which ended in my being received into her own household as her secretary.

I should have been delighted with this position if I had not remembered how my sister, who had gone there as her favourite, had fallen to the situation of chambermaid, and if I had not realised that my mistress's affection would probably be as short-lived as it was intemperate. It proved to be so indeed; it was succeeded by a hatred as violent as her attachment had been; and after subjecting me to every indignity she finally disposed of me by placing me in the household of the Duchess of Maine, at Sceaux.

Here I inhabited a tiny room, without windows or fireplace, and so low that it was impossible to stand upright. I was given sewing to do, but my first piece of work proved my incapacity, and my extremely short-sight made me equally helpless in waiting on the Duchess. I was astonished at the patience with which she bore my awkwardness, but my fellow-servants, with whom I was most unpopular, were less merciful. The hard and thankless existence, so different from anything which I had been accustomed, threw me into a profound depression, until I began to cherish the idea of taking leave of life.

But gradually my situation altered for the better. Her Serene Highness the Duchess began to take notice of me, and became accustomed to speak to me and to take interest and pleasure in my replies. She had now succeeded in raising her family to rank equal to her own, and by a famous edict her children and their descendants had been brought within the succession to the crown. Her delight in amusements and in pageants was now at its highest, and it happened that the Abbé de Vaubrun, designing a spectacular piece in honor of Night, confided to me the task of writing and delivering an epilogue in that character. My stage-fright spoiled my elocution, but from that day I was entrusted with the organisation of these magnificent entertainments, and the last of them was entirely designed and written by myself. By this means I came to take a quite different place in the household.

Political Intrigues

King Louis XIV. had been failing for some time, though every one pretended not to notice it; and the Duchess of Maine, ever anxious for the greatness of her family, was very eager to know his testamentary intentions. Enough was ascertained, by the help of Madame de Maintenon, to show that the King's dispositions were in favour of the Duke of Orleans, and the mistake was made of confiding to the Duke his future advantage. As the illness progressed, a council of regency was formed with the Duke of Orleans at its head, and when the King died the Duke was appointed Regent by Parliament, and the Duke of Maine was entrusted with the education of the young King.

The Duchess of Maine, who had come up to Paris for this anxious time, suffered a good deal from insomnia, and now called me in to read to her every night. But there was more conversation than reading, and she poured out to me in entire confidence all her secrets, projects, complaints and regrets. This touching confidence made me very deeply attached to her; and when she and her husband removed to the Tuilleries to superintend the King's education, they took me with them.

In defence of the interests of her family in the succession to the Crown, which were threatened by the Duke of Orleans, Cardinal Polignac and others undertook the preparation of a very learned memoir, based on a great mass of historical and legal precedents; the Duchess threw herself into the most laborious researches to assist them, and I was set to study ancient volumes and to correspond with all kinds of authorities. The great work was finished at last; it was a fine, well-written production; but it did not repay the trouble it had cost. The question was decided against the family of Maine, the edict conferring on them the succession to the Crown was revoked, and the rank of princes of the blood was taken from them.

It is impossible to describe the sorrow of my mistress at this sudden overthrow of the fortunes of her family. She was wholly unable to acquiesce in it, and her illtreatment in France suggested to her the idea of seeking help from the King of Spain. The Baron de Walef, who was going to that court, undertook to represent her case there, and the Duchess of Maine held secret interviews with the Spanish ambassador in Paris. Several other persons became implicated in these intrigues; the Duchess became more deeply compromised than she had at first intended; and her interests became interwoven with other chimerical projects, including the restoration of the Pretender in England. These movements became known to the Duke of Orleans, and my mistress's intrigues were soon brought to an end.

On December 9, 1718, we were informed that the house of the Spanish Ambassador was surrounded by troops, and a day or two later we learned that our arrest, on the charge of inciting to revolution, might be expected at any moment. On the 29th, we were awakened early in the morning to find the house full of soldiers; the Duchess was carried off to imprisonment at Dijon, and the Duke of Maine was immured in the citadel of Dourlans in Picardy.

In the Bastille

I was taken in a carriage with three musketeers, to a little bridge before a wall, and delivered to the governor of the Bastille, who sent me to a large empty room, the walls of which were covered with charcoal drawings executed by former prisoners. A little chair was brought me, a bundle of wood was lighted on the hearth, one small candle was fixed to the wall, and I heard half a dozen locks and bolts closing the door that shut me off from mankind. The first hour, which I spent gazing at my crackling fire, was the most desolate of all my imprisonment.

Then the governor appeared, with my attendant Mademoiselle Rondel; I was rejoiced to find that she was to relieve my solitude, and to hear from her that she had managed to hide all my papers after my capture. Our room was presently furnished with beds, table and chairs; on the following day we were given books and a pack of cards; our meals were tolerable, and except for our captivity we were comfortable enough.

The two judges charged with the interrogation of the prisoners in our affair, of whom there seemed to be a considerable number, came daily, and held their interviews in a room immediately below ours; so that Rondel could see through the window one of our acquaintances after another being brought across the court to be examined. My time did not come for many days, and I spent long hours racking my brain for the answers which I ought to give. The fear of the questions by torture began to force itself on my mind; and though I thought I could face pain or even death I was doubtful whether I should be able to keep silence under that dreadful ordeal.

After these weeks of suspense I was called before the judges, and was asked whether the Duchess of Maine had not great confidence in me and whether I had not been aware of her treasonable correspondence and intrigues. The line I took was to represent my services to my mistress as having been of a very humble nature; I insisted that I knew nothing of her private affairs, and had seen and heard nothing that could at all compromise her loyalty to the Government. This appeared to satisfy them for the present, and after enquiring whether I was well treated in prison they dismissed me.

I did not suffer from ennui in the Bastille; I devised for myself many little occupations; and soon a surreptitious correspondence with the Chevalier de Menil, who had been imprisoned for participation in our affair, gave interest to the days. We were even permitted occasional interviews by favour of one of the subordinate officials, and before we regained our liberty I had promised to be his wife.

The Regent at last became anxious to bring to an end the whole episode of the Duchess of Maine's intrigue; but he wished first to secure a full admission of guilt from the principal actors in it. The Duchess was promised her complete liberty if she would send him a frank confession in writing, which should be seen by no one but himself. Finding herself in a position to secure the freedom of all those whom she had imperilled, she sent the Duke of Orleans the required paper, in which she disclosed everything in detail and with entire sincerity.

I was examined again without making any disclosure, but after receiving the written command of the Duchess I wrote out a declaration of all that I knew and was a few days later set at liberty, after two years of captivity. I went down at once to Sceaux, where I was affectionately received by my mistress.

Returning to Paris two days later, to fetch my things from the Bastille, I called at the Convent of the Presentation, and found in the parlour the Chevalier de Menil. I was astonished at his manner, no less than by what he said; it was evidently that his only desire was to break his engagement with me. I realised that the man was without honour or kindness, and yet it was difficult to detach my affections from him.

It was about a year later that M. Dacier was introduced to me, after the death of his wife, by the Duchess de La Ferté, and an ardent desire for liberty from my condition of servitude led me to accept his proposal of marriage, subject only to be the permission of my Duchess. This she was reluctant to give, and the matter was still under discussion when we heard of M. Dacier's sudden death.

The rest of my life, though it has been a long one, contains little of interest. I found myself without any object to live for, and a strange deadness of feeling came over me, harder to bear than illness or death. I had a distaste for existence and a horror of the world, and desired nothing more than to hide myself away. A little pension had been secured for me; my mistress had fallen dangerously ill; I wished to leave Sceaux in order to run away from a new attachment which was gaining power over me; and the thought of entering a Carmelite house became a settled project. But I was refused even this last refuge; the prioress deciding that I had no vocation for the religious life.

I spent several years without coming to any harmony either with myself or with fortune. Several offers of marriage were made to me, but I could not bring myself to accept any of them, until a sudden fancy for the sweet simplicities of country life led me to agree to a marriage with M. de Staal.

A few days after my marriage I heard of the death of the Duchess of Maine. I never knew a more perfectly reasonable woman. She was all feeling; even her thoughts were really sentiments; she was lively without moodiness, impassioned without violence, always animated; sweet and sensible. There was a vivid warmth about her, that made her a perfectly gracious friend.

EARL STANHOPE

Life of William Pitt

The biographer of Pitt was a grandson of the Lord Mahon, afterwards Earl of Stanhope, who married, in 1774, the great statesman's eldest sister. Philip Henry Stanhope was born at Walmer on January 30, 1805, and entered the House of Commons as Lord Mahon in 1831. He took a prominent part in the foundation of the National Portrait Gallery, and the Historical Manuscripts Commission, and the promotion of successful archaeological investigations on the site of Troy. His literary labours were considerable and important. Chief among them were the "History of England from the Peace of Utrecht to the Peace of Versailles," the "History of Queen Anne's Reign," and the "Life of the Right Honourable William Pitt." The last named, published in 1861-2, is one of the most authoritative of political biographies, compiled with a gravity and care characteristic of its author, and of abiding value as a standard book of reference for one of the greatest personalities and one of the most stirring periods of English history. Earl Stanhope died on December 24, 1875.

I.--The Boy Statesman

William Pitt, the elder, afterwards Earl of Chatham, married in 1754 Lady Hester Grenville. William Pitt, their second son, was born on May 28, 1759, at Hayes, near Bromley, in Kent.

In his boyhood, from the earliest years, William Pitt evinced to all around him many tokens of intellectual promise and ambition; but his parents were frequently distressed by his delicate health. It was no doubt on this account that he was not sent to any public or private school. Lord Chatham was extremely careful of the education of his family; and, without any disparagement to young William's tutor, it was certainly from his father that he profited most.

William was at fourteen so forward in his studies that he was sent to Cambridge, commencing his residence at Pembroke Hall in October 1773. His health at this period gave cause for great alarm. A serious illness at Cambridge, however, proved a turning-point; for long afterwards he enjoyed fairly good health. Early hours, daily exercise on horseback, and liberal potations of port wine--his elixir of strength at this time, although it helped in later years to undermine his constitution--made him far stronger after his illness than before it.

In 1778, after the death of his father, he was entered at Lincoln's Inn, and was called to the Bar in 1780. But he had little opportunity of practising as a barrister, for his parliamentary ambitions were soon fulfilled. In the autumn of 1780 he was an unsuccessful candidate for Cambridge University; but through the influence of Sir James Lowther he was returned in the same year for Appleby, and took his seat in the Commons on January 23, 1781.

Lord North was still at the head of affairs, and the Opposition consisted of two parties: the aristocratic Whigs, whose leader was the Marquis of Rockingham, but whose true guiding spirit was Charles James Fox; and a smaller band of the old adherents of Lord Chatham, under Lord Shelburne. To this party Pitt, as a matter of course, attached himself. His first speech was made on February 26, in support of Burke's bill for economical reform. He completely fulfilled the high expectations that had been formed of the son of so illustrious a father. Not only did he please, it may be said that he astonished the House.

Two speeches later in the session confirmed the distinction of the young orator. In 1782, after a long series of Opposition attacks, Lord North resigned; but in the new arrangements Pitt was not included. He had determined that he would serve his sovereign as a cabinet minister, or not at all. For a time he devoted his efforts, without success, to the reform of the representation of the House of Commons. But in July 1782 Lord Rockingham died; there was a cabinet split, due to a quarrel between Fox and Shelburne; the latter became First Lord of the Treasury, and Pitt, at the age of twenty-three, was offered and accepted the post of Chancellor of the Exchequer.

The newly-formed ministry was soon exposed to hot attacks by the coalition of the parties of Fox and North, and Pitt, in attacking this "baneful alliance," made one of the greatest speeches of his career. But the ministry was defeated; Lord Shelburne resigned; and the king, advised by Shelburne, invited Pitt to become Prime Minister. After anxious consideration he refused.

The Fox and North coalition now assumed office. This union of extremes was unpopular in the country, although powerful in parliamentary strength. Pitt tried once more to pass a measure of parliamentary reform; and during the recess he paid a visit to France--the one foreign journey of his life.

When parliament resumed its sittings, in the autumn of 1783, Fox's India Bill was passed by the Commons, but rejected by the Lords. The king, who was vehemently opposed to the bill, demanded the resignation of Fox and North, and on December 19 invited Pitt, now aged twenty-four, to become Prime Minister. This time the invitation was not refused.

Pitt had great difficulty in forming a cabinet, and was the only cabinet minister in the Commons. His main support in that house was Henry Dundas, treasurer of the navy--his life-long friend. On facing parliament at the opening of 1784, Pitt's purpose was to delay a dissolution until the coalition's unpopularity in the country had reached its height, and with this end he patiently endured defeat after defeat. In March he deemed that the right moment had come, and his judgement was rewarded at the General Election by a triumphant majority.

Pitt was Chancellor of the Exchequer as well as First Lord of the Treasury, and during the years of peace that followed, his successes were largely financial. He established a series of financial reforms that not only increased the favour in which his ministry was held, but undoubtedly enabled the country to bear the terrible strain that was afterwards to be placed upon it. In his attempt to adjust commercial relations with Ireland he was less successful; he was obliged, besides, to abandon his schemes of parliamentary reform, and his exertions, in concert with his friend Wilberforce, to destroy the slave traffic ended in disappointment--even although in this he had the hearty support of his rival, Fox.

Young as he was, and victorious as he had become, he was never tempted to presume upon his genius, or relax in his application. He allowed himself but little holiday. He spent a good deal of such time as he could spare at Holwood, a property he had bought near Bromley; and occasional visits to Brighton, and to his mother's residence at Burton Pynsent, in Somersetshire, made up the greater part of his travels.

II.--The Regency Problem

Not only had Pitt's administration rehabilitated English finances; it had gained for England a strong measure of European support. In 1788 there was concluded what was virtually a triple defensive alliance with Prussia and Holland; and with France herself, should she be willing to remain at peace, there was a treaty of commerce to engage her in more friendly relations.

But towards the end of the year Pitt was confronted with what seemed a certainty of loss of office. King George III., after a long period of ill health, was found to be definitely suffering from mental alienation. A regency became necessary, and the person clearly marked out for the office was the Prince of Wales. But the prince was the political associate of Fox, and there was no doubt that his first step on accession to power would be the dismissal of Pitt.

Pitt saw the prospect before him, and did not attempt to shirk it. But he did propose certain restrictions on the regency in order that the king, should he recover his reason, might without difficulty resume his power.

When parliament assembled in December, Fox declared boldly that the prince had as much right to assume sovereignty during the king's incapacity as he would have in the event of the king's death. Pitt, exulting in his rival's indiscreet departure from Whig principles, retorted that the assertion of such a right, independent of the decision of the two houses, was little less than treason to the constitution. Fox's attitude was unpopular, and Pitt's resolutions, and the Regency Bill that followed, were carried through the Commons.

Towards the end of February, the third reading of the Regency Bill was impending in the Lords. Pitt had proposed that the difficulty about procuring the royal assent to the measure should be overcome by empowering the chancellor by a joint vote of both houses to put the Great Seal to a commission for giving the assent. But this expedient was unnecessary. By February 22 the king was completely recovered. The Regency Bill fell to the ground, and all the hopes which the Opposition had reared upon it.

The day of thanksgiving for the king's recovery is regarded by Lord Macaulay as the zenith in Pitt's political life. "To such a height of power and glory," he says, "had this extraordinary man risen at twenty-nine years of age. And now," he adds, perhaps less justly, "the tide was on the turn."

III.--The Struggle with France

Pitt was able to declare, in the session that preceded the dissolution of 1790, that "we are adding daily to our strength, wealth, and prosperity," and, as a result of the elections, his parliamentary majority was more than confirmed.

But symptoms of the coming stress were already manifest. The minister was anxiously watching the course of the revolution in France; and, while far from sharing the enthusiasm of Fox for the new principles, he did not endorse the fierce hostility of Burke.

"I cannot regard with envious eyes," he said, "any approximation in neighbouring states to those sentiments which are the characteristics of every British subject."

But the development of events soon made it clear that the new France had become a danger to the peace of Europe. As long as possible Pitt avoided war, which was ultimately forced upon him in 1793 by France's attack upon Holland, to which we were bound by treaty obligations.

From that time, until the peace in 1802, English naval enterprises were generally successful, and English military enterprises generally failed. Pitt has often been blamed for the faults of his country's generals; but it is assuredly true that he did all that a civilian could do to secure success in the field.

The heavy cost of the war, increased as it was by the subsidies paid to Austria, and afterwards to Russia, compelled an entire departure from Pitt's old financial methods. Each year brought an increase of taxation and an increase of debt; and at the beginning of 1797 the directors of the Bank of England, in dire perplexity, told Pitt that the state, for all his expedients, was threatened with insolvency. Pitt did not falter. An order in council was issued, suspending cash payments at the bank. Thus was established a gigantic system of paper credit, giving us power to cope with no less gigantic foes. Cash payments were not resumed until 1819.

Pitt had not only to cope with enemies without, but with sedition within. Societies formed for propagating the principles of the revolution advocated the subversion of the constitution under the pretence of parliamentary reform; the populace, angered by the privations caused by the clearness of food, listened readily to the agitators; riots were frequent, but the most mischievous form taken by sedition was that of armed conspiracy. Against these evils Pitt contended by royal proclamations, prosecutions, and, above all, by the suspension of the Habeas Corpus Act. In his firm suppression of disorder Pitt was loyally supported by large majorities in both houses, and the country generally was on his side. But his domestic policy, his foreign policy, and his finance were unsparingly attacked by Fox and a small band of devoted followers--followers who did not abate in their resolution when their leader, weary of the unequal conflict, retired for a time from public life.

In the busy and anxious year 1796, there was a report that Pitt was on the point of marriage. During his short intervals of leisure at Holwood, he often visited his neighbour, Lord Auckland, at Beckenham, and was much attracted by Lord Auckland's eldest daughter, the Hon. Eleanor Eden. This strong attachment did not proceed to a proposal and a marriage. Pitt wrote to Lord Auckland avowing his affection, but explaining that in the circumstances of pecuniary difficulty in which he was involved, he would not presume to make the lady an offer. Lord Auckland acknowledged the explanation as adequate, and thus honourably ended the only "love-passage" in the life of Pitt.

Considering that Pitt's income as minister was £6,000 a year, and that he derived an additional £3,000 a year from the Lord Wardenship of the Cinque Ports, his pecuniary troubles may seem hard to explain. He had no family, and no expensive tastes. But he was so intent upon the national exchequer that he neglected his private accounts, with the consequence that he was plundered by his domestics. His expenses were not checked, and his debts continued to grow.

IV.--Resignation

In the year 1800 Pitt was able to achieve a momentous change in the affairs of Ireland. The chronic discontent of that country, largely due to the resentment of the Catholics at their exclusion from the rights of citizenship, had been fanned by the importation of revolutionary ideas; and there were hopes, once or twice on the point of realisation, of a French invasion of the island. In 1798 a rebellion broke out, but was suppressed with promptness, and, it must be added, in many instances with cruelty. But to Pitt the suppression of the insurrection was only the first part of his duty. He thought that to revert to the old system would be a most shallow policy. A new, and comprehensive, and healing method must be tried--an Act of Union, which should raise the minds of Irishmen from local to imperial aims--which should blend the two legislatures, and, if possible, also the two nations, in one.

In 1800 the project was fulfilled--not without fierce resistance in the Irish Parliament, and not without a certain distribution of favours to those for whose support the government was anxious; although the allegations made on this subject seem to be exaggerated. Having accomplished the union, Pitt laid plans for a further reform which led, early in the following year, to his retirement from office.

He proposed the emancipation of the Catholics by the substitution of a political for the religious test of fitness for citizenship. Although the Anglican bishops and clergy and many laymen were strongly opposed to Catholic emancipation, Pitt would probably have been able to carry his scheme had it not been for royal antagonism. The king believed, erroneously but passionately, that by consenting to such a measure he would violate his coronation oath.

His majesty expressed his opinions on the subject so publicly and so vehemently that on January 31, 1801, Pitt felt compelled to ask leave to resign unless he were allowed to pursue his course on the Catholic question. The king required the abandonment of the scheme, and on February 3 Pitt resigned office. Thus abruptly ended his renowned administration of more than seventeen years.

The new Prime Minister was Mr. Addington, formerly Speaker of the Commons. Several of Pitt's colleagues remained in the ministry, although others withdrew from it; and Pitt himself gave general support to the government--support which was offered with especial warmth, and possessed especial value, during the hotly criticised peace negotiations with the First Consul Bonaparte in 1801 and 1802. Although Pitt had been obliged when in office to refuse several inadequate offers of peace, he had always been prepared to end the war under honourable conditions. The distinction of ending the war did not fall to his share; but his services were not forgotten. On May 7, 1802, the House of Commons carried by overwhelming numbers a motion, "That the Right Hon. William Pitt has rendered great and important services to his country, and especially deserves the gratitude of this house." And on May 28, 1802, Pitt's birthday, more than 800 persons assembled at a memorable banquet in honour of "the pilot that weathered the storm."

Until the renewal of war in 1803 Pitt took little-part in public affairs. Most of his time was spent at Walmer Castle, with occasional visits to Bath for the sake of his health, which had been uncertain since an attack of serious illness in 1797. He remained in constant communication with his political friends, and sometimes during the earlier part of his retirement aided the ministry with his advice. But with the progress of time he found himself less and less able to support Addington and his colleagues.

In May 1803 the uneasy peace came to an end. The constant aggressions of Bonaparte and his dominating tone made friendly relations impossible. There was a widespread feeling in the country that now that the storm had recommenced the old pilot should be called to the helm. Pitt returned to the Commons after the declaration of war, and forcibly criticised some of the financial and defensive measures of the ministry.

In 1804 the ministry showed itself wholly unequal to the strain upon it; and the situation was complicated by a temporary return of the king's malady. Pitt not only renewed his opposition to Addington, but made it plain that he was prepared to take part in a strong and comprehensive administration, including even Fox, that should be formed to rescue the crown and country from the dangers to which they were exposed under the Addington ministry.

A series of combined attacks was directed against the government during the month of April. Although Addington was not defeated in the Commons, he saw his majority steadily diminish; and on April 26 he resolved to resign. On the 30th, the Lord Chancellor intimated to Pitt his majesty's desire to receive the plan of a new administration.

V.--The Last Ministry

The king's opposition made the inclusion of Fox in the new ministry impossible. His hostility to Fox, however, was not simply on political grounds; he believed him to be responsible for the excesses of the Prince of Wales. Pitt was in consequence obliged to be content with a restricted choice of ministers, and had to face a powerful opposition in parliament. Addington was persuaded to join the ministry early in 1805.

During the summer of 1804 Bonaparte and his host lay menacingly at Boulogne, awaiting that command of the channel "for six hours," which the great warrior recognised as essential to his plans. Meanwhile, Pitt laboured to form another coalition, and, at the cost of heavy subsidies, was successful. Russia, Austria, and Sweden joined in the league against Napoleon; Prussia still hesitated.

In the summer of 1805 Napoleon was again at Boulogne, but his plan of invasion was wrecked by the failure of the French fleet to reach the Channel. When Napoleon learned that the fleet had gone south, and that the attack upon England had been thwarted, he straightway marched his army to mid-Europe. Pitt had staked everything on the new coalition, and the surrender of the Austrians at Ulm was news of the utmost bitterness to him. But a splendid corrective came soon afterwards in the crowning naval victory of Trafalgar. Although the nation's feelings were divided between joy at the triumph and grief at the death of the illustrious victor, Pitt's popularity, which had been somewhat uncertain, was enormously enhanced by the event. The Lord Mayor proposed his health as "the saviour of Europe."

Pitt's reply was nearly as follows: "I return you many thanks for the honour you have done me, but Europe is not to be saved by any single man. England has saved herself by her exertions, and will, I trust, save Europe by her example." With only these two sentences the minister sat down. They were the last words that Pitt ever spoke in public.

He was suffering much at this time from gout, and his general health was undermined by anxiety. In December he journeyed to Bath, and at Bath there reached him the news of the destruction of his coalition at Austerlitz. The battle was the cause of his death. He was struck down by a severe internal malady and he was in a state of extreme debility when on January 11, 1806, he returned home to the house he had taken on Putney Heath. It is said that as he passed along to his bedroom, he observed a map of Europe hanging on the wall, upon which he turned to his niece and mournfully said: "Roll up that map. It will not be wanted these ten years."

For a few days the doctors had hopes that he might recover, but on the 22nd it became evident that he could not live for twenty-four hours. Early in the morning of the 23rd he died.

"At about half-past two," wrote the Hon. James Hamilton Stanhope, who was at his bedside, "Mr. Pitt ceased moaning, and did not make the slightest sound for some time. Shortly afterwards, in a tone I never shall forget, he exclaimed: 'Oh, my country! How I love my country!' From that time he never spoke or moved, and at half-past four expired without a groan or struggle. His strength being quite exhausted, his life departed like a candle burning out."

ARTHUR PENRHYN STANLEY

The Life of Thomas Arnold, D.D.

Arthur Penrhyn Stanley was born at Alderley Rectory, Cheshire, on December 13, 1815. He was educated at Rugby under Arnold, and at Oxford, where Tait, the future Archbishop of Canterbury, was his tutor. Entering holy orders, he was appointed select preacher in 1845; became Canon of Canterbury in 1851; and in 1863 succeeded Trench as Dean of Westminster. He died on July 18, 1881, and by Queen Victoria's commands his remains were laid beside those of his wife, Lady Augusta Bruce, in Henry VII.'s Chapel, Westminster. Of all his works, perhaps his most important contribution to English literature is the "Life of Arnold," which was published two years after the death of the famous master of Rugby. To the task of writing the book Stanley devoted all his energies, steering clear, however, of any attempt to form an opinion of his own upon Arnold's life and character, while achieving a result that not only assured his own position at Oxford, but brought him well into the front rank of contemporary writers. The religious animosity at Oxford was uncongenial to Stanley, and it was only the prospect of Dr. Arnold occupying the Chair of Modern History that reconciled him to his surroundings.

I.--Youth and Early Manhood

Thomas Arnold, seventh child and youngest son of William and Martha Arnold, was born June 13, 1795, at East Cowes, Isle of Wight, where his father was collector of customs. His early education was undertaken by a sister; and in 1803 he was sent to Warminister School, in Wiltshire. In 1807 he went to Winchester, where, having entered as a commoner and afterwards become a scholar of the college, he remained till 1811. In after life he always cherished a strong Wykehamist feeling, and, during his headmastership at Rugby, often recurred to his knowledge there first acquired, of the peculiar constitution of a public school.

He was then, as always, of a shy and retiring disposition; but his manner as a child, and till his entrance at Oxford, was marked by a stiffness and formality, the very reverse of the joyousness and simplicity of his later years. He was unlike those of his own age, with pursuits peculiar to himself; and the tone and style of his early letters are such as might have been produced by living chiefly with his elders, and reading, or hearing read, books suited to a more advanced age. Both as boy and young man he was remarkable for a difficulty in early rising amounting almost to a constitutional infirmity; and though in after life this was overcome by habit, he often said that early rising was a daily effort to him.

The beginning of some of his later interests may be traced in his earlier amusements and occupations. He never lost the recollection of the impression produced upon him by the excitement of naval and military affairs, of which he naturally saw and heard much by living at Cowes in the time of the Napoleonic war; and with his playmates he would sail rival toy fleets or act the battles of the Homeric heroes with improvised spears and shields. He was extremely fond of ballad poetry, and his earliest compositions all ran in that direction. At Winchester he was noted for his forwardness in history and geography; and there also he gave indications of that mnemonic faculty which in later years showed itself in minute details, extending to the exact state of the weather on particular days, or the exact words or passages he had not seen for twenty years. The period of his home and school education was too short to exercise much influence on his after life, but he always looked back upon it with tenderness.

In 1811 he was elected a scholar of Corpus Christi College, Oxford; in 1814 he took a first class in classics; in 1815 he was made a Fellow of Oriel; and he gained the Chancellor's prizes for the Latin and English essays in 1815 and 1817. During his later time at Oxford he took private pupils and read extensively in the libraries. Meanwhile, he had been led gradually to fix on his future life course. In December, 1818, he was ordained deacon and next year settled at Laleham, where, in August, 1820, he married Mary Penrose, daughter of the rector of Fledborough, Notts.

At Laleham he remained for nine years, coaching private pupils for the universities. Here were born six of his nine children; the youngest three, besides one who died in infancy, were born at Rugby. During this period an essential change and growth of Arnold's character became manifest. The warm feelings of his youth gave place to the fixed earnestness and devotion which henceforth took possession of him. His former indolent habits, his morbid restlessness and occasional weariness of duty, indulgence of vague schemes without definite purpose, intellectual doubts as to accepted religious beliefs--all seem to have vanished for ever.

It was now that the religious aspect of his character came to be emphasised. In common acts of life, public and private, the depths of his religious convictions very visibly appeared. And while it is impossible to understand his religious belief except through the knowledge of his life and writings on ordinary subjects, it is impossible on the other hand, to understand his life and writings without bearing in mind how vivid was his realisation of those truths of religion on which he most habitually dwelt. It was this which enabled him to undertake labours which, without such a power, must have crushed or enfeebled the spiritual growth which in him they seemed only to foster. His letters at this time show better than anything else how he was, though unconsciously to himself, maturing for the arduous duties he afterwards undertook. It was now, too, that he first became acquainted with Niebuhr's "History of Rome," which revolutionised his views of history, and, later, served as a model for his own "History of Rome."

II.--Headmaster of Rugby

Arnold was not without his visions of ambition and extensive influence from the first, but he liked Laleham, and always looked back with fond regret to his time there. "I have always thought," he wrote in 1823, "with regard to ambition, that I should like to be *aut Caesar aut nullus;* and as it is pretty well settled for me that I shall not be Caesar, I am quite content to live in peace as *nullus.*" But the fates had ordered it otherwise. Friends had long been urging him to seek a larger sphere of usefulness; and when, in August, 1827, the headmastership of Rugby became vacant, he applied for the post.

He had himself little hope of success. The testimonials he sent in were few, but all spoke strongly of his qualifications. Among them was a letter from Dr. Hawkins, the future Provost of Oriel, in which the prediction was made that if Arnold were elected he would change the face of education throughout the public schools of England. The impression produced upon the trustees by this letter and by the other testimonials was such that Arnold was immediately appointed. In June, 1828, he received priest's orders; in April and November of the same year took his degrees of B.D. and D.D., and in August entered on his new office.

The post was in many respects suited to his natural tastes--to his love of tuition, which had now grown so strongly upon him that he declared sometimes that he could hardly live without such employment; to the vigour and spirits which fitted him rather to deal with the young than the old; to the desire of carrying out his favourite ideas of uniting things secular with things spiritual, and of introducing the highest principles of action into regions comparatively uncongenial to their reception. He had not, however, accepted it without grave doubts about his fitness. In a private letter he says:

I confess that I should very much object to undertake a charge in which I was not invested with pretty full discretion. According to my notions of what large schools are, founded on all I know and all I have ever heard of them, expulsion should be practised much oftener than it is. Now, I know that trustees, in general, are averse to this plan, because it has a tendency to lessen the numbers of the school, and they regard quantity more than quality. In fact, my opinions on this point might, perhaps, generally be considered as disqualifying me for the situation of master of a great school; yet I could not consent to tolerate much that I know is tolerated generally, and, therefore, I should not like to enter on an office which I could not discharge according to my own views of what is right.

At Rugby, Arnold from the first maintained that in the actual working of the school he must be completely independent, and that the remedy of the trustees, if they were dissatisfied, was not interference, but dismissal. It was on this condition that he took the post; and any attempt to control either the administration of the school or his own private occupations he felt bound to resist as a duty not only to himself but the master of every foundation school in England. The remonstrances which he encountered, particularly from his fixed determination always to get rid of unpromising subjects, were vehement and numerous; but he repeatedly declared that on no other conditions could he hold his appointment, or justify the existence of the public school system in a Christian country.

"My object," he wrote, just before taking up duty, "will be, if possible, to form Christian men, for Christian boys I can scarcely hope to make; I mean that, from the natural imperfect state of boyhood, they are not susceptible of Christian principles in their full development upon their practice, and I suspect that a low standard of morals in many respects must be tolerated amongst them, as it was on a larger scale in what I consider the boyhood of the human race."

This is the keynote of his whole system. As he put it, what he looked for in the school was, first, religious and moral principles; second, gentlemanly conduct; and third, intellectual ability. Intellectual training was never for a moment underrated, but he always thought first of his charges as schoolboys who must grow up to be Christian men. His education, in short, "was not based upon religion, but was itself *religious*." For cleverness as such, Arnold had no regard. "Mere intellectual acuteness," he used to say, "divested as it is, in too many cases, of all that is comprehensive and great and good, is to me more revolting than the most helpless imbecility, seeming to be almost like the spirit of Mephistopheles." Often when this intellectual cleverness was seen in union with moral depravity, he would be inclined to deny its existence altogether.

A mere plodding boy was, above all others, encouraged by him. At Laleham he had once got out of patience, and spoken sharply to a pupil of this kind, when the pupil looked up in his face and said, "Why do you speak angrily, sir? Indeed, I am doing the best that I can." Years afterwards he used to tell the story to his children, and said, "I never felt so much ashamed in my life--that look and that speech I have never forgotten." And though it would, of course, happen that clever boys, from a greater sympathy with his understanding, would be brought into closer intercourse with him, this did not affect his feeling of respect, and even of reverence, for those who, without ability, were distinguished for high principle and industry. "If there be one thing on earth which is truly admirable, it is to see God's wisdom blessing an inferiority of natural powers where they have been honestly, truly and zealously cultivated."

III.--As Teacher and Preacher

Arnold had always been painfully impressed by the evils of the public school system, according to which a number of boys are left to form an independent society of their own, in which the influence they exert over each other is far greater than that exerted by the masters. He writes, in 1837:

> Of all the painful things connected with my employment, nothing is equal to the grief of seeing a boy come to school innocent and promising, and tracing the corruption of his character from the influence of the temptations around him, in the very place which ought to have strengthened and improved it. But in most cases those who come with a character of positive good are benefited; it is the neutral and indecisive characters which are apt to be decided for evil by schools, as they would be, in fact, by any other temptation.

This very feeling led him to catch with eagerness at every means by which the trial might be shortened or alleviated. He believed that the change from childhood to manhood might be hastened without prematurely exhausting the faculties of body and mind; and it was on this principle that he chiefly acted. He desired the boys to cultivate true manliness as the only step to something higher. He treated them as gentlemen, and appealed and trusted to their common sense and conscience.

Lying to the masters he made a grave offence. He placed implicit confidence in a boy's assertion, and then, if a falsehood were discovered, punished it severely. In the higher forms any attempt at further proof of an assertion was immediately checked. "If you say so, that is quite enough; of course, I believe your word"; and there grew up in consequence a general feeling that "it was a shame to tell Arnold a lie: he always believed you." Few scenes can be recorded more characteristic of him than when, in consequence of a disturbance, he had been obliged to send away several boys, and when, in the midst of the general spirit of discontent which this excited, he stood in his place before the assembled school and said, "It is *not* necessary that this should be a school of three hundred, or one hundred, or of fifty boys; but it is necessary that it should be a school of Christian gentlemen."

Arnold's method of teaching was founded on the principle of awakening the intellect of every individual boy. Hence it was his practice to teach by questioning. As a general rule, he never gave information, except as a kind of reward for an answer, and often withheld it altogether, or checked himself in the very act of uttering it, from a sense that those whom he was addressing had not sufficient interest or sympathy to receive it. His explanations were at short as possible--enough to dispose of the difficulty and no more; and his questions were of a kind to call the attention of the boys to the real point of every subject and to disclose to them the exact boundaries of what they knew or did not know. With regard to the younger boys, he said: "It is a great mistake to think that they should *understand* all they learn; for God has ordered that in youth the memory should act vigorously, independent of the understanding--whereas a man cannot usually recollect a thing unless he understands it."

At Rugby he made it an essential part of the headmaster's office to preach a sermon every Sunday in the school chapel. "The veriest stranger," he said, "who ever attends service in this chapel does well to feel something more than common interest in the sight of the congregation here assembled. But if the sight so interests a mere stranger, what should it be to ourselves, both to you and to me?" More than either matter or manner of his preaching was the impression of himself. Even the mere readers of his sermons will derive from them the history of his whole mind, and of his whole management of the school. But to his hearers it was more than this. It was the man himself, there more than in any other place, concentrating all his various faculties and feelings on one sole object, combating face to face the evil which, directly or indirectly, he was elsewhere perpetually struggling.

His personal interest in the boys was always strong. "Do you see," he on one occasion said to an assistant-master who had recently come, "those two boys walking together? I never saw them together before; you should make an especial point of observing the company they keep; nothing so tells the changes in a boy's character."

IV.--Influence of the Great Teacher

But the impression which Arnold produced upon the boys was derived not so much from any immediate intercourse or conversation with them as from the general influence of his whole character, displayed consistently whenever he appeared before them. This influence, with its consequent effects, was gradually on the increase during the whole of his stay. From the earliest period, indeed, the boys were conscious of something unlike what they had been taught to imagine of a schoolmaster, and by many a lasting regard was contracted for him. In the higher forms, at least, it became the fashion, so to speak, to think and talk of him with pride and affection. As regards the permanent effects of his whole system, it may be said that not so much among his own pupils, or in the scene of his actual labours, as in every public school throughout England is to be sought the chief and enduring monument of Arnold's headmastership at Rugby.

Of Arnold's general life at Rugby there is no need to say much; for although the school did not occupy his whole energies, it is almost solely by his school work that he is remembered. He took a not unimportant part in the political and theological discussions of his time, and various literary enterprises also engaged his attention. In theology he entertained very broad views. One great principle he advocated with intense earnestness was that a Christian people and a Christian Church should be synonymous. That use of the word "Church" which limits it to the clergy, or which implies in the clergy any particular sacredness, he entirely repudiated.

He was convinced that the founders of our constitution in Church and State did truly consider them to be identical; the Christian nation of England to be the Church of England; the head of that nation to be, for that very reason, the head of the Church. This view placed him in antagonism to the High Church party; but, as a matter of fact, he neither belonged, nor felt himself to belong, to any section of the English clergy. Politically, he held himself to be a strong Whig; but that he was not, in the common sense of the word, a member of any party is shown by the readiness with which all parties alike, according to the fashion of the time, claimed or renounced him as an associate.

Arnold did not like the flat scenery of Warwickshire He described himself as "in it like a plant sunk in the ground in a pot." His holidays were always spent away from Rugby, either on the Continent, or, in later years, at his Westmoreland home, Fox How, a small estate between Rydal and Ambleside, which he purchased in 1832. He was just about to leave

Rugby for Fox How when his life was mournfully and suddenly ended by an attack of angina pectoris, on June 12, 1842. Only the year before he had been appointed by Lord Melbourne Regius Professor of Modern History at Oxford.

Arnold's principal works are six volumes of sermons, a three-volume edition of Thucydides, the Oxford "Lectures on Modern History," and the three-volume "History of Rome," which, by his unfortunate death, was broken off at the Second Punic War. To the last-named he looked as the chief monument of his historical fame.

AGNES STRICKLAND

Life of Queen Elizabeth

Agnes Strickland, born in London on August 19, 1796, with her sister Elizabeth began in 1840 the publication of the immense series of historical biographies of which the "Lives of the Queens of England" formed the first and most important group. In that group the "Elizabeth" is recognised as holding the highest rank. It is an essentially feminine study of one of the most remarkable of women; not a history, for historical events are treated as of infinitely less importance than picturesque personal details and miscellaneous gossip, but presenting altogether an admirable picture of the outward seeming of those spacious days, and a discriminating and judicious portrait of the maiden queen herself. The author's views, however, would not always be endorsed by a masculine critic. Agnes Strickland died on July 13, 1874. The literature relating to the life and times of Queen Elizabeth would form a library of contemporary records. Many volumes of state papers have been published: Camden's "Annals of Elizabeth" is the classical account of her. Creighton's "Queen Elizabeth" and volumes VII. to XII. of Froude's "History of England" are the leading modern works; and no one who wishes to know anything of the great queen can afford to neglect Hume's "Courtships of Queen Elizabeth," which will also be found in these pages (see Hume).

I.--The Lady Elizabeth

Queen Elizabeth first saw the light at Greenwich Palace, where, says Heywood, "she was born on the eve of the Virgin's nativity, and died on the eve of the Virgin's annunciation." The christening ceremony was gorgeous and elaborate, but, with the downfall of her mother, Anne Boleyn, she ceased to be treated as a princess. She seems to have owed much to the judicious training of Lady Margaret Bryan, in whose charge she was. Later, she was associated with Prince Edward, four years her junior; both displayed an extraordinary precocity and capacity for learning.

On Henry's death, she resided with his widow, Catharine Parr, who married the Lord Admiral, Thomas Seymour. That ambitious nobleman, brother of the Protector, certainly designed, when Catharine died, to marry Elizabeth; an intention which was among the causes of his execution under attainder. His relations with her had already been unduly familiar, but there was no warrant for the scandalous stories that were repeated; and although Elizabeth all her life was naturally disposed to an excessive freedom of manners, she now became a pattern of decorum. But she was probably more in love with Seymour, as a girl of fifteen, than with anyone else in after life; though, on his death, she called him "a man of much wit and very little judgement."

Ascham is full of praises of her learning and her wide reading, both in Greek and Latin, which is displayed somewhat pedantically in her letters; her propriety and simplicity of apparel in these days is in curious contrast to the extravagances of her wardrobe in later life.

Mary treated her conspicuously as a sister; she refused, however, to abjure her Protestantism. Her position became extremely difficult, as the French, the Spaniards, and the Protestant party each sought to involve her in plots for their own ends. These culminated in Wyat's rebellion. The inevitable suspicions attaching to her caused her to be lodged in the Tower; but, in spite of the machinations of the Spanish party and the distrust of Mary, the evidence produced failed to warrant her condemnation.

Yet she was kept in rigorous confinement, her life continuing to be in danger for a month after Wyat himself had been executed. She was then removed to Richmond, but refused to purchase liberty at the price of marriage to a foreign prince, Philibert of Savoy--a scheme intended as a cover for Mary's determination to marry Philip, the Prince of Spain. Finally, she was transferred to Woodstock, where she was held a close prisoner.

Policy now led her to profess acceptance of the Roman religion, but in very ambiguous fashion. Probably it was through the intercession of Philip--now her brother-in-law, whose policy at this time was to conciliate the English people--that she was set at liberty and readmitted to court at Christmas.

At the end of the next year Elizabeth was at Hatfield, under the gentle surveillance of Sir Thomas Pope. She continued to be involved in grave dangers by perpetual plots, in which she was far too shrewd to let herself be implicated; and she guarded herself by a continued profession of Romanism to the hour of her accession on her sister's death.

As the hour of Mary's death approached, there was no doubt of Elizabeth's succession, though there was alarm as to possible complications. On November 17, 1558, the Chancellor announced to Parliament that Mary was dead, and Elizabeth queen. She held her first council at Hatfield two days later, when William Cecil took his place as her chief counsellor; on her entry into London, the position which was to be occupied by Lord Robert Dudley, afterwards Earl of Leicester, was already conspicuous.

The coronation, which took place in January, was a magnificent pageant, in which Elizabeth openly courted the favour and affection of her subjects; and it became at once apparent that the breach with Rome was reopened. The supremacy of the crown was reasserted, the all but empty bench of bishops was filled up with reformers; and, in answer to the Commons, Elizabeth very clearly implied her intention of reigning a virgin queen. She had already declined Philip of Spain's offer of his widowed hand; and now the fact that Mary Stuart stood next in the succession--with a better title than Elizabeth's own, if her legitimacy were challenged--became of immense importance.

Accordingly, an express declaration of her legitimate right to the throne was procured from Parliament. For some time pageants and popular displays were the order of the day. But, in spite of Elizabeth's own declarations, all her council were convinced that the safety of the realm demanded her marriage; and suitors began to abound. Arran appears--who now stood very near the throne of Scotland. Pickering, Arundel, Dudley, all seemed possible aspirants. The Austrian Archduke Charles, cousin of Philip of Spain, and Eric of Norway, were candidates. She played with them all, and the play was made more grim by the tragic death of Dudley's wife, Amy Robsart.

II.--Mary Stuart and Saint Bartholomew

The proposals for Elizabeth's own hand were now diversified by her interest in those for the hand of the Queen of Scots; for it was of immense importance to the Queen of England that Mary should not wed a foreign prince who might support her claim to the English throne. Mary professed willingness to be guided by her "sister," but was insulted by Elizabeth's offer of her own favourite, Dudley, who was made Earl of Leicester. Melville, the courtly Scots ambassador, had much ado to answer Elizabeth's questions about his mistress's beauty and accomplishments in a manner agreeable to the English queen. Mary solved her own problem, only to create a new one, by marrying her cousin, Lord Darnley. Elizabeth was bitterly aggrieved when a son--afterwards James I.--was born to them. She herself continued to agitate Cecil and the council by the favours she lavished on Leicester. But the renewed entreaties of Parliament, that steps might be taken to secure the succession, led to what threatened to be a serious quarrel.

Amongst these high matters, the records of her majesty's wardrobe, and the interests of Cecil in capturing for her service a tailor employed by Catherine de Medici, form an entertaining interlude. But tragedy was at hand; the murder of Darnley, Mary's marriage to the murderer Bothwell, her imprisonment at Loch Leven, Elizabeth's perturbation--for she was sincere in her fear of encouraging subjects to control monarchs by force of arms-- was diversified by a last negotiation for her marriage with the Archduke Charles, which broke down over his refusal to abjure his religion.

Then came a turn of the wheel; Mary escaped from Loch Leven, her followers were dispersed at Langside, and she fled across the Solway to throw herself on Elizabeth's protection and find herself Elizabeth's prisoner.

The Scottish queen was consigned to Bolton; an investigation was held at York, when Mary's accusers were allowed to produce, and Mary's friends were not allowed to test, their evidence of her complicity in Darnley's murder. At that stage the investigations were stopped; but the Duke of Norfolk, the head of the commission, was not deterred from pressing the design of marrying Mary himself. Mary was placed in the charge of Shrewsbury and his termagant spouse, Bess of Hardwick.

From this time for fifteen years, Elizabeth was perpetually playing at proposals for her own marriage with one or other of the French King's brothers, to keep the French court from a *rapprochement* with Spain. Suspicions of Norfolk's intentions led to his arrest, and this precipitated the rising in favour of Mary under the Catholic northern earls of Northumberland and Westmoreland; an insurrection promptly and cruelly crushed. In the spring of 1570 the Pope issued a bull of deposition; and the plots on behalf of Mary as Catholic claimant to the throne thickened.

In 1571 it appeared that Elizabeth was set on the marriage with Henry of Anjou, nineteen years her junior, the brother who stood next in succession to the throne of Charles IX. of France--a marriage not at all approved by her council, and very little to Henry's own taste. It was at this time that the conduct of negotiations in Paris was entrusted to Francis Walsingham.

The relations between the queen and the Commons were exemplified by her attempt to exclude an obnoxious member, Strickland, met by the successful assertion of their privileges on the part of the House.

In this year the plot known as Ridolfi's was discovered, and it is to be noted that Elizabeth herself ordered the rack to be used to extort information. The result was condemnation of Norfolk to the block. The recalcitrance of Henry of Anjou led to his definitely withdrawing from his courtship, while the young Alençon became the new subject of matrimonial negotiation.

Elizabeth played with the new proposal, as usual, relying always on her ability to back out of the negotiations, as in previous cases, by demanding of her suitor a more uncompromising acceptance of Protestantism than could be admitted. The whole affair, however, was apparently brought to a check by the massacre of St. Bartholomew, with the perpetration of which it seemed impossible for the most powerful of Protestant monarchs to associate herself.

Cecil--now Lord Burleigh--would have used the occasion for the destruction of Mary Stuart; but the device for doing so irreproachably by handing her over to her own rebels, was frustrated--though Elizabeth concurred--by the refusal of the Scots lords to play the part which was assigned to them. The Alençon affair was soon in full swing again, the young prince writing love-letters to the lady whom he had not seen.

III.--The Hour of Mary's Doom

Elizabeth's fondness for pageantry--partly out of a personal delight in it, partly from a politic appreciation of its value in making her popular--especially pageantry at some one else's expense, was illustrated in the gorgeous doings at Kenilworth, depicted (with sundry anachronisms) in Scott's novel.

These gaieties were the embroidery on more serious matters, for the Netherlands had for some time been engaged in their apparently desperate struggle with the power of Spain, and now actually invited the Queen of England to assume sovereignty over them--an offer which she was too acute to accept.

Yet we cannot pass over a highly characteristic incident. When the queen's majesty had a bad toothache, the protestations of her whole council failed to persuade her to face the extraction of the tooth, till the Bishop of London invited the surgeon to operate first on him in her presence, with satisfactory results. We must also record how the ugly little Alençon, or Anjou as he was now called, arrived unexpectedly to woo her in person, charmed her by his chivalrous audacity in doing so, and won from her the appropriate name of "Little Frog."

Whether she really wished to marry her "frog" is extremely doubtful. She made all the more parade of her desire to do so, since the extreme antipathy of the council and the nation to the project would secure her a retreat to the last. The expectation of the marriage caused the Netherlanders to offer Anjou the sovereignty which she had rejected; with the idea of thus securing the united support of England and France. But when matters reached the point of negotiation for an Anglo-French league, with the marriage as one of the articles, Elizabeth, of course, could not be brought to a definite answer, and after long delay Anjou found himself obliged to return to the Netherlands, neither accepted nor rejected. His subsequent death put an end to this, her last, matrimonial comedy.

At last an English force was actually sent to help the Netherlanders, under the command of Leicester. His conduct there led to his recall. Another favourite stood high in the queen's good graces--Walter Raleigh. Probably it was with a view to ousting this rival that Leicester brought his stepson Essex into the queen's notice.

But now the hour of Mary's doom was approaching. A plot was set on foot for the assassination of Elizabeth, into which Anthony Babington, whose name it bears, was drawn. Walsingham, possessed of complete information from the beginning, through his spies, nursed the plot carefully; letters from Mary were systematically intercepted and copied till the moment came for striking; the conspirators were arrested, and suffered the extreme penalty of the treason laws; and Elizabeth consented to have Mary herself at last brought to trial. She was refused counsel; the commission condemned her. Parliament demanded the execution of the death sentence. Elizabeth had her own misgivings.

She was afraid of the responsibility. Leicester suggested poison, but Burleigh and Walsingham stood by the law. A special embassy of remonstrance came from France; Mary wrote a dignified letter, not an appeal for her life, which moved the queen to tears; protests from the King of Scotland only aroused indignation; Elizabeth was frightened by rumours of fresh plots and of a French invasion.

At last she signed the death warrant, brought to her by Secretary Davison; the Chancellor's seal was attached, and the council, fearing some evasion on Elizabeth's part, issued the commission for Mary's execution without further reference to the queen; she was kept in ignorance of the fact till the tragedy was completed. She was furious with the council, but powerless against their unanimity. She could venture to make a scapegoat of Davison, and made a vain attempt to clear herself of responsibility in a letter to James, which failed to soothe the burst of indignation with which the news was received in Scotland. But the one thing she feared--a coalition of France, Spain, and Scotland--was made impossible by the antagonisms of the former and the weakness of the last.

Another crisis was at hand. Philip of Spain, claiming the throne of England as a descendant of John of Gaunt, was preparing the great Armada; Pope Sixtus V. was proclaiming a crusade against the heretic queen. Drake sailed into Cadiz harbour, and "singed the don's whiskers," but the vast preparations went on. A lofty spirit animated the queen and the people. London undertook to provide double the number of ships and men demanded from her. The militia was gathered at Tilbury, under Leicester. Howard of Effingham was Lord Admiral, with Drake as vice-admiral; in the enthusiasm of the moment, Elizabeth bestowed knighthood on a valorous lady, Mary, the wife of Sir Hugh Cholmondeley.

A report that the Armada had been destroyed by a gale, which actually drove it into Corunna for repairs, caused Elizabeth, with her usual parsimony, to order four great vessels to be dismantled; Howard retained them instead, at his own charges. On July 19, 1588, the Armada was sighted off the Lizard, and for eighteen days the naval heroes were grappling with that "invincible" fleet. Elizabeth herself visited the camp at Tilbury, rode through the lines, wearing a corselet and a farthingale of amazing dimensions, while a page bore her helmet, and addressed her soldiers in stirring words.

The victory was celebrated by medals bearing the device of a fleet in full sail, with the words *Venit, vidit, fugit* ("it came, it saw, it fled"), and of the dispersal by fireships with the words, *Dux femina facti* ("a woman led the movement").

IV.--Elizabeth's Closing Years

The defeat of the Armada was followed by an expedition to Lisbon, to wrest Portugal from Spain; owing to inadequate equipment it failed, after a promising beginning, the Portuguese lending no help. Essex managed to escape from court and join the expedition, messengers ordering him to return being too late. For this he was forgiven; but when he secretly married the widow of Sidney, and daughter of Walsingham, Elizabeth was furiously angry.

Not Essex, but Norris was sent to command a force dispatched to the aid of Henry of Navarre, who was now fighting for the crown of France. Essex, however, was subsequently sent, at Henry's own request. His absence was utilised by Burleigh to secure the advancement of his own astute son, Robert Cecil, who secured the royal favour by the ingenuity of his flattery.

When Essex finally returned from France, he was received with the utmost favour; but in the interval he had been transformed into an intriguing politician. Parliament, which had not been called for four years, met in 1593, and there was an immediate collision with the Crown. Elizabeth's tone was much more despotic than of old. Petitions for the settlement of the succession were met by the arbitrary imprisonment of Wentworth and other members.

Essex favoured the popular party, but had not the courage to head it; he was moved not by patriotism, but by jealousy of the Cecil ascendancy. The queen, when she had passed the age of sixty, was as determined as ever to pose as a youthful beauty, and her courtiers had no reluctance in assuming the tone of despairing lovers. No one played this part more persistently than Raleigh, who, when relegated to the Tower for marrying, proclaimed his misery, not at being separated from his bride, but at being shut out of the radiant presence of the queen.

Essex and Raleigh were associated in two expeditions, one directed with complete success against Cadiz, the other being a complete failure. The Burleigh faction succeeded in getting for Raleigh whatever credit there was in both cases, though Essex was better entitled to it.

But it was Ireland that wrought the ruin of Essex. A dispute in the council on the subject caused the queen to box the favourite's ears, which caused him to retire in resentment for many months. Soon after his return to court, he brought upon himself his own appointment to the lord-deputyship of Ireland. His conduct there displeased her; from her scolding letters, he concluded that his enemies in the council were undermining his position in his absence. He deserted his post, hurried to London, and burst, travel-stained as he was, into Elizabeth's chamber. For the moment she appeared disposed to forgive him, but was not long in deciding that his insolence must be punished, and he was placed in confinement.

So he continued for about a year, in spite of appeals to the queen. The adverse party in the council had the predominance. At last, however, he was granted a degree of liberty, and Francis Bacon tried to conciliate Elizabeth towards her former favourite. But the unfortunate man allowed his resentment to carry him into dangerous courses. His house became a rendezvous of the discontented. Finally, a futile attempt on his part to raise the citizens of London in his favour consummated his ruin. He was soon a prisoner; his condemnation was now a foregone conclusion; Elizabeth signed the warrant with fingers which did not tremble; and, to the universal astonishment, the favourite was executed.

Elizabeth's meeting with her last parliament displays in a marked degree the tact which never deserted her when she thought fit to employ it. Their protest against the practice of monopolies, instead of rousing her ire, brought from her a notably gracious promise to redress the grievances complained of. This was in 1601. In the next year, when she became sixty-nine, there was no relaxation in her gaieties; but under the surface, Elizabeth was old and sad.

Her popularity had never been the same since the death of Essex; and the memory of the man she had cherished and finally sent to his doom, well-deserved as that was, was a perpetual source of grief to her. In March 1603, she was stricken with her last fatal illness. Yet she would not go to bed. At last she gave in; she knew herself dying long before she admitted it.

It was uncertain whether even in her last moments she would acknowledge the right of any successor to her throne, but a gesture was interpreted as favouring the King of Scots. Finally, she sank into a sleep from which she never awoke. So passed away England's Elizabeth.

JONATHAN SWIFT

Journal to Stella

The "Journal to Stella," which extends over the years 1710 to 1713, was first published in 1766 and has often been republished since. The manuscripts are preserved in the British Museum. It was at Sir William Temple's home, Moor Park in Surrey, that Swift came to know Esther Johnson, or "Stella," who was fourteen years younger than himself. In 1699 Temple died, and Stella, with her friend, Rebecca Dingley, came to Ireland at Swift's request. Their relation has been made a great mystery. It will perhaps always be doubtful whether he was nominally married to her secretly; the evidence is on the whole against the existence of such a bond. But to the further question--why did he not take her to live as his wife--a sufficient reply may be found in his abnormal nature. In the "Journal" the word "Presto" refers to Swift himself (see FICTION); "MD" to Stella.

LONDON, Sept. 9, 1710.

I got here last Thursday, after five days' travelling, weary the first, almost dead the second, tolerable the third, and well enough the rest; and am now glad of the fatigue, which has served for exercise; and I am at present well enough. The Whigs were ravished to see me, and would lay hold on me as a twig while they are drowning, and the great men making me their clumsy apologies, etc. But my Lord Treasurer received me with a great deal of coldness, which has enraged me so, I am almost vowing revenge. I have not yet gone half my circle; but I find all my acquaintance just as I left them. Everything is turning upside down; every Whig in great office will, to a man, be infallibly put out; and we shall have such a winter as hath not been seen in England.

The Tatler expects every day to be turned out of his employment; and the Duke of Ormond, they say, will be Lieutenant of Ireland. I hope you are now peaceably in Presto's lodgings; but I resolve to turn you out by

Christmas; in which time I shall either have done my business, or find it not to be done. Pray be at Trim by the time this letter comes to you; and ride little Johnson, who must needs be now in good case. I have begun this letter unusually, on the post-night, and have already written to the Archbishop; and cannot lengthen this. Henceforth I will write something every day to MD, and make it a sort of journal; and when it is full, I will send it, whether MD writes or no; and so that will be pretty: and I shall always be in conversation with MD, and MD with Presto; and so farewell.

LONDON, NOV. 11, 1710.

I dined to-day in the City, and then went to christen Will Frankland's child; Lady Falconbridge was one of the godmothers; this is a daughter of Oliver Cromwell, and extremely like him by the picture I have seen. My business in the City was to thank Stratford for a kindness he has done me. I found Bank stock fallen thirty-four to the hundred, and was mighty desirous to buy it. I had three hundred pounds in Ireland, and I desired Stratford to buy me three hundred pounds in Bank stock and that he keep the papers, and that I would be bound to pay him for them; and, if it should rise or fall, I should take my chance and pay him interest in the meantime. I was told money was so hard to get here, and no one would do this for me. However, Stratford, one of the most generous men alive, has done this for me: so that three hundred pounds cost me three hundred pounds and thirty shillings. This was done a week ago, and I can have five pounds for my bargain already. I writ to your Mother to desire Lady Giffard would do the same with what she owes me, but she tells your mother she has no money. I would to God, all you had in the world was there. Whenever you lend money, take this rule, to have two people bound, who have both visible fortunes; for they will hardly die together; and, when one dies, you fall upon the other, and make him add another security. So, ladies, enough of business for one night. Paaaaast twelve o'clock; nite, nite deelest MD. I must only add, that, after a long fit of rainy weather, it has been fair two or three days, and is this day grown cold and frosty; so you must give poor little Presto leave to have a fire in his chamber morning and evening too; and he will do as much for you. Shall I send this to-morrow? Well I will, to oblige MD. 'Tis late, so I bid you good-night.

CHELSEA, June, 1711.

I went at noon to see Mr. Secretary at his office, and there was Lord Treasurer; so I killed two birds, etc., and we were glad to see one another and so forth. And the Secretary and I dined at Sir William Wyndam's, who married Lady Catherine Seymour, your acquaintance, I suppose. There were ten of us at dinner. It seems, in my absence, they had erected a Club, and made me one; and we made some laws to-day, which I am to digest and add to, against next meeting. Our meetings are to be every Thursday. We are yet but twelve; Lord Keeper and Lord Treasurer were proposed; but I was against them, and so was Mr. Secretary, though their sons are of it, and so they are excluded; but we design to admit the Duke of Shrewsbury. The end of our Club is to advance conversation and friendship, and to reward deserving persons with our interest and recommendation. We take in none but men of wit or men of interest; and if we go on as we begin, no other Club in this town will be worth talking of. This letter will come three weeks after the last, so there is a week lost; but that is owing to my being out of town.

Well, but I must answer this letter of our MD's. Saturday approaches, and I han't written down this side. Oh, faith, Presto has been a sort of lazy fellow: but Presto will remove to town this day se'night: the Secretary has commanded me to do so: and I believe he and I shall go some days to Windsor, where he will have leisure to mind some business we have together. To-day our Society (it must not be called a Club) dined at Mr. Secretary's: we were but eight. We made some laws, and then I went to take my leave of Lady Ashburnham, who goes out of town to-morrow.

Steele has had the assurance to write to me that I would engage my Lord Treasurer to keep a friend of his in an employment. I believe I told you how he and Addison served me for my good offices in Steele's behalf; and I promised Lord Treasurer never to speak for either of them again.

We have plays acted in our town; and Patrick was at one of them, oh, oh. He was damnably mauled one day when he was drunk, by a brother-footman, who dragged him along the floor on his face, which looked for a week after as if he had the leprosy, and I was glad enough to see it. I have been ten times sending him back to you; yet now he has new clothes and a laced hat, which the hatter brought by his orders, and he offered to pay for the lace out of his wages.

I must rise now and shave, and walk to town, unless I go with the Dean in his chariot at twelve: and I have not seen that Lord Peterborough yet. The Duke of Shrewsbury is almost well again, but what care you? You do not care for my friends. Farewell, my dearest lives and delights: I love you better than ever, if possible, as hope saved, I do, and ever will. God almighty bless you ever, and make us happy together! I pray for this twice every day; and I hope God will hear my poor hearty prayers. Remember, if I am used ill and ungratefully, as I have formerly been, 'tis what I am prepared for, and I shall not wonder at it. Yet I am now envied, and thought in high favour, and have every day numbers of considerable men teasing me to solicit for them.

And the Ministry all use me perfectly well; and all that know them say they love me. Yet I can count upon nothing, nor will, but upon MD's love and kindness. They think me useful; they pretended they were afraid of none but me, and that they resolved to have me; they have often confessed this: yet all this makes little impression on me--Pox of these speculations! They give me the spleen; a disease I was not born to. Let me alone, sirrahs, and be satisfied: I am, as long as MD and Presto are well. Little wealth, and much health, and a life by stealth: that is all we want; and so farewell, dearest MD; Stella, Dingley, Presto, all together; now and for ever all together. Farewell again and again.

LONDON, July, 1711.

I have just sent my 26th, and have nothing to say, because I have other letters to write (pshaw, I began too high) but to-morrow I will say more, and fetch up this line to be straight This is enough at present for two dear saucy naughty girls.

Morning. It is a terrible rainy day. Patrick lay out all last night, and is not yet returned: faith, poor Presto is a desolate creature; neither servant, nor linen, nor anything.

I was at Court and Church to-day: I am acquainted with about thirty in the drawing-room, and I am so proud I make all the Lords come up to me; one passes half an hour pleasant enough. We had a dunce to preach before the queen to-day, which often happens. Windsor is a delicious situation, but the town is scoundrel. The Duke of Hamilton would needs be witty, and hold up my train as I walked upstairs. It is an ill circumstance that on Sundays much company always meet at the great tables. The Secretary showed me his bill of fare, to encourage me to dine with him. "Poh," said I, "show me a bill of company, for I value not your dinner."

In my conscience. I fear I shall have the gout. I sometimes feel pains about my feet and toes: I never drank till within these two years, and I did it to cure my head. I often sit evenings with some of these people, and drink in my turn; but I am resolved to drink ten times less than before; but they advise me to let what I drink be all wine, and not to put water in it. Tooke and the printer stayed to-day to finish their affair. Then I went to see Lord Treasurer, and chid him for not taking notice of me at Windsor. He said he kept a place for me yesterday at dinner, and expected me there; but I was glad I did not go, because the Duke of Buckingham was there, and that would have made us acquainted; which I have no mind to.

I have sent a noble haunch of venison this afternoon to Mrs. Vanhomrigh; I wish you had it sirrahs. I dined gravely with my landlord, the Secretary.

The queen was abroad to-day to hunt; but finding it disposed to rain, she kept in her coach, which she drives herself, and drives furiously, like Jehu, and is a mighty hunter, like Nimrod. Dingley has heard of Nimrod, but not Stella, for it is in the Bible. Mr. Secretary has given me a warrant for a buck; I can't sent it to MD. It is a sad thing, faith, considering how Presto loves MD, and how MD would love Presto's venison for Presto's sake. God bless the two dear Wexford girls!

There was a drawing-room to-day at Court; but so few company, that the queen sent for us into her bedchamber, where we made our bows, and stood about twenty of us round the room, while she looked at us round with her fan in her mouth, and once a minute said about three words to some that were nearest to her, and then she was told dinner was ready, and went out.

LONDON, Dec. 1, 1711.

To-morrow is the fatal day for the Parliament meeting, and we are full of hopes and fears. We reckon we have a majority of ten on our side in the House of Lords; yet I observe Mrs. Masham a little uneasy. The Duke of Marlborough has not seen the queen for some days past; Mrs. Masham is glad of it, because she says he tells a hundred lies to his friends of what she says to him: he is one day humble, and the next day on the high ropes.

This being the day Parliament was to meet, and the great question to be determined, I went with Dr. Freind to dine in the City, on purpose to be out of the way, and we sent our printer to see what was our fate; but he gave us a most melancholy account of things. The Earl of Nottingham began and spoke against a peace, and desired that in their address they might put in a clause to advise the queen not to make a peace without Spain; which was debated, and carried by the Whigs by about six voices: and this has happened entirely by my Lord Treasurer's neglect, who did not take timely care to make up his strength, although every one of us gave him caution enough. Nottingham has certainly been bribed. The question is yet only carried in the Committee of the whole House, and we hope when it is reported to the House to-morrow, we shall have a majority.

This is a day that may produce great alterations and hazard the ruin of England. The Whigs are all in triumph; they foretold how all this would be, but we thought it boasting. Nay, they said the Parliament should be dissolved before Christmas, and perhaps it may: this is all your d----d Duchess of Somerset's doings. I warned them of this nine months ago, and a hundred times since. I told Lord Treasurer I should have the advantage of him; for he would lose his head, and I should only be hanged, and so carry my body entire to the grave.

I was this morning with Mr. Secretary: we are both of opinion that the queen is false. He gave me reasons to believe the whole matter is settled between the queen and the Whigs. Things are now in a crisis, and a day or two will determine. I have desired him to engage Lord Treasurer to send, me abroad as Queen's Secretary somewhere or other, where I will remain till the new Ministers recall me; and then I will be sick for five or six months, till the storm has spent itself. I hope he will grant me this; for I should hardly trust myself to the mercy of my enemies while their anger is fresh.

Morning. They say the Occasional Bill is brought to-day into the House of Lords; but I know not. I will now put an end to my letter, and give it into the post-house with my own fair hands. This will be a memorable letter, and I shall sigh to see it some years hence. Here are the first steps towards the ruin of an excellent Ministry; for I look upon them as certainly ruined; and God knows what may be the consequence.--I now bid my dearest MD farewell; for company is coming, and I must be at Lord Dartmouth's office by noon. Farewell, dearest MD; I wish you a merry Christmas; I believe you will have this about that time. Love Presto, who loves MD above all things a thousand times. Farewell again, dearest MD.

LONDON, Dec. 20, 1711.

I was with the Secretary this morning, and, for aught I can see, we shall have a languishing death: I can know nothing, nor themselves neither. I dined, you know, with our Society, and that odious Secretary would make me President next week; so I must entertain them this day se'night at the Thatched House Tavern: it will cost me five or six pounds; yet the Secretary says he will give me wine.

Saturday night. I have broken open my letter, and tore it into the bargain, to let you know that we are all safe: the queen has made no less than twelve Lords to have a majority; nine new ones, the other three peers' sons; and has turned out the Duke of Somerset. She is awaked at last, and so is Lord Treasurer: I want nothing now but to see the Duchess out. But we shall do without her. We are all extremely happy. Give me joy, sirrahs. This is written in a coffee-house.

LONDON, Feb. 26, 1712.

I was again busy with the Secretary. I dined with him, and we were to do more business after dinner; but after dinner is after dinner--an old saying and a true, "much drinking, little thinking." We had company with us, and nothing could be done, so I am to go there again to-morrow.

To-day in the morning I visited upwards: first I saw the Duke of Ormond below stairs, and gave him joy of being declared General in Flanders; then I went up one pair of stairs, and sat with the duchess; then I went up another pair of stairs, and paid a visit to Lady Betty; and then desired her woman to go up to the garret, that I might pass half an hour with her, for she was young and handsome, but she would not.

Tell Walls that I spoke to the Duke of Ormond about his friend's affairs. I likewise mentioned his own affair to Mr. Southwell. But oo must not know zees sings, zey are secrets; and we must keep them flom nauty dallars. I was with Lord Treasurer to-day, and hat care oo for zat? Monday is parson's holiday, and oo lost oo money at cards; ze devil's device. Nite, nite, my two deelest logues.

LONDON, April 6, 1713

I was this morning at the rehearsal of Mr. Addison's play, called "Cato," which is to be acted on Friday. There were not above half a score of us to see it. We stood on the stage, and it was foolish enough to see the actors prompted every moment, and the poet directing them; and the drab that acts Cato's daughter, in the midst of a passionate part, calling out "What's next?" I went back and dined with Mr. Addison.

Nothing new to-day; so I'll seal up this to-night. Pray write soon.... Farewell, deelest MD, MD, MD. Love Presto.

LYOF N. TOLSTOY

Childhood, Boyhood, Youth

Childhood (1852), Boyhood (1854), and Youth (1855-57)--
Tolstoy's first literary efforts--may be regarded as semi-
autobiographical studies; if not in detail, at least in the wider
sense that all his books contain pictures more or less accurate
of himself and his own experiences. No plot runs through
them; they simply analyse and describe with extraordinary
minuteness the feelings of a nervous and morbid boy-
-a male Marie Bashkirtseff. They are tales rather of the
developments of the thoughts, than of the life of a child,
with a pale background of men and events. The distinct
charm lies in the sincerity with which this development is
represented.

I.--Childhood

August 12, 18--, was the third day after my tenth birthday anniversary.
Wonderful presents had been given me. My tutor, Karl Ivanitch, roused
me at seven by striking at a fly directly over my head with a flapper made
of sugar paper fastened to a stick. He generally spoke in German, and in
his kindly voice exclaimed, "Auf, Kinder, auf; es ist Zeit. Die Mutter ist
schon im Saal." ("Get up, children, it is time. Your Mother is already in the
drawing-room.")

Dyadka Nikolai, the valet of us children, a neat little man, brought in
the clothes for me and Volodya, who was imitating my sister's governess,
Marya Ivanova, in mocking, merry laughter. Somewhat sternly presently
Karl Ivanitch called from the schoolroom to know if we were nearly ready
to begin our lessons.

In the schoolroom, on one shelf was our promiscuous assortment of
books, on another, the still more miscellaneous collection which our dear
old tutor was pleased to call his library. I remember that it included a
German treatise on cabbage gardens, a history of the Seven Years' War, and
a work on hydrostatic. Karl Ivanitch spent all his spare time in reading his
beloved books, but he never read anything beyond these and the Northern
Bee. After early lessons our tutor conducted us downstairs to greet Mamma.

She was sitting in the parlour, in front of the samovar, pouring out tea. To the left of the divan was the old English grand piano, on which my dark-complexioned sister, Liubotchka, eleven years old, was painfully practising Clementi's exercises. Near her Marya Ivanova, with scowls on her face, was loudly counting, and beating time with her foot. She frowned still more disagreeably at Karl as he entered, but he appeared to ignore this and kissed my mother's hand with a German salutation. After mutually affectionate greetings Mamma told us to go to our father and to ask him to come to her before he went to the threshing floor.

We found Papa angrily discussing business affairs with Yakov Mikhailof, the chief concern being apparently about money from Mamma's estate at Khabarovka, her native village. A large sum was due to the council, and Yakov pleaded that it would be difficult to raise it from the sale of hay and the proceeds of the mill. "For example," said he, "the miller has been twice to ask me for delay, swearing by Christ the Lord that he has no money. What little cash he had he put into the dam."

Yakov was a serf, and was a most devoted and assiduous man, excessively economical in managing his master's affairs, and constantly worried himself over the increase of his master's property at the expense of that of his mistress.

For some days we had been expecting something unusual, from preparations which we saw going on for some journey, but an announcement from Papa at length surprised us terribly. He greeted us one morning with the remark that it was time to put an end to our idleness, and that as he was going that evening to Moscow, we were to go with him and to live there with our grandmother, Mamma remaining on the estate with the girls.

My thoughts were mingled, for I was very grieved for the sake of Mamma, yet I felt pleasure at the idea that we were grown up. For poor Karl Ivanitch I was extremely sorry, as he would be discharged. On my way upstairs I saw Papa's favourite greyhound, Milka, basking in the sunshine on the terrace, and ran out, kissed her on the nose and caressed her, saying, "Farewell, Milotchka. We shall never see each other again." Then, altogether overcome with emotion, I burst into tears.

My father was a chivalrous character of the last century, who regarded with contempt the people of the present century. His two chief passions were cards and women. He was tall and commanding, bald, with small eyes ever twinkling vivaciously, and a lisping utterance. He knew how to exercise a spell over people of every grade, and in the highest society he was held in great esteem. He seemed born to shine in his brilliant position, and was an expert in the management of all things that could conduce to comfort and pleasure.

A lover of music, he sang to his own piano accompaniment operatic songs, but had no liking for Beethoven's sonatas and other scientific compositions. His principles grew more fixed as years rolled on; he judged actions as being good or bad accordingly as they procured him happiness and pleasure, or otherwise; he talked persuasively; and he could represent the same deed as either an innocent piece of playfulness or of abominable villainy.

Happy days of childhood that can never be recalled! What memories I yet cherish of them. I see Mamma just as plainly as when she so long since was talking to some one at the tea-table, while I, in my high chair, grew drowsy. Presently she stroked my hair with her soft hand, saying, "Get up, my darling, it is time to go to bed. Get up, my angel."

I spring up and embrace her, and exclaim, "Dear, dear Mamma, how I love you!" With her sad and fascinating smile she places me on her knees, is silent awhile, and then speaks. "So you love me very much? Love me always and never forget me. If you lose your Mamma, Nikolinka, you will not forget her?"

She kisses me still more lovingly, and I cry with tears of love and rapture flooding my face, "Oh, do not say that, my darling, my precious one." Will that freshness, that happy carelessness, that thirst for love which made life's only requirements, ever return? Where are those pure tears of tenderest emotion? The angel of consolation came and wiped them away. Do the memories alone abide?

About a month after we had removed to Moscow, Grandmamma received a visit from Princess Kornakova, a woman of forty-five, with disagreeable gray-green eyes, but sweetly curved lips, bright red hair, and insalubrious face. In spite of these peculiarities her aspect was noble. I took a dislike to her because I found from her talk that she was given to beating her own children, and thought that other people's children, especially boys, needed to be whipped.

Another visitor was Prince Ivan Ivanitch, distinguished for his noble character, handsome person, splendid bravery and extraordinary good fortune. He belonged to a powerful family, and lived in accordance with principles of the strictest religion and morality. Though somewhat reserved and haughty, in demeanour, he was full of kindly feeling. Prince Ivan Ivanitch was a highly cultured man of most versatile accomplishments. Our Grandmamma was evidently delighted to see him, and his magnificent aspect and her liking for him inspired me with unbounded admiration and reverence.

He asked why Mamma had not come to Moscow. "Ah," was the reply, "she would have come if possible, but they have no income this year."

"I do not understand," replied the Prince. "Her Khabarovka is a wonderful estate, and it must always bring in a fine revenue."

"I will tell you," said Grandmamma, sadly. "It seems to me that all the pretexts are made simply to enable him to live a gay life here, while she, angel of goodness that she is, suspects nothing. She believes him in everything."

This conversation should not have been overheard by me, but, having overheard it, I crept out of the room.

On the 16th of April, nearly six months later, serious news came from Mamma. She wrote to Papa that she had contracted a chill, which had caused a fever, that this was over, but had left her in such utter weakness that she would never rise from her bed again, although those about her were not aware of such a condition. She wished him to come to her at once and to bring her two boys with him. She prayed that God's holy will might be done.

On April 25th we reached our Petrovskoe home. Papa had been very sad and thoughtful during the journey. We at once learned from the steward that Mamma had not left her room for six days. I shall never forget what I saw when we entered Mamma's room. She was unconscious. Her eyes were open, but she saw nothing. We were led away. Mamma soon passed away.

She was dead, the funeral obsequies took place, and then our life went on much as before. We rose, had our repasts, and retired to rest at the same hours. Three days after the funeral the whole household removed to Moscow. Grandmamma only learned what had happened when we arrived, and her grief was terrible. She lay unconscious for a week, and the doctor feared for her life, for she would not eat, speak, or take medicine. When she recovered somewhat, her first thought was of us children. She cried softly, spoke of Mamma, and tenderly caressed us.

II.--Boyhood

On our arrival in Moscow a change had taken place in my views of things. My sentiment of reverence for Grandmamma had changed to one of sympathy. As she covered my cheeks with kisses I realised that each kiss expressed the thought "She is gone; I shall never see her more." Papa had very little to do with us in Moscow, coming to us only at dinner time, and lost much in my eyes, with his ostentatious dress, his stewards, his clerks, and his hunting and business expeditions.

Between us and the girls also an invisible barrier seemed to rise. We were proud of our trousers and straps, and they of their petticoats, which increased in length. Their showier Sunday dress made it manifest that we were no longer in the country. But soon commenced a period of my life of which it is difficult to trace a record. Rarely during memories of it do I find moments of the genuine warmth of feeling which so frequently illumined the earliest years of my life.

Vivid is the recollection of Volodya's entrance at the university. He was barely two years my senior in age. The day of his first examination arrived, and he presented a handsome appearance in his blue uniform with brass buttons and lacquered boots. The examination lasted ten days, and Volodya, having passed brilliantly, returned on the last day no longer in blue coat and grey cap, but in student uniform, with blue embroidered collar, three-cornered hat, and a gilt dagger by his side. Joy and excitement reigned in the whole household. For the first time since Mamma's death, Grandmamma drank champagne, and weeps with joy as she looks at Volodya, who henceforth rode in his own equipage, receives friends in his own rooms, smokes tobacco, goes to balls.

But soon another incident happened which is engraven on memory. The dear old Grandmamma was growing daily weaker, and one morning the announcement thrilled us that she was dead. Again, the house was full of mourning. In a few months I should be preparing to enter the university. I was by degrees emerging from my boyish moods, with the exception of one--a tendency to metaphysical dreaminess, which was fated to do me much injury in after years.

At this period an intimacy commenced between me and a very remarkable man, Prince Dmitri Nekhliudoff. He was a tall and commanding figure, with an extraordinary intellect. Whenever he found me alone, we seated ourselves in some secluded corner and found mutual delight in metaphysical discussions. With ecstasy in those moments I soared higher and higher into the realms of thought. This strange friendship grew. We agreed to confess everything to each other, and thus we should really know each other and not be ashamed; but, in order that we should not be in any fear of strangers, we vowed never to say anything to anybody else about each other. And we kept the vow. As may be imagined, the influence of my friend over me was greater than mine over him. I adopted his fervent ideas, which included lofty aspirations for the reformation of all mankind.

III.--Youth

I was nearly sixteen, and from that time I date the beginning of youth. Under various professors I studied, though by no means willingly, to prepare for the university. At length, on April 16, I went for the first time to the great hall of the university. For the first time in my life I wore a dress coat. The bright hall was filled with a brilliant crowd of hundreds of young men in gymnasium costumes and dress coats, stately professors moving freely about among the tables. On that day I was examined in history and answered questions in Russian history in brilliant style, for I knew the subject well. I received five marks. Similar success rewarded my efforts at the examination in mathematics, for the professor told me I had answered even better than was required, and on this occasion I received five points.

Everything went splendidly till I came to the Latin examination. The Latin professor was spoken of in accents of terror, for he had the reputation of taking a fierce delight in plucking candidates. My success so far had made me feel proudly confident, and as I could translate Cicero and Horace without the lexicon and was proficient in Zumpt's Grammar, I thought I might equal the rest. But not so. The professor amicably passed one of my young acquaintances, although the youth was palpably deficient in his answers. I afterwards learned that he was the student's protector.

When my turn came, immediately afterwards, the professor turned on me in truly savage demeanour. "That is not it; that is not it at all," exclaimed he. "This is not the way to prepare for higher education. You only want to wear the uniform and to boast of being first."

The demeanour of this professor so affected me that my confusion was complete. I only received two marks, and the injustice so depressed me that I lost all ambition and allowed the remaining examinations to proceed without making any effort. I made up my mind that it was unwise to aim at being first, and I resolved to adhere to this sentiment in the university.

My father married again. He was forty-eight when he took Avdotya Epifanova as his second wife. She was a beautiful woman, whom Mamma used to call Dunitchka. But I had suspected nothing until Papa actually announced to us that he was going to marry her. The wedding was to take place in a fortnight. I and Volodya returned to Moscow at the beginning of September, and on the following day I went to the university for my first lecture.

It was a magnificent, sunny day, and as I entered the auditorium I felt lost in the throng of gay youths flitting about through the doors and among the corridors. Belonging to no particular group I felt isolated, and then even angry, and I remember in my heart that this first day was a dismal occasion for me. I looked at the professor with an ironical feeling, for he commenced his lecture with an introduction which, to my mind, was without sense. I decided at this first lecture that there was no need to write down everything that each professor said, and to this principle I adhered.

Though during my course I made many pleasant acquaintances, and so felt less isolated than at first, I indulged in little real comradeship. But during the winter my attention was much engrossed with affairs of the heart, for I was in love three times. Yet I was overwhelmed with shyness, fearing that my love should be discovered by its object. With two of the young ladies, indeed, I had already been in love previously. Of one of them I was now enamoured for the third time. But I knew that Volodya also regarded her with passionate ecstasy. I felt that it would certainly not be agreeable to him to learn that two brothers were in love with the same young woman.

Therefore I said nothing to him of my love. But great satisfaction was afforded to my mind by the fact that our love was so pure, and that each would be ready, if needful, to make a sacrifice for the sake of the other. But that self-abnegation did not, after all, extend to Volodya, for when he heard that a certain diplomat was to marry the girl, he was disposed to slap his face and to challenge him to a duel. It happened that I had only spoken once to the young lady, and my love passed away in a week, as I made no effort to perpetuate it.

During that winter I was quite disenchanted with the social pleasures to which I had looked forward when I entered the university, in imitation of my brother Volodya. He danced a great deal, and Papa also went with his young wife to balls. But at the first one which I attended I was so shy that I declined the invitation of the Princess Kornakova to dance, declaring that I did not dance, though I had come to her evening party with the express intention of dancing a great deal. I remained silently in one place the whole evening.

Avdotya's passionate love for Papa was evident in every word, look, and action. We were always hypocritically polite to her, called her *chère maman*, and noted that at first she was fond of calling herself stepmother, and that she plainly felt the unpleasantness of her position. Her disposition was very amiable and she was in no way exacting.

My first examination at length arrived. It was on differential and integral calculus. I was indifferent and abstracted, but a feeling of some dread passed over me when the same young professor who had questioned me at the entrance examination looked me in the face. I answered so badly that he looked at me compassionately, and said quietly but firmly that as

I should not pass in the second class I had better not present myself for examination. I went home and remained weeping in my room for three days over my failure. I even looked out my pistols, in order that they might be at hand if I should feel a wish to shoot myself. Finally, I saw my father and begged him to permit me to enter the hussars, or to go to the Caucasus.

Though he was not pleased, yet, when he saw how deep was my grief he sought to comfort me by saying that it was not so very bad, and that arrangements might be made for a different course of study. After a few days I became composed, but did not leave the house till we departed for the country. I may some day relate the sequel in the happier half of my youth.

[Tolstoy has never published the continuation, but it is generally considered that he represents himself in Constantine Levin, the hero of the greatest of his stories, and that thus we gain an insight into his mature thoughts.]

My Confession

Count Lyof N. Tolstoy in writing this work expressed himself in such independent terms that it could not be published in Russia, but was issued in Geneva in 1888, by the firm of Elpidine, who had printed in 1886 his "What is my Life," and in 1892 brought out his "Walk in the Light." The books thus issued in the original Russian version outside of the famous author's native land are all purely spiritual, and are written in the most elevated tone. But Tolstoy's mode of interpreting the Scriptures is not approved by the Holy Synod of the Eastern Orthodox Church, or Russo-Greek Communion, and thus most of his treatises which come within the strictly religious category are classed amongst the "Forbidden Books" of modern Russian literature. In this "Confession" Tolstoy emphatically strikes the keynote which is the *motif* of all his didactic writings. It is an affirmation of the principle that the pure spirit of religion, apart from external dogma, is the really precious factor of life. He follows the same strain in his "What I Believe," and his "Christianity of Christ." The following synopsis is translated and summarised from the original Russian.

I.--Evil Early Years

Though reared in the faith of the Orthodox Eastern, or Russo-Greek Church, I had by the time when, at the age of eighteen, I left the university ceased to believe what I had been taught. My faith could never have been well grounded in conviction. I not only ceased to pray, but also to attend the services and to fast. Without denying the existence of God, yet I cherished no ideas either as to the nature of God or the teaching of Christ.

I found that my wish to become a good and virtuous man, whenever the aspiration was in any way expressed, simply exposed me to ridicule; while I instantly gained praise for any vicious behaviour. Even my excellent aunt declared that she wished two things for me. One was that I should form a liaison with some married lady; the other that I should become an adjutant to the Tsar.

I look back with horror on the years of my young manhood, for I was guilty of slaying men in battle, of gambling, of riotous squandering of substance gained by the toil of serfs, of deceit, and of profligacy. That course of life lasted ten years. Then I took to writing, but the motive was grovelling, for I aimed at gaining money and flattery.

My aims were gratified, for, coming to St. Petersburg at the age of 26, I secured the flattering reception I had coveted from the authors most in repute. The war, about which I had written much from the field of conflict, had just closed. I found that a theory prevailed amongst the "Intelligentia" that the function of writers, thinkers, and poets was to teach; they were to teach not because they knew or understood, but unconsciously and intuitively. Acting on this philosophy, I, as a thinker and poet, wrote and taught I knew not what, received large remuneration for my efforts with the pen, and lived loosely, gaily, and extravagantly.

Thus I was one of the hierarchs of the literary faith, and for a considerable time was undisturbed by any doubts as to its soundness; but when three years had been thus spent, serious suspicions entered my mind. I noted that the devotees of this apparently infallible principle were at variance amongst themselves, for they disputed, deceived, abused, and swindled each other. And many were grossly selfish, and most immoral.

Disgust supervened, both with myself and with mankind in general. My error now was that though my eyes were opened to the vanity and delusion of the position, yet I retained it, imagining that I, as thinker, poet, teacher, could teach other men while not at all knowing what to teach. To my other faults an inordinate pride had been added by my intercourse with these *litterateurs*. That period viewed retrospectively seems to me like one of a kind of madness. Hundreds of us wrote to teach the people, while we all abused and confuted one another. We could teach nothing, yet we sent millions of pages all over Russia, and we were unspeakably vexed that we seemed to gain no attention whatever, for nobody appeared to listen to us.

II.--Groping in Darkness

I travelled in Europe at this period, before my marriage, still cherishing in my mind the idea of general perfectibility, which was so popular at that time with the "Intelligentia." Cultured circles clung to the theory of what we call "progress," vague though are the notions attaching to the term. I was horrified with the spectacle of an execution in Paris, and my eyes were opened to the fallacy underlying the theory of human wisdom. The doctrine of "progress" I now felt to be a mere superstition, and I was further confirmed in my conviction by the sad death of my brother after a painful illness of a whole year.

My brother was kind, amiable, clever, and serious; but he passed away without ever knowing why he had lived or what his death meant for him. All theories were futile in the face of this tragedy. Returning to Russia I settled in my rural home and began to organise schools for the peasants, feeling real enthusiasm for the enterprise. For I still clung to a great extent to the idea of progress by development. I thought that though highly cultured men all thought and taught differently and agreed about nothing, yet in the case of the children of the mujiks the difficulty could easily be surmounted by permitting the children to learn what they liked.

I also tried through my own newspaper to indoctrinate the people, but my mind grew more and more embarrassed. At length I fell sick, rather mentally than physically. I went off to the Steppes to breathe the pure air and to take mare's milk and to live the simple life. I married soon after my return to my estate. As time passed on I became happily absorbed in the interests of wife and children, largely forgetting during a happy interval of fifteen years the old anxiety for individual perfection. For this desire was superseded by that of promoting the welfare of my family.

All this time, however, I was writing busily, and was gaining much money as well as winning great applause. And in everything I wrote I persistently taught what was for me the sole truth--that our chief object in life should be to secure our own happiness and that of our family. Then, five years ago, supervened a mood of mental lethargy. I grew despondent; my perplexity increased, and I was tormented by the constant recurrence of such questions as--"Why?" and "What afterwards?" And by degrees the questions took a more concrete form. "I now possess six thousand 'desyatins' of land in the government of Samara, and three hundred horses--what then?" I could find no answer. Then came the question, "What if I could excel Shakespeare, and Molière, and Gogol, and become the most celebrated the world has ever seen--what then?" Answer, there was none; yet I felt that I must find one in order to go on living.

Life had now lost its meaning, and was no longer real to me. I was a healthy and happy man, and yet so empty did life seem to me that I was afraid of being tempted to commit suicide, even though I had not the slightest intention to perpetrate such a deed. But, fearing lest the temptation might come upon me I hid a rope away out of my sight, and ceased carrying a gun in my walks.

III.--The Spirit of Despair

It was in my 50th year that the question "What is life" had reduced me to utter despair. Various queries clustered round this central interrogation. "Why should I live? Why should I do anything? Is there any signification in life that can overcome inevitable death?" I found that in human knowledge no real answer was forthcoming to such yearnings. None of the theories of the philosophers gave any satisfaction. In my search for a solution of life's problem I felt like a traveller lost in a forest, out of which he can find no issue.

I found that not only did Solomon declare that he hated life, for all is vanity and vexation of spirit; but that Sakya Muni, the Indian sage, equally decided that life was a great evil; while Socrates and Schopenhauer agree that annihilation is the only thing to be wished for. But neither these testimonies of great minds nor my own reasoning could induce me to destroy myself. For a force within me, combined with an instinctive consciousness of life, counteracted the feeling of despair and drew me out of my misery of soul. I felt that I must study life not merely as it was amongst those like myself, but as it was amongst the millions of the common people. I reflected that knowledge based on reason, the knowledge of the cultured, imparted no meaning to life, but that, on the other hand, amongst the masses of the common people there was an unreasoning consciousness of life which gave it a significance.

This unreasoning knowledge was the very faith which I was rejecting. It was faith in things I could not understand; in God, one yet three; in the creation of devils and angels. Such things seemed utterly contrary to reason. So I began to reflect that perhaps what I considered reasonable was after all not so, and what appeared unreasonable might not really be so.

I discovered one great error that I had perpetrated. I had been comparing life with life, that is, the finite with the finite, and the infinite with the infinite. The process was vain. It was like comparing force with force, matter with matter, nothing with nothing. It was like saying in mathematics that A equals A, or O equals O. Thus the only answer was "identity."

Now I saw that scientific knowledge would give no reply to my questions. I began to comprehend that though faith seemed to give unreasonable answers, these answers certainly did one important thing. They did at least bring in the relation of the finite to the infinite. I came to feel that in addition to the reasoning knowledge which I once reckoned to be the sole true knowledge, there was in every man also an unreasoning species of knowledge which makes life possible. That unreasoning knowledge is faith.

What is this faith? It is not only belief in God and in things unseen, but it is the apprehension of life's meaning. It is the force of life. I began to understand that the deepest source of human wisdom was to be found in the answers given by faith, that I had no reasonable right to reject them, and that they alone solved the problem of life.

IV.--Mistakes Apprehended

Nevertheless my heart was not lightened. I studied the writings of Buddhism, Islam, and Christianity. I also studied actual religious life by turning to the orthodox, the monks, and the Evangelicals who preach salvation through faith in a Redeemer. I asked what meaning was given for them to life by what they believed. But I could not accept the faith of any of these men, because I saw that it did not explain the meaning of life, but only obscured it. So I felt a return of the terrible feeling of despair.

Being unable to believe in the sincerity of men who did not live consistently with the doctrines they professed, and feeling that they were self-deceived, and, like myself, were satisfied with the lusts of the flesh, I began to draw near to the believers amongst the poor, simple, and ignorant, the pilgrims, monks, and peasants. I found that though their faith was mingled with much superstition, yet with them the whole life was a confirmation of the meaning of life which their faith gave them.

The more I contemplated the lives of these simple folk, the more deeply was I convinced of the reality of their faith, which I perceived to be a necessity for them, for it alone gave life a meaning and made it worth living. This was in direct opposition to what I saw in my own circle, where I marked the possibility of living without faith, for not one in a thousand professed to be a believer, while amongst the poorer classes not one in thousands was an unbeliever. The contradiction was extreme. In my class a tranquil death, without terror or despair, is rare; in that lower class, an uneasy death is a rare exception. I found that countless numbers in that lower mass of humanity had so understood the meaning of life that they were able both to live bearing contentedly the burdens of life, and to die peacefully.

The more I learned of these men of faith the more I liked them, and the easier I felt it so to live. For two years I lived in their fashion. Then the life of my own wealthy and cultured class became repellent to me, for it had lost all meaning whatever. It seemed like empty child's play, while the life of the working classes appeared to me in its true significance.

Now I began to apprehend where I had judged wrongly. My mistake was that I had applied an answer to my question concerning life which only concerned my own life, to life in general. My life had been but one long indulgence of my passions. It was evil and meaningless. Therefore such an answer had no application to life at large, but only to my individual life.

I understood the truth which the Gospel subsequently taught me more fully, that men loved darkness rather than light, because their deeds were evil. I understood that for the comprehension of life, it was essential that life should be something more than an evil and meaningless thing revealed by reason. Life must be considered as a whole, not merely in its parasitic excrescences. I felt that to be good was more important than to believe. I loved good men. I hated myself. I accepted truth. I understood that we were all more or less mad with the love of evil.

I looked at the animals, saw the birds building nests, living only to fly and to subsist. I saw how the goat, hare, and wolf live, but to feed and to nurture their young, and are contented and happy. Their life is a reasonable one. And man must gain his living like the animals do, only with this great difference, that if he should attempt this alone, he will perish. So he must labour for the good of all, not merely for himself.

I had not helped others. My life for thirty years had been that of a mere parasite. I had been contented to remain ignorant of the reason why I lived at all.

There is a supreme will in the universe. Some one makes the universal life his secret care. To know what that supreme will is, we must obey it implicitly. No reproaches against their masters come from the simple workers who do just what is required of them, though we are in the habit of regarding them as brutes. We, on the contrary, who think ourselves wise, consume the goods of our master while we do nothing willingly that he prescribes. We think that it would be stupid for us to do so.

What does such conduct imply? Simply that our master is stupid, or that we have no master.

V.--Feeling Versus Reason

Thus I was led at last to the conclusion that knowledge based on reason is fallacious, and that the knowledge of truth can be secured only by living. I had come to feel that I must live a real, not a parasitical life, and that the meaning of life could be perceived only by observation of the combined lives of the great human community.

The feelings of my mind during all these experiences and observations were mingled with a heart-torment which I can only describe as a searching after God. This search was a feeling rather than a course of reasoning. For it came from my heart, and was actually opposed to my way of thinking. Kant had shown the impossibility of proving the existence of God, yet I still hoped to find Him, and I still addressed Him in prayer. Yet I did not find Him whom I sought.

At times I contended against the reasoning of Kant and Schopenhauer, and argued that causation is not in the same category with thought and space and time. I argued that if I existed, there was a cause of my being, and that cause was the cause of all causes. Then I pondered the idea that the cause of all things is what is called God, and with all my powers I strove to attain a sense of the presence of this cause.

Directly I became conscious of a power over me I felt a possibility of living. Then I asked myself what was this cause, and what was my relation to what I called God? Simply the old familiar answer occurred to me, that God is the creator, the giver of all. Yet I was dissatisfied and fearful, and the more I prayed, the more convinced I was that I was not heard. In my despair I cried aloud for mercy, but no one had mercy on me, and I felt as if life stagnated within me.

Yet the conviction kept recurring that I must have appeared in this world with some motive on the part of some one who had sent me into it. If I had been sent here, who sent me? I had not been like a fledgling flung out of a nest to perish. Some one had cared for me, had loved me. Who was it? Again came the same answer, God. He knew and saw my fear, my despair, and so I passed from the consideration of the existence of God, which was proved, on to that of our relation towards him as our Redeemer through His Son. But I felt this to be a thing apart from me and from the world, and this God vanished like melting ice from my eyes. Again I was left in despair. I felt there was nothing left but to put an end to my life; yet I knew that I should never do this.

Thus did moods of joy and despair come and go, till one day, when I was listening to the sounds in a forest, and was still on that day in the early springtide seeking after God in my thoughts, a flash of joy illumined my soul. I realised that the conception of God was not God Himself. I felt that I had only truly lived when I believed in God. God is life. Live to seek God and life will not be without Him. The light that then shone never left me. Thus I was saved from self-destruction. Gradually I felt the glow and strength of life return to me. I renounced the life of my own class, because it was unreal, and its luxurious superfluity rendered comprehension of life impossible. The simple men around me, the working classes, were the real Russian people. To them I turned. They made the meaning of life clear. It may thus be expressed:--

Each of us is so created by God that he may ruin or save his soul. To save his soul, a man must live after God's word by humility, charity, and endurance, while renouncing all the pleasures of life. This is for the common people the meaning of the whole system of faith, traditionally delivered to them from the past and administered to them by the pastors of the Church.

PASQUALE VILLARI

The Life of Girolamo Savonarola

Pasquale Villari was born October 3, 1827, at Naples. At the age of twenty he produced his first literary effort, a Liberal manifesto against Neapolitan Bourbonism, which necessitated his flight from his native city. He retreated to Florence and there wrote his work on "Savonarola," which at once achieved fame and was translated into French, German, and English. His next great book was his "Macchiavelli." Villari had been appointed Professor of History at Nice, but left that city for a similar position at Florence. He entered political life in 1862, and has sat as a Parliamentary Deputy several times. In 1884 he was made senator, and in 1891 he was minister of public instruction in the Rudini Cabinet. Villari's essays on Dante are much esteemed. His treatise on "The First Two Centuries of Florentine History" is considered a standard work. All his books have been translated into our language by his English wife, Linda Villari, who is herself an accomplished authoress.

I.--1452-1494

The House of Savonarola derived its ancient origin from the city of Padua. In the beginning of the fifteenth century the family removed to Ferrara where, on September 21, 1452, the subject of this biography, Girolamo Savonarola, first saw the light. He was the third of seven children of his parents. The lad became the favourite of his grandfather, Michele, who wished to see him become a great physician, and devoted most assiduous care on the task of training his intellect. But unfortunately the grandfather soon passed away, and Girolamo's studies were then directed by his father, who began to instruct him in philosophy.

The natural sciences were then only branches of philosophy, and the latter, though employed as preliminary to the study of medicine, was purely scholastic. The books which came into the hands of the young Savonarola were the works of St. Thomas Aquinas and the Arabic commentaries on Aristotle. He was specially fascinated with the works of St. Thomas, but besides literature he studied music. He also composed verses.

All particulars, however, of Savonarola's boyhood are unfortunately lacking. But we can form a vivid idea of the surroundings which must have influenced him. Ferrara was then the splendid capital of the House of Este, with 100,000 inhabitants and a court which was one of the first in Italy, and was continually visited by princes, emperors, and popes. The lad must have witnessed gorgeous pageants, like the two which occurred on visits of Pope Pius II., in 1459 and 1460. But during all this period Savonarola was entirely absorbed in studying the Scriptures and St. Thomas Aquinas, allowing himself no recreation save playing sad music on his lute, or writing verses expressing, not without force and simplicity, the griefs of his heart.

The contrasts that the youth witnessed between the magnificence ostentatiously displayed and the evidences of tyranny in palaces and castles in whose dungeons were immured numerous victims, clanking their chains, made indelible impressions on his mind. Conducted once by his parents to the ducal palace at Ferrara, he firmly refused ever to enter its doors again. With singular spiritual fervour in one so young, Savonarola surrendered his whole heart and soul to religious sentiments and exercises. To him worldly life, as he saw all Ferrara absorbed in its gaieties, became utterly repellent, and a sermon to which he listened from an Augustinian friar determined him to adopt the monastic life.

April 24, 1475, when his parents were absent from home attending the festival of St. George, he ran away to Bologna and presented himself at the Monastery of St. Dominic, begging that he might be admitted for the most menial service. He was instantly received, and at once began to prepare for his novitiate. In this retreat he submitted himself to the severest penances and discipline and displayed such excessive zeal and devotion as to win the admiration of the monks, who at times believed him to be rapt in a holy trance.

II.--1475-1481

Savonarola's sojourn at Bologna in the Dominican Monastery lasted for seven years, during which his spirit was occupied not only with faith and prayer, but with deep meditation on the miserable condition of the Church. His soul was stirred to wrathful indignation. The shocking corruption of the Papacy, dating from the death of Pius II. in 1464, was to reach its climax under Alexander VI. The avarice of Paul II. was soon noted by all the world, and so boundless was the profligacy of his successor, Sixtus IV., that no deed was too scandalous for him to commit.

The state of Italy as well as of the Church was miserable, and the soul of the young monk was filled with horror-stricken grief, relieved only by study and prayer. He had been much occupied in instructing the novices, but now he was promoted to the function of preacher. In 1481 he was sent by his superiors to preach in Ferrara. Nothing is known of the effect of the sermons he delivered at that time and place. Savonarola had not yet developed his gifts of oratory. He was driven from Ferrara by an outbreak of war with the Venetians, and repaired to Florence, where, in the Monastery of St. Mark the brightest as well as the saddest years of his life were to be spent. The Monastery contained the first public library established in Italy, which was kept in excellent order by the monks.

Savonarola was half intoxicated with joy during his first days in Florence. He was charmed by the soft lines of the Tuscan hills and the beauty of the Tuscan speech. Lorenzo the Magnificent had been ruling Florence for many years and was then at the climacteric of his fame. Under his sway everything appeared to prosper. Enemies had been imprisoned or banished, and factions had ceased to distract the city. Lorenzo's shameless licentiousness was condoned by reason of his brilliancy, his patronage of art and literature, and his lavish public entertainments.

Greek scholars, driven westward by the fall of Constantinople, sought refuge at the Florentine court. The fine arts flourished and a Platonic Academy was established. It was even proposed that the Pope should canonise Plato as a saint. In fact that period witnessed the inauguration of modern culture.

III.--1481-1490

After the first few days in Florence, Savonarola again began to experience the feeling of isolation. For he speedily detected the unbelief and frivolity under the surface of the intellectual culture of the people. Even in St. Mark's Monastery there was no real religion. Savonarola was soon invited to preach the Lenten sermons in St. Lorenzo. His discourses produced no special effect, for the Florentines preferred preachers who indulged in Pagan quotations and rhetorical elegancies rather than in expatiating in the precepts of Christianity. But a stirring event was at hand.

Savonarola was sent by his superiors to Reggio to attend a Chapter of the Dominicans. During the discussion he was suddenly impelled to rise to his feet and to plunge into a powerful declamation against the corruptions of the Church and the clergy which transfixed his hearers with astonishment. This outburst was a revelation of his extraordinary powers. It instantly secured his fame and from that moment many sought his acquaintance.

Savonarola's mind from that moment became strangely excited and it is not surprising that he should have seen many visions. He on one occasion saw the heavens open. A panorama of the calamities of the Church passed before him and he heard a voice charging him to proclaim them to the people. In that year, 1484, Pope Sixtus died. The election of his successor, Innocent VIII. destroyed the hopes of honest men. For the new Pope no longer disguised his children under the appellation of nephews, but openly acknowledged them as his sons, conferring on them the title of princes.

We may imagine the storms of emotion excited in the soul of Savonarola. Fortunately, he was sent to preach Lenten sermons at San Gimignano, the "City of the Grey Towers" in the Siennese hills. Here he found his true vocation. His words flowed freely and were eloquent and effective. Next he was sent to Brescia, where his predictions of coming terrors and his exhortations to repentance produced a profound impression. During the sack of that same city in 1512 by the fierce soldiers of Gaston de Foix, when 6,000 citizens were slain, the stricken people vividly remembered the Apocalyptic denunciations and predictions of the preacher from Ferrara.

Through the wonderful success of these Lenten sermons the name of Savonarola became known throughout Italy, and he no longer felt uncertain as to his proper mission. Yet, the more popular he became the greater was his humility and the more ardent was his devotion to prayer. He seemed when engaged in prayer frequently to lapse into a trance, and tradition even alleges that at such times a bright halo was seen to encircle his head.

IV.--1491

Returning to Florence, Savonarola by his Lenten sermons in 1491 drew immense crowds to the Duomo. From that moment he became the paramount power in the pulpit. His vivid imagery and his predictions of coming troubles seemed to produce a magical effect on the minds of the people. But this growing influence was a source of considerable vexation to Lorenzo de' Medici and his friends. Savonarola vehemently denounced the greed of the clergy and their neglect of spiritual life for the sake of mere external ceremonialism, and he with equal insistence inveighed against the corruption of public manners. As Lorenzo was already considered a tyrant by many of the citizens, and as he was universally charged with having corrupted the magistrates and appropriated the public and private funds, it was generally inferred that Savonarola had had the audacity to make allusion to him.

This only enhanced the Friar's reputation and in July, 1491, he was elected Prior of St. Mark's. The office made him both more prominent than before and also more independent. He showed this to be the case by at once refusing to go according to custom to do homage to the Magnificent, declaring that he owed his election to God alone, and to God only would he vow obedience. Lorenzo was deeply offended, yet he judged it discreet rather to win the new Prior over by kindness than to wage war with him.

The Seignior only deepened Savonarola's contempt by sending rich gifts to the convent and by sending five of the chief citizens to him in order to induce him to modify the strain of his preaching. The gifts were immediately distributed among the poor, and Savonarola in a pulpit allusion observed that a faithful dog does not cease barking in his master's defence because a bone is flung him. To the five citizens, who hinted to the Prior that he might be sent into exile, he replied that they should bid Lorenzo do penance for his sins, for God was no respecter of persons and did not spare the princes of the earth.

Wonderful was the effect of Savonarola's preaching on the corrupt and pagan society of Florence. His natural, spontaneous, heart-stirring eloquence, with its exalted imagery and outbursts of righteous indignation, was entirely unprecedented in that era of pedantry and simulation of the classic and heathen oratory. The scholastic jargon indulged in by the preachers of the time was utterly unintelligible to the common people. Savonarola's voice was the only one that addressed the multitude in familiar and fascinating tones and in an accent that evinced true affection for the people. They knew that he alone fought for truth and was fervently devoted to goodness. Thus he was the one truly eloquent preacher of the time, who restored pulpit preaching to its pristine honour, and he well deserves to be styled the first orator of modern times.

V.--1492-1494

A wasting disease from which Lorenzo suffered had by the beginning of April, 1492, made such inroads as to end all hopes of his recovery. The Magnificent turned his thoughts to religion and suddenly asked to confess to Savonarola. Though astonished at the request, the Prior acceded to it and found Lorenzo in great agitation, which he sought to calm by reminding the sick man of the goodness and mercy of God.

A painful scene ensued. Savonarola added that three things were needful. First, a living faith in God's mercy. Secondly, Lorenzo must restore all his ill-gotten wealth, or at least command his sons to do it in his name. Lastly, he must restore liberty to the people of Florence. The sick man, collecting all his remaining strength, angrily turned his back on his Confessor, who at once left his presence. On April 8, 1492, the Magnificent, in an agony of remorse, breathed his last. On July 25 of the same year Pope Innocent VIII. expired.

The next Pope, Alexander VI., was notorious for his avarice and his profligacy. The announcement of his elevation to the papal chair was received throughout Italy with dismay. The worst apprehensions were soon fulfilled, for the Pope proved to be guilty of shocking extortion, the object of which was to provide more lavishly for his dissolute children.

This deplorable state of things caused men to look wistfully to Savonarola. The times he had foretold seemed to be at hand, and the excitement was intensified by two visions which he declared had been manifested to him as celestial revelations. He had seen a sword in the sky and had heard voices proclaiming mercy to the righteous and retribution to the wicked.

In the other vision a black cross hung over the city of Rome, stretching its arms over the whole earth. On it was written, "The Cross of God's wrath." But from Jerusalem rose a golden cross, inscribed, "The Cross of God's compassion." Discontent was growing in Florence. The insolence and the rapacity of Pietro de' Medici increased. In the autumn of that year Savonarola delivered a famous course of sermons on Noah's Ark, warning all to take refuge from the coming flood in the mystical Ark of mercy. The flood came indeed, for suddenly all Florence was startled as if by a thunderclap by the news that a foreign army was pouring over the Alps for the conquest of Italy. The terror was overwhelming. Italy was unprepared, for the princes had no efficient armies for resistance.

The invader was the new King of France, the young and adventurous Charles VIII. His army was a model to all Europe in the art of war. It possessed weapons of the latest invention and its main strength lay in its splendid infantry. Florence was entered without a blow, and King Charles demanded as a ransom a far larger sum than the Republic could pay. He remained day after day in the city, showing no inclination to depart. Then was manifested a proof of the wonderful influence of Savonarola's personality.

The Prior being earnestly entreated by the citizens to ask the French king to depart, he readily undertook the mission and presented himself to Charles, who, surrounded by his barons, received him cordially and listened graciously to his proposal. Savonarola admonished him not to bring ruin on the city and the anger of the Lord on himself.

The Prior's overtures were completely successful, for on November 28, the king departed with his army. And now all was changed in Florence. The partisans of the Medici had vanished magically and Savonarola ruled the city at the head of the popular party. He speedily proposed a new form of government suggesting as the best model, a Grand Council like that of Venice. The new Government was formed of a Grand Council and a Council of Eighty answering to an Assembly of the People and a Senate. All the proposals of the Prior were adopted, and laws were framed almost in his own words.

Germs of civil discord were not lacking, and these soon developed so as to divide Florence into factions, the two chief of these being the Whites, who were favourable to popular liberty, and the Greys, who were adherents of the Medici. The latter were dangerous and treacherous enemies of Savonarola and of the Republic. For a time the Prior's preaching confounded his foes, for it completely changed the aspect of the city. The women cast off their jewels and dressed simply; young profligates were transformed into sober, religious men, the churches were filled with people at prayer, and the Bible was diligently read.

Now came danger from without. The departure of the French had endangered the security of Florence. The Pope and Venice desired the reinstatement of the fallen tyrant Pietro de' Medici, and he prepared to attack the city. But he was foiled by the energy to which the Prior roused the Florentines for measures of defence. Meantime, Savonarola once more displayed his noble independence by spurning the offer on the part of the Pope of a Cardinal's hat. And terrible in their vehemence and audacity were his denunciations against the vices of Rome, delivered in his Lenten sermons of 1496.

In his usual strain, but with increasing power, Savonarola graphically and vividly described the woes of Italy, as though he were gifted with prophetic vision. One of his sermons was interdicted by the Pope, but the preacher modified nothing and defied the Vatican. And now, while the enthusiasm of his followers was developing into fanaticism, the hatred of his enemies was approaching a climax, and the war was waxing furious.

The fame of this marvellous preacher was now extending throughout the world by means of his printed sermons. Even the Sultan of Turkey commanded them to be translated into Turkish for his own study. Of course the individual aim of Savonarola was simply to be the regenerator of religion. The Florentines, however, adulated him as the real founder of the free Republic. Hence they displayed immense ardour in defending him against the Pope, seeing that thus they were upholding their own freedom, because the Pope was aiming at reinstating the Medici in Florence.

The Pope had hoped that the Prior would moderate his tone, but this was only more aggressive than ever, and threatening messages arrived from the Vatican. Attempts by his friends, some of them of high and influential position, to defend him, only the more enraged Pope Alexander Borgia. He summoned a consistory of fourteen Dominican theologians who were ordered to investigate Savonarola's conduct and doctrine. The strange issue was he was charged with having been the cause of all the misfortunes that had befallen Pietro de' Medici.

After Lent the Prior went to preach a course of sermons at Prato, and on his return to Florence he delivered a sermon in the Hall of the Greater Council in the presence of all the magistrates and leading citizens of the city, in which he openly and courageously defied all the wrath of Alexander Borgia. Then he once more set himself to the work of serving the Republic, though, as the sequel shows, he was fated to meet with a base reward.

Commerce and industry had been paralysed in Florence by the incessant commotions of past years. The immense sums paid to the French king had together with sums spent on war drained the public resources and lowered the credit of the Republic. And now famine was threatened, for the people in the rural districts were pinched with hunger. The starving peasantry began to flock in great numbers into the city, so that the misery increased. Terror was occasioned by a few cases of death from plague. Florence was at war with Pisa, but without success, for many of her mercenary soldiers were deserting and the forces besieging Pisa were dwindling for lack of supplies.

Fresh adversities were in store for the Florentines. Though the rumours of a second invasion of Italy by King Charles proved unfounded, for he renounced all idea of returning, new enemies arose. The Emperor Maximilian was marching towards the frontier, and the Pope felt encouraged to enter into open war with the Florentines. His forces and the troops from Sienna actually attempted an incursion into the territories of the Republic, but they suffered repeated repulses, and at length were put to flight. But this conflict weakened still more the forces before Pisa, at which city Maximilian arrived with 1,000 foot soldiers, receiving a cordial welcome from the Pisans.

The Florentines did not quail before the storm. Their courage never failed. They collected fresh stores and sent abundant provisions to the camp. But the hatred of the Pope grew more intense, especially against Savonarola, who, however, had not returned to the pulpit, being actuated by a wish not to accentuate the situation. For the general misery in Florence daily increased and the plague was extending its ravages. The hospitals were full. And the faction against Savonarola, named the Arrabbiati, seemed positively to regard the distress with glee, for these fanatics went about crying aloud, "At last we can all perceive how we have been deceived! This is the happiness that the Friar predicted for Florence!" Moreover they proclaimed that now was the time to overthrow the Government.

But the Seigniory entreated Savonarola to come forth again from his retirement. He entered the pulpit on October 28, but only to look on people whose faces were marked by distress and terror. Yet his sermons administered such comfort to the citizens who in the majority still adhered to him, though the Arrabbiati mocked at his words. Temporary relief was at hand, for suddenly, as if by a miracle, ships arrived from Marseilles bringing long-expected reinforcements and supplies of corn. The people were frantic with joy and solemn thanksgivings were offered in the churches.

The Pope was now designing measures to entrap the Prior. A new Vicar-General was appointed with power which would invest him with such authority over Savonarola that the latter would lose his independence. But he displayed no disposition to yield to Rome. On the contrary, he delivered in the Duomo those eight magnificent, fearless, and immortal sermons which intensified the bitter struggle with Rome, while for the time being they made the great Reformer's name and authority again ascendant, and rendered the popular party once more master of the situation, notwithstanding the strategy of the Pope and the machinations of the factions.

VII.--1497-1498

During Lent, 1497, Savonarola continued his course of sermons on Ezekiel, and in these discourses he said much that bore on the conflict with Rome, now daily growing more virulent. He inveighed against the temporal wealth of the Church and launched many accusations against Rome. The impression produced was the deeper because of the general presentiment in men's minds of the coming uprising of Christendom against the abominations of Rome.

Savonarola now daily expected to be excommunicated and he was determined to defy the Pope. The plague increased in Florence and the Seigniory prohibited preaching in the churches for a time, but Savonarola persisted in preaching on Ascension Day. The factions were infuriated. They denied the pulpit with filth and draped it with the skin of an ass, and threatened the life of the Prior. His friends implored him not to preach at the risk of his life. He refused to yield, but a fearful riot took place in the church which was talked of through all Italy.

The storm was now gathering. The fury of the factions increased, as also did the wrath of the Pope. At length, on May 13, the excommunicatory brief was despatched from Rome, directed against a "certain Fra Girolamo Savonarola who had disseminated pernicious doctrines to the scandal and grief of simple souls." The event threw all Florence into confusion. The Arrabbiati were triumphant. But the city was filled with lamentation and disorder. The rabble rejoiced. The churches were quickly deserted; the taverns were filled; immorality returned as if magically; and again women attired in dazzling finery paraded the streets. In less than a month, so rapid was the transformation, Florence seemed to have relapsed into the days of the Magnificent, and piety and patriotism were alike forgotten.

Meantime, the Prior was calm and composed and took measures for his defence. He wrote an Epistle against surreptitious excommunication, addressed to all Christians beloved of God. He followed it by a second letter, also breathing courage and defiance. A conflict ensued. The Arrabbiati sent accusations against the Prior to Rome, while the Seigniory sought to vindicate him, most of the members, newly elected, being his friends. The plague grew so terrible that on some days there were a hundred deaths. In the autumn it abated, and gradually disappeared. Savonarola's energy in fighting the pestilence was unwearied throughout.

The Prior soon commenced to preach again. On Christmas Day he put an end to all suspense as to his policy by thrice performing high mass, afterwards leading his monks in solemn procession through St. Mark's Square. He continued to issue new tracts and to preach regularly. But on February 26 the Pope announced that Savonarola's preaching should be tolerated no longer. The Prior was conscious that the end was near. His last sermon was delivered, after he had preached in Florence for eight years, on March 18, 1498. His adherents were terrified, and seemed to vanish.

On April 8, Palm Sunday, the Arrabbiati attacked St. Mark's Convent. Savonarola was seized and bound by a brutal rabble, and he and two of his monks were lodged in prison. Cruel proceedings followed. For a whole month he was brought day after day to examination and he was repeatedly subjected to torture. The Pope's Commissioners were never able to extract from him any confession of guilt. Savonarola was from first to last unflinchingly consistent with himself.

On May 22 sentence of death was passed on Savonarola, on Fra Silvestro, and on Fra Domenico. They prepared to face death firmly and well. The tragedy was enacted next morning. Three platforms had been erected on the steps of the Ringhiera, on which sat the Bishop of Vasona, the Apostolic Commissioners, and the Gonfaliero with the Council of Eight. On a gibbet in the form of a cross hung three chains, and combustibles were piled beneath. Sad and solemn was the silence of the vast throng assembled in the Piazza, excepting where members of the factions were raging like wild beasts and venting indecent blasphemies.

The three friars were publicly stripped of their monkish robes and degraded. Tranquilly they mounted the scaffold, the dregs of the populace assailing them with vile words. But silence reigned at the moment of the execution. As soon as life was extinct the flames were kindled beneath the bodies of the three victims. The tragic and awful spectacle elicited bitter grief amongst the people on the one side, while cries of wild exultation were raised on the other.

JOHN WESLEY

Journal

John Wesley, who was born June 17, 1703, at Epworth, and who died in London March 2, 1791, was the son of a Lincolnshire rector. His history covers practically the whole of the eighteenth century, of which he was one of the most typical personalities, as he was certainly the most strenuous figure. His career was absolutely without parallel, for John Wesley, as an itinerating clergyman, and as the propagator of that mission of Methodism which he founded, travelled on his preaching tours for forty years, mostly on horseback. He paid more turnpike fees than any man that ever bestrode a horse, and 8,000 miles constituted his annual record for many a year, during each of which he preached on the average 5,000 times. John Wesley received a classical education at Charterhouse and Christ Church, Oxford, and all through his wonderful life of endurance and adventure, of devotion and consecration, remained a scholar and a gentleman. His "Journal" is valuable for its pictures of the England of his day, as well as for his own simple and unpretending record of his experiences. Wesley made religion his business and incorporated it into the national life. Of him Mr. Augustine Birrell says:--"No man lived nearer the centre than John Wesley. Neither Clive nor Pitt, neither Mansfield nor Johnson. You cannot cut him out of our national life. No single figure influenced so many minds, no single voice touched so many hearts. No other man did such a life's work for England."

The Holy Club

In November 1729, at which time I came to reside at Oxford, Mr. Morgan, my brother, myself, and one more, agreed to spend three or four evenings in a week together. Our design was to read over the classics, which we had before read in private, on common nights, and on Sunday some book in divinity. In the summer following, Mr. M. told me he had called at the gaol, to see a man who was condemned for killing his wife; and that, from the talk he had with one of the debtors, he verily believed it would do much good, if any one would be at the pains of now and then speaking with them.

This he so frequently repeated, that on August 24, 1730, my brother and I walked with him to the castle. We were so well satisfied with our conversation there, that we agreed to go thither once or twice a week; which we had not done long, before he desired me to go with him to see a poor sick woman in the town.

I next proposed to Mr. Gerard, the Bishop of Oxford's chaplain, who took care of any prisoners condemned to die, that I intended to preach in the prison once a month, if the bishop approved. Our design was approved and permission was granted. Soon after a gentleman of Merton College, who was one of our little company, now consisting of five persons, acquainted us that he had been much rallied the day before for being a member of the Holy Club, and that it was become a common topic of mirth at his college, where they had found out several of our customs, to which we were ourselves utter strangers.

I corresponded with my father, and from him received encouragement, so that we still continued to meet as usual, and to do what service we could to the prisoners, and to two or three poor families in the town.

A Missioner to Georgia

1735. Oct. 14. Mr. Benjamin Ingham, of Queen's College, Oxford; Mr. Charles Delamotte, son of a London merchant, my brother Charles, and myself, took boat for Gravesend, in order to embark for Georgia. Our end in leaving our country was singly this, to save our souls; to live wholly to the glory of God. In the afternoon we found the "Simmonds" off Gravesend, and immediately went on board.

Oct. 17. I began to learn German, in order to converse with the 26 Germans on board. On Sunday I preached extempore and then administered the Lord's supper to seven communicants.

Oct. 20. Believing the denying ourselves might be helpful, we wholly left off the use of flesh and wine, and confined ourselves to vegetable food, chiefly rice and biscuit.

1736. Feb. 5. After a passage in which storms were frequent, between two and three in the afternoon, God brought us all safe into the Savannah river. We cast anchor near Tybee Island, where the groves of pines along the shore made an agreeable prospect, showing, as it were, the bloom of spring in the depth of winter.

Sunday, March 7. I entered upon my ministry at Savannah. I do here bear witness against myself, that when I saw the number of people crowding into the church, the deep attention with which they received the word, and the seriousness that sat on all their faces, I could hardly believe that the greater part of them would hereafter trample under foot that word, and say all manner of evil falsely against him that spake it.

March 30. Mr. Delamotte and I began to try, whether life might not be as well sustained by one sort as by a variety of food. We chose to make the experiment with bread, and were never more vigorous and healthy than while we tasted nothing else.

June 30. I hoped a door was opened for my main design, which was to preach the gospel to the Indians, and I purposed to go immediately to the Choctaws, the least polished, that is, the least corrupted of the tribes. On my informing Lieutenant-Governor Oglethorpe of our wish, he objected, alleging not only danger from the French, but also the inexpediency of leaving Savannah without a minister. These objections I related to our brethren, who were all of opinion, "We ought not to go yet."

Warrant for Wesley's Arrest

July 3. Preaching at Charlestown, immediately after communion I mentioned to Mrs. Williamson (Mr. Causton's niece) some things I thought reprovable in her behaviour. At this she appeared extremely angry.

Aug. 7. I repelled Mrs. Williamson from the holy communion. And next day Mr. Recorder, of Savannah, issued out a warrant for my arrest. Mr. Jones, the constable, served the warrant, and carried me before Mr. Bailiff Parker and Mr. Recorder. I was told that I must appear at the next court. Mr. Causton came to my house and declared that the affront had been offered to him; that he espoused the cause of his niece; that he was ill-used, and that he would have satisfaction if it was to be had in this world.

To many persons Mr. Causton declared that "Mr. Wesley had repelled Sophy from holy communion purely out of revenge, because he had made proposals of marriage to her which she had rejected, and married Mr. Williamson." But when the case came on the grand jury, having heard the charge, declared themselves thoroughly persuaded that it was an artifice of Mr. Causton's designed "rather to blacken the character of Mr. Wesley, than to free the colony from religious tyranny, as he had been pleased to term it."

Oct. 7. I consulted my friends whether God did not call me to return to England. I had found no possibility of instructing the Indians. They were unanimous that I ought to go, but not yet. But subsequently they agreed with me that the time was come.

In London Again

1738. Feb. 1. Landed at Deal. It is now two years and almost four months since I left my native country. After reading prayers and explaining a portion of Scripture to a large company at the inn, I left Deal, and came in the evening to Feversham. I here read prayers and explained the second lesson to a few of those who were called Christians, but were indeed more savage in their behaviour than the wildest Indians I have yet met with.

Feb. 26. Sunday. I preached at six in the morning at St. Lawrence's, London; at ten, in St. Catherine Cree's; and in the afternoon at St. John's, Wapping. I believe it pleased God to bless the first sermon most, because it gave most offence.

March 4. I found my brother at Oxford, and with him Peter Böhler; by whom, in the great hand of God, I was, on Sunday, the 5th, clearly convinced of unbelief, of the want of that faith whereby alone we are saved. Immediately it struck into my mind, "Leave off preaching. How can you preach to others who have not faith yourself?" I asked Böhler whether he thought I should leave it off or not. He answered, "By no means." I asked, "But what can I preach?" He said, "Preach faith till you have it; and then, because you have it, you will preach faith."

Accordingly, Monday, 6, I began preaching this new doctrine, though my soul started back from the work. The first person to whom I offered salvation through faith alone, was a prisoner under sentence of death.

On Tuesday 25, I spoke clearly and fully at Blendon to Mr. Delamotte's family of the nature and fruits of faith. Mr. Broughton and my brother were there. Mr. Broughton's great objection was, he could never think that I had not faith, who had done and suffered such things. My brother was very angry, and told me I did not know what mischief I had done by talking thus. And, indeed, it did please God to kindle a fire which I trust shall never be extinguished.

On May 1 our little society began, which afterwards met in Fetter Lane. May 3. My brother had a long and particular conversation with Peter Böhler. And it now pleased God to open his eyes; so that he also saw clearly what was the nature of that one true living faith, thereby alone, "through grace we are saved."

Sunday 7. I preached at St. Lawrence's in the morning; and afterwards at St. Catherine Cree's. I was enabled to speak strong words at both; and was therefore the less surprised at being informed I was not to preach any more in either of those churches. I was likewise after preaching the next Sunday at St. Ann's, Aldersgate, and the following Sunday at St. John's, Wapping and at St. Bennett's, Paul's Wharf, that at these churches I must preach no more.

1739. March 28. A letter from Mr. Whitefield, and another from Mr. Seward, pressed me to come to Bristol. I reached Bristol March 31 and met Mr. Whitefield there. I could scarcely at first reconcile myself to the strange way of preaching in the fields, of which he set me the example, for all my life I should have thought the saving of souls almost a sin, if it had not been done in a church; but I now proclaimed in the highways the glad tidings of salvation speaking in the open air to about three thousand people.

May 9. We took possession of a piece of ground in the Horse Fair, Bristol, where it was designed to build a room large enough to contain both the societies of Nicholas and Baldwin Street; and on May 12 the first stone was laid with thanksgiving. The responsibility of payment I took entirely on myself. Money I had not, it is true, nor any human prospect of procuring it; but I knew "the earth is the Lord's and the fulness thereof."

Beau Nash Argues with Wesley

June 5. There was great expectation at Bath of what a noted man was to do to me there. Many appeared surprised and were sinking apace into seriousness when their champion came up to me and asked by what authority I did these things. I replied, "By the authority of Jesus Christ, conveyed to me by the Archbishop of Canterbury, when he laid his hands on me." He said, "This is contrary to the Act of Parliament; this is a conventicle. Besides, your preaching frightens people out of their wits."

"Give me leave, Sir, to ask, is not your name Nash?" "My name is Nash." An old woman said to him, "You, Mr. Nash, take care of your body; we take care of our souls; and for the food of our souls we come here." He replied not a word, but walked away.

"All the World My Parish"

All this time I had many thoughts concerning my manner of ministering; but after frequently laying it before the Lord, I could not but adhere to what I had some time since written to a friend--"I look on all the world as my parish; thus far I mean, that, in whatever part I am of it, I judge it meet to declare to all who are willing to hear, the glad tidings of salvation."

June 14. I went with Mr. Whitefield to Blackheath, where were, I believe, 12,000 people. He a little surprised me by desiring me to preach in his stead; and I was greatly moved with compassion for the rich that were there, to whom I made a particular application. Some of them seemed to attend, while others drove away their coaches from so uncouth a preacher.

Sunday 24. As I was riding to Rose Green, near Bristol, my horse suddenly pitched on his head, and rolled over and over. I received no other hurt than a little bruise on my side; which for the present I felt not, but preached without pain to seven thousand people.

Sept. 16. I preached at Moorfields to about ten thousand, and at Kennington Common to near twenty thousand. At both places I described the real difference between what is generally called Christianity and the real old Christianity, which under the new name of Methodism is now everywhere spoken against.

The Colliers of Kingswood

Nov. 27. Few persons have lived in the west of England who have not heard of the colliers of Kingswood, famous for neither regarding God nor man. The scene is changed. Kingswood does not now, as a year ago, resound with cursing and blasphemy. Peace and love reign there since the preaching of the Gospel in the spring. Great numbers of the people are gentle, mild, and easy to be entreated.

1745. July 3. At Gwennap, in Cornwall, I was seized for a soldier. As I was reading my text a man rode up and cried "Seize the preacher for his Majesty's service." As the people would not do it, he leaped off his horse, and caught hold of my cassock, crying, "I take you to serve his Majesty." He walked off with me and talked with me for some time, but then let me go.

In Ireland

1748. April 9. I preached in Connaught, a few miles from Athlone. Many heard, but, I doubt, felt nothing. The Shannon comes within a mile of the house where I preached. I think there is not such another river in Europe. It is here ten miles wide, though only thirty miles from its source. There are many islands in it, once well inhabited, but now mostly desolate. In almost every one is a ruined church; in one, the remains of no fewer than seven.

1750. May 21. At Bandon the mob burnt me in effigy. Yet, though Dr. B. tried to stir up the people against me more and more, and a clergyman, said to be in drink, opposed me, and some young gentlemen came on the scene with pistols in their hands, I was enabled to preach. God gave me great peace in Bandon, in spite of these efforts against me.

May 31. I rode to Rathcormuck. There being a great burying in the afternoon, to which people came from all parts, I preached after Mr. Lloyd had read the service. I was exceedingly shocked at (what I had only heard of before) the Irish howl which followed. It was not a song, as I supposed, but a dismal, inarticulate yell, set up at the grave by four shrill-voiced women, hired for the purpose. But I saw not one that shed a tear; for that, it seems, was not in their bargain.

Clothing French Prisoners

1759. Oct. 1. At Bristol. I had ridden in about seven months not less than 2,400 miles. On Monday, Oct. 15, I went to Knowle, a mile from Bristol, to see the French prisoners. About 1,100 were there confined, with only a little dirty straw to lie on, so that they died like rotten sheep. I was much affected, and after I had preached the sum of £18 was contributed immediately, which next day we made up to £24. With this we bought linen and woollen cloth, and this was made up into clothing for the prisoners. Presently after, the Corporation of Bristol sent a large quantity of mattresses and blankets. And it was not long before contributions were set on foot in London, and other parts of the country; so that I believe that from this time they were pretty well provided with the necessaries of life.

Gwennap's Famous Amphitheatre

1766. Sept. 14. I preached in the natural amphitheatre at Gwennap; far the finest I know in the kingdom. It is a round, green hollow, gently shelving down, about 50 feet deep; but I suppose it is 200 feet across one way, and nearly 300 the other. I believe there were full 20,000 people; and, the evening being calm, all could hear.

1770. April 21. I rode slowly on this and the following days through Staffordshire and Cheshire to Manchester. In this journey, as well as in many others, I observed a mistake that almost universally prevails; and I desire all travellers to take good notice of it, which may save them from both trouble and danger. Near 30 years ago I was thinking, "How is it that no horse ever stumbles while I am reading?" (History, poetry, and philosophy I commonly read on horseback, having other employment at other times.) No account can possibly be given but this: because then I throw the reins on his neck. I then set myself to observe; and I aver, that in riding above 100,000 miles I scarce ever remember my horse (except two, that would fall head over heels anyway) to fall, or make a considerable stumble, while I rode with a slack rein. To fancy, therefore, that a tight rein prevents stumbling, is a capital blunder.

1771. Jan. 23. For what cause I know not to this day, my wife set out for Newcastle, purposing "never to return." *Non eam reliqui: non dimisi: non revocabo.* (I did not desert her: I did not send her away: I will not recall her.)

The American War

1775. In November I published the following letter in Lloyd's "Evening Post":

"Sir--I have been seriously asked from what motive I published my *Calm Address to the American Colonies*? I seriously answer, Not to get money;

not to get preferment; not to please any man living; least of all to inflame any; just the contrary. I contributed my mite towards putting out the flame that rages. This I have more opportunity to see than any man in England. I see with pain to what a height this already rises, in every part of the nation. And I see many pouring oil into the flame, by crying out, 'How unjustly, how cruelly, the King is using the poor Americans; who are only contending for their liberty, and for their legal privileges.'

"Now there is no possible way to put out this flame, or hinder its rising higher and higher, but to show that the Americans are not used either cruelly or unjustly; that they are not injured at all, seeing they are not contending for liberty (this they had, even in its full extent, both civil and religious); neither for any legal privileges; for they enjoy all that their charters grant. But what they contend for is, the illegal privilege of being exempt from parliamentary taxation. A privilege this, which no charter ever gave to any American colony yet; which no charter can give, unless it be confirmed both by King, Lords, and Commons; which in fact our Colonies never had; which they never claimed till the present reign; and probably they would not have claimed now, had they not been incited thereto by letters from England. One of these was read, according to the desire of the writer, not only at the Continental Congress but likewise in many congregations throughout the Combined Provinces. It advised them to seize upon all the King's officers; and exhorted them, 'Stand valiantly, only for six months, and in that time there will be such commotions in England that you may have your own terms.' This being the real state of the question, without any colouring or exaggeration, what impartial man can either blame the King, or commend the Americans? With this view, to quench the fire, by laying the blame where it was due, the 'Calm Address' was written.

Your humble servant,

JOHN WESLEY."

City Road Chapel Begun

1777. April 21. The day appointed for laying the foundation of the new chapel. The rain befriended us much, by keeping away thousands who proposed to be there. But there were still such multitudes, that it was with great difficulty I got through them, to lay the first stone. Upon this was a plate of brass (covered with another stone) on which was engraved, "This was laid by Mr. John Wesley, on April 21, 1777." Probably this will be seen no more, by any human eye; but will remain there, till the earth and the works thereof are burned up.

1778. Dec. 17. Having been many times desired, for near forty years, to publish a magazine, I at length complied, and now began to collect materials for it. If it once begin, I incline to think it will not end but with my life. Just at this time there was a combination among many of the postchaise drivers on the Bath road, especially those that drove in the night, to deliver their passengers into each other's hands. One driver stopped at the spot they had appointed, when another waited to attack the chaise. In consequence of this many were robbed; but I had a good Protector still. I have travelled all roads, by day and by night, for these forty years, and never was interrupted yet.

June 28. I am this day 75 years old; and I do not find myself, blessed be God, any weaker than I was at 25. This also hath God wrought.

Attended by Felons

1779. July 21. When I came to Coventry, I found notice had been given for my preaching in the park; but the heavy rain prevented. I sent to the Mayor, desiring the use of the town-hall. He refused; but the same day gave the use of it to a dancing-master. I then went to the women's market. Many soon gathered together and listened with all seriousness. I preached there again the next morning, and again in the evening. Then I took coach for London. I was nobly attended: behind the coach were ten convicted felons, loudly blaspheming and rattling their chains; by my side sat a man with a loaded blunderbuss, and another upon the coach.

1780. May 20. In Scotland. I took one more walk through Holyrood House, the mansion of ancient kings. But how melancholy an appearance does it make now! The stately rooms are dirty as stables; the colours of the tapestry are quite faded; several of the pictures are cut and defaced. The roof of the royal chapel is fallen in; and the bones of James V., and the once beautiful Lord Dankley, are scattered about like those of sheep or oxen. Such is human greatness. Is not "a living dog better than a dead lion?"

1782. May 14. Some years ago four factories were set up at Epworth. In these a large number of young women and boys and girls were employed. The whole conversation of these was profane and loose to the last degree. But some of them stumbling in at the prayermeeting were suddenly cut to the heart. These never rested till they had gained their companions. The whole scene was changed. In three of the factories no more lewdness was found: for God had put a new song in their mouth, and blasphemies were turned to praise. Those three I visited to-day, and found religion had taken deep root in them. No trifling word was heard among them, and they watch over each other in love.

Enters His 80th Year

June 26. I preached at Thirsk; 27, at York. Friday, 28, I entered my 80th year; but, blessed be God, my strength is not "labour and sorrow." I find no more pain or bodily infirmities than at 25. This I still impute, 1. To the power of God, fitting me for what He calls me to. 2. To my still travelling four or five thousand miles a year. 3. To my still sleeping, night or day, whenever I want it. 4. To my rising at a set hour. And 5. To my constant preaching, particularly in the morning.

1783. Dec. 18. I spent two hours with that great man, Dr. Johnson, who is sinking into the grave by a gentle decay.

1784. June 28 (Epworth). To-day I entered on my 82nd year, and found myself just as strong to labour, and as fit for any exercise of body and mind, as I was 40 years ago. I am as strong at 81 as I was at 21; but abundantly more healthy, being a stranger to the headache, toothache, and other bodily disorders which attended me in my youth.

1785. Jan. 25. I spent two or three hours in the House of Lords. I had frequently heard that this was the most venerable assembly in England. But how I was disappointed! What is a lord, but a sinner, born to die!

1786. Jan. 24. I was desired to go and hear the King deliver his speech in the House of Lords. But how agreeably I was surprised. He pronounced every word with exact propriety. I doubt whether there be any other King in Europe, that is so just and natural a speaker.

His 86th Christmas

1789. Dec 25. Being Christmas Day, we began the service in the new chapel at four in the morning, as usual, where I preached again in the evening after having officiated in West Street at the common hour. Sunday, 27, I preached in St. Luke's, our parish church, to a very numerous congregation. So are the tables turned that I have now more invitations to preach in churches than I can accept.

JOHN WOOLMAN

Journal

John Woolman, American Quaker evangelist, author of this autobiography, was born in West Jersey in 1720 and followed the trade of a tailor. But all his interests lay in the practice of piety, and in the uncompromising application of religious Principles to the problems of social life. He advocated incessantly two principal reforms--that members of the Society of Friends should separate utterly from the possession of slaves, and that they should return to their primitive simplicity and moderation in the use of worldly things. Like many economists before and after him, he saw in luxury, extravagance and ostentation, the true cause of all poverty and oppression; and a tract of his entitled "A Word of Remembrance and Caution to the Rich," first published in 1793, was republished a hundred years later by the Fabian Society. His most important treatise, published in 1754, entitled "Some Considerations on the Keeping of Negroes," was one of the earliest indications of the growing Abolitionist feeling in New England. His voyage across the Atlantic in May and Tune, 1772, to visit the English Quakers, was followed by his death from small-pox, in the city of York, on October 7 in the same year. The "Journal," which is marked by great simplicity and sincerity, was published shortly afterwards and has been issued in many subsequent editions.

I.--The Curse of Slavery

Having reached manhood, I wrought at my trade as a tailor; carefully attended meetings for worship and discipline; and found an enlargement of gospel love in my mind, and therein a concern to visit friends in the settlements of Pennsylvania, Virginia and other parts. I expressed it to my beloved friend, Isaac Andrews, who then told me that he had drawings to the same places. I opened the case in our monthly meeting, and friends expressing their unity therewith, we obtained certificates to travel as companions.

Two things were remarkable to me in this journey. First, in regard to my entertainment; when I ate, drank and lodged free of cost with people who lived in ease on the hard labour of their slaves, I felt uneasy, and this uneasiness returned upon me, at times, through the whole visit. Secondly, this trade of importing slaves from their native country being much encouraged among them, and the white people and their children so generally living without much labour, was frequently the subject of my serious thoughts. And I saw in these southern provinces so many vices and corruptions, increased by this trade and this way of life, that it appeared to me as a dark gloominess hanging over the land; and though now many willingly run into it, yet in future the consequence will be grievous to posterity.

About this time, believing it good for me to settle, and thinking seriously about a companion, my heart was turned to the Lord and He was pleased to give me a well-inclined damsel, Sarah Ellis, to whom I was married the 18th day of the 8th month, in the year 1749.

II--Among the Indians

Having many years felt love in my heart towards the natives of this land, who dwell far back in the wilderness, whose ancestors were the owners of the land where we dwell, and being at Philadelphia in 1761, I fell in company with some of those natives who live on the east branch of the river Susquehannah, at an Indian town called Wehaloosing, 200 miles from Philadelphia; and in conversation with them by an interpreter, as also by observations on their character and conduct, I believed some of them were acquainted with that divine power which subjects the rough and froward will of the creature.

At times I felt inward drawings toward a visit to that place, and laid it before friends at our monthly and quarterly, and afterwards at our general spring meeting; and having the unity of friends, I agreed to join certain Indians, in 1763, on their return to their town. So I took leave of my family and neighbours, and with my friend Benjamin Parvin, met the Indians.

About four miles from Fort Allen we met with an Indian trader, lately come from Wyoming; and in conversation with him I perceived that many white people do often sell rum to the Indians, which is a great evil: first, their being thereby deprived of the use of their reason, and their spirits being violently agitated, quarrels often arise which end in mischief; again their skins and furs, gotten through much fatigue in hunting, with which they intended to buy clothing, when they become intoxicated, they often sell at a low rate for more rum, and afterwards are angry with those who, for the sake of gain, took advantage of their weakness. To sell to people that which we know does them harm, manifests a hardened and corrupt heart.

We crossed the western branch of the Delaware, having laboured hard over the mountains called the Blue Ridge, and pitched our tent near the banks of the river. Near our tent, on the sides of large trees peeled for that purpose, were various representations of men going to, and returning from the wars, and of some killed in battle, this being a path used by warriors. As I walked about viewing those Indian histories, painted in red and in black; and thinking on the innumerable afflictions which the proud, fierce spirit produceth in the world; thinking on the toils and fatigues of warriors, travelling over mountains and deserts; and of their restless, unquiet state of mind, who live in this spirit, and of the hatred which mutually grows up in the minds of the children of those nations engaged in war; during these meditations, the desire to cherish the spirit of love and peace among these people arose very fresh in me.

As I rode, day after day, over the barren hills, my thoughts were on the alterations of the circumstances of the natives since the coming of the English. The lands near the sea are conveniently situated for fishing; the lands near the rivers are in many places fertile and not mountainous. Those natives have, in some places, for trifling considerations, sold their inheritance so favourably situated; and in other places, have been driven back by superior force. By the extending of English settlements, and partly by English hunters, the wild beasts they chiefly depend upon for a subsistence are not so plentiful as they were; and people too often open a door for them to waste their furs, in purchasing a liquor which tends to the ruin of them and their families.

III.--Across the Atlantic

Having been for some time under a religious concern to cross the seas, in order to visit friends in England, after weighty consideration I thought it expedient to inform friends, at our monthly meeting at Burlington, of it; who, having unity with me therein, gave me a certificate; and I afterwards communicated the same to our general meeting, and they likewise signified their unity by a certificate, dated the 24th day of the third month, 1772, directed to friends in Great Britain.

I was informed that my beloved friend Samuel Emlen, intended to go to London, and had taken a passage in the cabin of the ship called Mary and Elizabeth; and I, feeling a draft in my mind towards the steerage of the same ship, went and opened to Samuel the feeling I had concerning it. My beloved friend wept when I spake to him; and he offering to go with me, we went on board, first into the cabin, a commodious room, and then into the steerage, where we sat down on a chest and the owner of the ship came and sat down with us. I made no agreement as to a passage in the ship; but on the next morning I went with Samuel to the house of the owner, to whom I opened my exercise in relation to a scruple I felt with regard to a passage in the cabin.

I told the owner that on the outside of that part of the ship where the cabin was, I observed sundry sorts of carved work and imagery; and that in the cabin I observed some superfluity of workmanship of several sorts; and that the monies received from the passengers are calculated to answer the expense of these superfluities; and that I felt a scruple with regard to paying my money to defray such expenses. After this, I agreed for a passage in the steerage, and went on board with Samuel Emlen on the first day of the fifth month.

My lodging in the steerage afforded me opportunities of seeing, hearing and feeling, with respect to the life and spirit of many poor sailors; and an inward exercise of soul hath attended me, in regard to placing out children and youth where they may be exampled and instructed in the fear of the Lord. Now, concerning lads being trained up as seamen, I believe a communication from one part of the world to some other parts of it, by sea, is at times consistent with the will of our heavenly Father; and to educate some youth in the practice of sailing, I believe may be right. But how lamentable is the present corruption of the world! How impure are the channels through which trade hath a conveyance! How great is that danger to which poor lads are now exposed, when placed on shipboard to learn the art of sailing!

IV.--Prices, Wages, and Religion

On landing at London I went straight to the yearly meeting of ministers and elders, which, by adjournments, continued near a week. I then went to quarterly meetings at Hertford, Sherrington, Northampton, Banbury and Shipston, and visited other meetings at Birmingham, Coventry, Warwick, Nottingham, Sheffield, Settle, and other places.

On inquiry, I found the price of rye about five shillings, wheat about eight shillings, per bushel; mutton threepence to fivepence per pound; bacon from sevenpence to ninepence; cheese from fourpence to sixpence; butter from eightpence to tenpence; house-rent, for a poor man, from twenty-five shillings to forty shillings per year, to be paid weekly; wood for fire very scarce and dear; coal in some places two shillings and sixpence per hundredweight but near the pits not a quarter so much. O may the wealthy consider the poor!

The wages of labouring men, in several counties toward London, is tenpence per day in common business; the employer finds small beer and the labourer finds his own food; but in harvest and hay times wages are about one shilling per day and the labourer hath all his diet. In the north of England poor labouring men do rather better than nearer London.

Industrious women who spin in the factories get some fourpence, some fivepence, and so on to tenpence per day, and find their own house-room and diet. Great numbers of poor people live chiefly on bread and water, and there are many poor children not even taught to read. May those, who have plenty, lay these things to heart!

Stage coaches frequently go upwards of an hundred miles in twenty-four hours; and I have heard friends say, in several places, that it is common for horses to be killed with hard driving. Post-boys pursue their business, each one to his stage, all night through the winter. Some boys, who ride long stages, suffer greatly on winter nights, and at several places I have heard of their being frozen to death. So great is the hurry in the spirit in this world, that in aiming to do business quickly, and to gain wealth, the creation, at this day doth loudly groan!